Property, Kin,

and Community on Truk

BY

WARD H. GOODENOUGH

Second Edition

ARCHON BOOKS
Hamden, Connecticut

Library of Congress Cataloging in Publication Data

Goodenough, Ward Hunt.
Property, kin, and community on Truk.

Bibliography: p.
1. Ethnology—Caroline Islands—Truk Islands.
2. Property—Caroline Islands—Truk Islands.
3. Kinship—Caroline Islands—Truk Islands. I. Title.
GN671.C3   1978   301.29′96′6   78-16193
ISBN 0-208-01696-1

THE PUBLICATION OF THE ORIGINAL PAPER AND THE FIELD WORK
ON WHICH IT WAS BASED HAVE BEEN MADE POSSIBLE THROUGH
GRANTS FROM THE OFFICE OF NAVAL RESEARCH, THE YALE UNI-
VERSITY DEPARTMENT OF ANTHROPOLOGY, AND THE WENNER-
GREN FOUNDATION FOR ANTHROPOLOGICAL RESEARCH, INC.

Originally published 1951 as
Yale University Publications in Anthropology
Number 46

Reprinted 1966 with permission as an Archon Book
in an unaltered and unabridged edition

Second edition published 1978
as an Archon Book, an imprint of
The Shoe String Press Inc,
Hamden, Connecticut 06514
©Ward H. Goodenough 1978

Printed in the United States of America

CONTENTS

3

4

ILLUSTRATIONS

TEXT FIGURES

GENEALOGICAL CHARTS

(following page 223)

TABLES

PREFACE TO THE SECOND EDITION

SINCE PUBLICATION of this monograph in 1951, the ethnographic literature on Truk has grown considerably, as revealed in the excellent bibliography of Micronesian ethnography compiled by Marshall and Nason (1975). Good summary statements have been provided by Fischer (1957) and Alkire (1977). These should be consulted by anyone who wishes access to the newer literature.

The community of Romonum itself has been further studied by John and Ann Fischer in 1949-50, by Marc Swartz in 1955-56, and in 1964-5 by myself and my wife. This monograph has not yet been superseded, however, and remains the principal source of information on Truk's social organization, in spite of its many shortcomings. Nevertheless, readers should bear in mind that this description is less applicable to communities in Truk other than Romonum than I thought it was when I wrote it. In its broad outlines regarding clan, lineage, and district organization it is representative, but considerable variation is now evident in such important features as the extent of incest taboos and preferential marriage. Therefore, except as specifically indicated otherwise, this account should be understood as an attempt to describe social relationships on Romonum Island and not necessarily those of Truk as a whole.

Because of the cost of making changes in the body of the text of the original edition, I have left it unchanged except to correct some mispellings and typographical errors. I have added as an appendix a household-by-household analysis of residence in marriage. I have also appended, with permission of the Cornell University Press, a paper assessing social change on Romonum as of my return visit in 1964-5. The latter paper also presents in summary form an overview of Truk's traditional social organization as I had come to understand it following my second period of study there.

As of 1964, the pattern of life in Truk had changed relatively little from what it had been seventeen years earlier. A few years later, however, administrative policy of the United States changed markedly. The budget of Micronesia was increased enormously. As a result, Truk's school system was greatly expanded at the secondary level. A new hospital was built and a new courthouse. There is now the beginning of a tourist industry. Peace Corps volunteers began coming in large numbers in early 1967, and Truk also became eligible for various United States federal programs, such as those dealing with community action and problems of the aged. At the same time, native Trukese have rapidly replaced Americans in most administrative positions in government and education. A growing number of young adults has received college education in Hawaii and on the United States mainland. The resulting changes in purchasing power and outlook have been considerable. These changes have affected Romonum less than Moen, which is the government seat and commercial center, but Romonum's people are much caught up in these developments.

At this time of writing, moreover, Micronesia, and Truk with it, is negotiating the

7

8

terms of its future political autonomy. The colonial era, which began with German pacification of Truk in 1903, is now coming to an end. Whatever the future holds for Truk's people, I wish them well.

Wallingford, Pennsylvania
November, 1977   W.H.G.

FOREWORD

By George P. Murdock

THIS volume represents the first major publication to issue from the participation of Yale University in the Coordinated Investigation of Micronesian Anthropology (CIMA), sponsored by the Pacific Science Board of the National Research Council during 1947 and 1948. As an integral part of a program of research and publication by Yale anthropologists on the culture of the Truk group, which in turn forms a part of a much larger plan for the systematic investigation of the Micronesian peoples administered by the United States under trusteeship from the United Nations, it deserves to be placed in its full historical setting.

In 1942, shortly after the entry of the United States into World War II, the Cross-Cultural Survey at Yale, on advice from the armed services, began to concentrate its research activities on the Micronesian islands occupied by Japan. The translation and classification of cultural materials was unable to keep pace with the progress of the war in the Pacific, however, and in 1943 the Navy Department undertook to expedite the program by substantial grants of research funds. At the same time three members of the staff—Dr. Clellan S. Ford, Dr. John W. M. Whiting, and the writer—received commissions as reserve officers and were assigned the task, with adequate assistance, of preparing a series of Civil Affairs Handbooks from materials in the files for use in the field by military government personnel. The information gathered by the Cross-Cultural Survey was summarized in four such handbooks, dealing respectively with the Marshall Islands, the East Caroline Islands, the West Caroline Islands, and the Mandated Marianas.

The preparation of the handbooks revealed serious lacunae and inadequacies in the scientific knowledge of the islands and their inhabitants. During the period of German control prior to World War I, to be sure, missionaries, administrators, and especially the Thilenius Expedition of 1908–10 had published a considerable body of ethnographic material, but this was confined largely to descriptions of native arts and crafts and to mythological beliefs and religious practices. Relatively little useful work had been done on such subjects as language, economy, land tenure, and social and political organization. Anthropological research by the Japanese after 1914 was negligible both in quantity and in quality. Thus, though the handbooks served adequately as guides for wartime military government, neither they nor the original files of organized source materials contained information detailed enough to cope successfully with many problems of postwar reconstruction and peacetime administration.

The Navy Department, in which administrative responsibility for the former Japanese Mandated Islands was initially vested, quickly recognized the urgent need for fuller information. An Economic Survey by a group of anthropologists and other scientists during the summer of 1946 answered some of the most immediate questions. In 1946, however, the Navy asked the National Research Council, through its Pacific Science Board, to organize a large-scale program of anthropological research in Micronesia. A generous contractual appropriation from the Office of Naval Research, supplemented by grants from the Wenner-Gren Foundation and cooperating institutions, made possible the initiation of the CIMA program, which sent 42 anthropologists and related scientists from 22 universities and other institutions into Micronesia during 1947 and 1948 for field researches ranging in time from three to twelve months each.

In the assignment of areas, the Truk group in the central Carolines was allocated to a team from Yale University led by the writer. Its other members were Dr. Isidore Dyen, Associate Professor of Malayan Languages at Yale, Mr. Clarence Wong of Honolulu, and three advanced graduate students in the Yale Department of Anthropology, Messrs. Thomas F. Gladwin, Ward H. Goodenough, and Frank M. LeBar. A tentative division of labor, subsequently somewhat modified in the field, was worked out whereby Dr. Dyen was to concentrate upon linguistics, Mr. Wong upon ethnobotany, Mr. LeBar upon the technological and economic aspects of the culture, Mr. Gladwin upon the life cycle and personality, Mr. Goodenough upon interaction patterns and religion, and the writer upon social organization and property.

In order to insure the most effective use of the six months to be spent in the field, the party devoted much of the second semester of the academic year 1946–47 to analyzing and assessing the existing literature on Truk. The abundant source materials had been translated and organized for the Navy during the war and were available in the files of the Cross-Cultural Survey (now the Human Relations Area Files). The information was compiled into a single tentative ethnography, a typescript copy of which was taken into the field by each member of the team. This procedure gave the party a solid background on the history, geography, and culture of Truk. It acquainted them with gaps and inconsistencies in the descriptive literature, and enabled them rapidly to confirm what was sound in the earlier work and thus to avoid unnecessary duplication of effort. It also facilitated rapport in the field and often helped elicit information that might otherwise have been difficult to obtain.

One example will illustrate its advantages. Mr. Goodenough, in questioning an excellent informant on the elaborate native system of divination by knots, encountered marked reluctance and evasion, since knot divination is carefully guarded knowledge among the Trukese. But when he confronted the informant with the fairly detailed account by Bollig (1927: 65–8) of certain aspects of the subject, this demonstration of unexpected comprehension broke down the barrier of reserve. The informant became interested in checking the accuracy of Bollig's report and went on to volunteer a considerable amount of new material.

The party left for Truk by Navy air transportation in June, 1947, stopping for a week in Honolulu to exchange plans and formulate common objectives with the members of teams going to other islands. Arriving at Moen Island, the administrative headquarters on Truk, the party spent several days seeking a good field site and finally selected the small island of Romonum (Ulalu) on the western side of the lagoon. With its population of 240, forming a single community on a land area of three-tenths of a square mile, Romonum proved an ideal place to gain an intensive understanding of Trukese culture. The minor variations in culture and social organization on the other islands of the atoll were later established by spot checks made on Pata, Tol, Moen, and Uman.

The first month on Romonum was devoted exclusively to gaining a grounding in the native language. During this period each member of the team worked several hours a day with an individual linguistic informant, and spent the rest of the time analyzing his transcriptions and discussing his findings and problems with his colleagues. Progress was expedited by the use of a short Trukese grammar (Elbert, 1947) and especially by the assistance of Dr. Dyen, whose general linguistic background and special knowledge of other Malayo-Polynesian languages enabled the team to master the Trukese phonemic system and some of the essential elements of the grammatical structure sufficiently well to initiate actual research—haltingly, to be sure—by the beginning of the second month. Constant practice and informal daily participation in community affairs brought rapid improvement, and by the end of the third month some members of the party, including Mr. Goodenough, had acquired considerable fluency and reasonable accuracy.

The fact that all investigation was conducted in the native language was due to necessity rather than choice. Only five or six natives in the entire Truk group had even a rudimentary command of English, and all were employed full time by the administration. There were occasions, particularly in the earlier months, when the ethnographers were seriously handicapped by the unavailability of interpreters. Perforce, however, they made a virtue of necessity, and in consequence acquired greater facility in Trukese, and with greater rapidity, than might otherwise have been the case. The fact that the party included an expert linguist was unquestionably an immense aid in surmounting the language barrier.

At the end of the first month of residence on Romonum the writer began his actual ethnographic research by undertaking a complete census of the island, recording the name, age, sex, marital status, and lineage affiliation of the members of every household. He then undertook the systematic mapping of the island, including its physiographic features, the location of all paths, dwellings, and other features, and ultimately the boundaries, use, and ownership of the named plots into which the land and adjacent waters are divided. Using the census data as a basis, he worked out the genealogies of the entire population as far back as memory carried, noting all marriages and shifts of residence and establishing all kinship connections. The information on land holdings was then correlated with the genealogies; each plot was traced backward through its succession of former owners, and the circumstances of each transfer noted. It proved possible to carry the genealogies and land records back about 150 years, or to approximately 1800, because of the fact that, under the complex Trukese system of land tenure, property claims frequently depend upon the retention of exact knowledge concerning such matters.

In both the genealogical work and the mapping and reconstruction of land holdings, primary dependence was placed upon Simiron, an intelligent elderly informant who was regarded as the island's leading authority on these subjects. He took great interest in the work and frequently corrected mistakes by checking with others on his own initiative. Other informants, of course, were used for corroboration and for resolving inconsistencies.

These procedures resulted in the accumulation of a vast body of relatively objective data on marriages, household composition, residence changes, and property transactions extending over a period of a century and a half, with the evidence always pinned to specific individuals and specific localities. From this material it was possible to verify and refine the verbal generalizations of informants concerning rules of marriage, residence, descent, inheritance, and succession, and to establish the exact circumstances under which exceptions or alternative norms prevail. The method threw into relief the processes by which new kin groups become established and old ones die. It revealed actual historical changes and sometimes corrected seemingly obvious but erroneous inferences as to change. Above all, it illuminated the social structure as a functioning system, not alone in the sense of exhibiting an integrated equilibrium at the period of observation, but also in the sense of adjusting dynamically through time in response to changing conditions. The results strongly suggest that the taking of censuses, the compilation of genealogies, and the recording of land holdings, long established as sound ethnographic techniques, are capable of utilization for establishing historical processes of cultural change, and need not be confined to the description and analysis of synchronic interrelationships as has been usual among "functional" anthropologists.

The research underlying the present report has involved considerable cooperative effort. The data gathered by Mr. Gladwin on marriage and socialization contributed significantly to the understanding of the social structure. Mr. LeBar, because land use was pertinent to his interest in economics, assisted in the basic mapping of the island. Mr. Goodenough found the investigation of religion less demanding than anticipated, and discovered that his other interests intermeshed so closely with social structure that he gravitated toward working with the writer. His help was particularly appreciated in the light of the rather staggering proportions which the accumulation of genealogical and property data began to assume. Assistance ripened into complete cooperation. The data gathered and interpretations made up to the time of the writer's departure from Truk in late November, 1947, thus represent the product of a joint effort. The status of the research and analysis up to that date is revealed in a stock-taking article (Murdock and Goodenough, 1947) written in the field just prior to the writer's return.

Thenceforward Mr. Goodenough carried on alone. He finished the investigation on Romonum, checked the results on other islands, and after his return to Yale analyzed and wrote up the material for his doctoral dissertation. Though the present volume reflects methods of field research initiated by the writer, and incorporates most of his own ethnographic findings, its factual content is to a large extent, and its organization and interpretations completely, the work of Mr. Goodenough. Comparison with the above-mentioned preliminary report will reveal how far he has carried the project beyond its joint phase, how much more deeply he has penetrated into the underlying organization of Trukese society, and how creatively he has expanded the methodology of structural analysis.

Other publications on Trukese culture will appear in this series as they become available. Mr. LeBar's analysis of the material culture, for example, is at an advanced stage of preparation. The publication of Mr. Gladwin's findings may, however, be delayed since he has remained in Truk since the field trip as an anthropological adviser to the civil administration.

PREFACE

THE techniques of field work upon which this study is based have been set forth by Dr. Murdock in the Foreword. Of special importance was the use of the "genealogical method" developed by Rivers (1906) for the investigation of kinship. Its application to the study of property relationships was likewise first recommended by Rivers (1914, I: 55). The method was fully exploited on Truk for both purposes. The responses elicited from informants respecting the use of kinship terms, the patterns of behavior between kinsmen, and organization of kin groups, and the rules governing marriage and the transfer of property were regularly tested against the behavior of specific individuals in the genealogical framework. This led to progressive refinement in the definition of cultural norms and to exposing the specific conditions under which alternative modes of behavior occur.

The initial period of intensive investigation on the island of Romonum yielded a degree of insight into Trukese social structure which enabled us to check our data against the situation on other islands with maximum efficiency within a relatively brief period. By the time we were ready to survey the other islands our presence was generally known throughout the atoll, as was the fact that we spoke Trukese and were persons of good will who would not abuse cooperation. The personal relations we had established with the people of Romonum enabled us to receive hospitality and help from their kinsmen on other islands. Negotiations with local authorities were thus made easy and informal during the last few weeks of traveling about.

In the final phase of his field work on Romonum, the author became a "brother" to a native informant of about his own age, Jejiwe, thereby increasing his participation in the social system of relationships and enabling him to test the conclusions which he had tentatively drawn. A happy result was the discovery of another type of kin group, one for which there is no specific name in Trukese and which will be referred to as a subsib in this report. It was to the subsib mates of his "brother" and his "brother's" wife that the writer was sent when making final checks on other islands. Discovery of this group immediately cleared up a number of false impressions of, and contradictory statements about, the named sibs on Truk.

Our attempts at participation also revealed unsuspected aspects of the internal organization of the extended family. Rules of conduct which informants had given frequently turned out to be inaccurate generalizations or approximate rules of thumb when the responses which the writer's behavior evoked proved quite different from those he had been told it would evoke. While in this way the writer unquestionably made a fool of himself in native eyes on more than one occasion, his *faux pas* provided a basis for straightening out many misconceptions which no amount of straight interviewing would have clarified. They revealed that many of his questions of informants had been beside the point, had failed to allow for necessary distinctions, or had left a confused impression as to what he was driving at.

Although "participant observation" enabled us to enhance the validity of some of our conclusions about Trukese social organization, a large proportion of the conclusions

13

to be presented here are based on analysis subsequent to the field work's completion, which it has not been possible to test against new data. It is intended, however, throughout this report to couch our description in terms which will readily enable tests of its validity to be made by anyone electing to do further ethnographic work on Truk.

Important for the orientation of our study was the Navy's sponsorship of the research and the interest it expressed in using the results to develop an informed administration in Micronesia. While it was made clear from the outset that participating ethnographers were free to study whatever aspects of Micronesian culture interested them, the prospect that our reports would be used as an aid in solving administrative problems introduced considerations which might otherwise have been neglected. In the study of property organization, for example, it required that a report on land tenure so formulate the principles of native property law that an administrator would be equipped to assess claims and settle disputes in whatever form they might arise, and to do this in such a way that the natives would feel that justice had been done in accordance with their principles.

To prepare a case book providing an example of every possible situation and a precedent for handling it was out of the question. Rarely would there occur two situations identical in all respects. Attention was therefore concentrated on the ways in which events are classified, defined, and canalized within the native cultural framework. In the case of property, we sought to isolate the culturally defined types of transactions which may occur. It was felt that once the rights and duties attendant on each type of transaction were understood, it would be possible to unravel the complex picture found on any given plot of land by tracing its history, just as a lawyer who knows our own principles of property law establishes the status of a holding through a "search of title." This process would in turn provide a means for validating our formulation of property principles. The possibility that our work might have practical applications, far from proving a handicap, served in the writer's opinion to raise his standards of scientific rigor and led to ethnographic results which in some instances far exceeded his expectations.

The problem of rendering an ethnographic account that can be of practical use to administrators boils down, we feel, to trying to give the reader a basis for learning to operate in terms of the culture described in somewhat the same manner that a grammar would provide him with a basis for learning to speak a language. To seek to do this implies that a culture is as susceptible of rigorous analysis and description as is any language. The demonstration of this proposition is, in fact, a long-range objective towards which the present study was undertaken as an exploratory step. The writer feels that the recent advances in methodological and conceptual rigor in descriptive linguistics present a serious challenge to descriptive ethnography; for patterned verbal behaviors, the basic data of linguistics, are but one branch of patterned behaviors in general, which are the basic data of ethnographic analysis.[1]

Regardless of its ultimate validity, our objective focuses attention not only on field techniques, but on subsequent analysis of field materials. For example, simply to

[1] For a provocative statement of the same view, see Levi-Straus (1945).

determine that residence on Truk is usually matrilocal with a few patrilocal exceptions, while it may serve to type Trukese residence as matrilocal for purposes of cross-cultural comparison,[2] will not help the reader to decide whether he should live in matrilocal or patrilocal residence, should he choose to marry a Trukese woman in Trukese fashion. To summarize materials in the form of statistical means or modes is inadequate for such purposes. While they characterize a sociological situation at a given time, they do not state the cultural rules whose application results in that situation. Wherever possible, therefore, the ensuing account of Trukese social organization has sought to formulate rules and state the conditions governing their application in such a way that none of the available information contradicts them at any point. As our analysis progressed, generalizations which failed to account for known cases were modified accordingly.

Like considerations have entered into the formulation of definitions. In the case of kin-groups, for example, we have sought so to define the Trukese lineage that everything to which the Trukese react as such is accounted for by our definition while everything else is excluded. As products of analysis, our definitions frequently fail to coincide with those given by informants, which were usually in the nature of rules of thumb. Should the writer be accused, therefore, of misrepresenting Trukese culture, his defense is that he does not intend to present it as the Trukese see it but as his analysis reveals it. It is not his aim to make the Trukese people "come to life" nor to pursue that will-o'-the-wisp, their culture "as it really is."

The order in which to present our materials has posed a serious problem. As might be expected, with each successive step of our analysis the order suggested by the internal consistency of our materials shifted. That finally arrived at is largely a function of the level of analysis attained. We mention this problem because some members of the "functional" school of anthropologists have taken the position that one can start with any phase of a culture and it will lead on to the next until the whole with the interrelation of all its parts is encompassed.[3] In their field work they have found that the interdependence of cultural elements tended to lead them, in the study of any single problem, into areas further and further removed from their point of departure. In recognition of this they have emphasized that cultures are fairly well integrated configurations whose elements dovetail to a remarkable degree. With this the writer has no quarrel. Description can indeed start almost anywhere if its purpose is to demonstrate that cultural elements must be seen in widely ramified contexts in order to understand their meaning. In the present study, however, having ascertained that the various elements of Trukese social organization are integrated so as to form a fairly consistent whole, we have sought to break the whole back into its parts again and reorder them in conformance with our aim of formulating as precise definitions and rules as possible. It is in this connection that the problem of order acquires significance within a functionalistic framework. Characteristics by which one element of Trukese culture had to

[2] See, for example, the brilliant cross-cultural analyses of Murdock (1949).

[3] This position, for instance, is explicitly illustrated by Arensberg (1937) in his examples of the "west room" and "the old man's curse."

be defined were frequently other elements in the culture, which in turn required definition. If this interrelatedness were completely circular, however, in the sense that every element depended for its rigorous definition directly or indirectly on every other element, any formulation of precise definitions and rules would be impossible and our treatment would perforce follow the more discursive pattern typical of functionalists' reports. For systematic description some logical starting point was needed.

As already indicated, a logical starting point could not be decided in advance on any *a priori* basis but had to emerge as an empirical finding from analysis. Several chapters of this report were drafted more than once before it became clear that the aspects of Trukese social structure described depended for their definition, directly or indirectly, on the system of property relationships. This experience has led the writer to conclude that the empirical determination of logical starting points is a requisite for rigorous ethnographic description.[4] It enhances the precision of functionalistic analysis in that those elements of a culture whose definition derives from the same logical starting point are by this fact differentiated sharply from elements whose definition must be derived from other starting points. This consideration suggests a method for isolating empirically what elements are functionally linked to a given set of in tial definitions to form what may be called a structural system within the larger culture.[5] Its success, however, depends on the degree to which one's definitions rigorously account for all the relevant facts available for analysis.

To all those who have helped make this study possible the writer is deeply indebted: to Mr. Harold J. Coolidge of the Pacific Science Board of the National Research Council for masterly coordination of the CIMA project; to the United States Navy for transportation to and from Truk; to Admiral C. H. Wright, Deputy High Commissioner of the Trust Territory of the Pacific, and the members of his staff for their helpfulness and consideration; to Commander H. D. Huxley and his administrative staff on Truk for their hospitality and interest and for the generous donation of their time to make comfortable our stay in the field; to the other members of the field party, who proved most helpful co-workers and excellent companions. Before we went to Truk, Dr. Edward T. Hall generously made available his own field notes for study, and Dr. Karl J. Pelzer and Mr. Samuel H. Elbert gave helpful advice as to the conditions we would encounter. Messrs. LeBar and Gladwin have kindly consented to the use of their data wherever relevant to an understanding of Trukese social structure. Many helpful suggestions have been given by Dr. John Useem, who read and criticized the manuscript.

Funds for this study were made available through the generosity of the Office of Naval Research, the Wenner-Gren Foundation for Anthropological Research, Inc., and the Department of Anthropology, Yale University. The work was also materially aided by a Sterling Fellowship from the Graduate School of Yale University, to whose faculty

[4] Its importance for the systematic description of technological processes has been demonstrated by Osgood (1940), whose presentation of Ingalik material culture similarly progresses from the logical starting point which the interrelationships of his materials required.

[5] Cf. the discussion of "social systems" by Linton (1936: 253–70).

this report was submitted in substantially its present form in partial fulfillment of the requirements for the degree of Doctor of Philosophy.

A special debt is owed to Dr. George P. Murdock and to the writer's wife, Ruth Gallagher Goodenough. Many of the data presented were collected by Dr. Murdock, who generously gave permission to incorporate them in full in this report. His stimulating guidance in the classroom and in the field, his keen criticism of the manuscript, the encouragement he has given, all have served to make of this study a wonderful educational experience for the writer. To Mrs. Goodenough goes the credit for holding the writer to his objectives, clarifying much of his thinking in its developmental stages, and providing the necessary encouragement and assistance to carry him over the hurdles of analysis.

Thanks, finally, are due to the people of Truk, in particular to the inhabitants of Romonum Island; to their chiefs, Cyyw and Taapen; to Jamiwo, Jejiwe, Kekin, Kinöwus, Puruuta, Siipen, Simiron, Siro, Söön and the residents of Fääggypë for their warm hospitality, good humor, and extreme patience.

Philadelphia, 1950.   WARD H. GOODENOUGH

INTRODUCTION
TRUK AND ITS PEOPLE

TRUK lies in the heart of the Caroline Islands in Micronesia and is located between 7°7' and 7°41' north latitude and 151°22' and 152°4' east longitude (Fig. 1). It is situated roughly at the center of what is known as the East Central Carolines or Greater Truk Area. Other islands and atolls in this area are the Mortlock or Nomoi Islands (including Satawan, Lukunor, and Etal), Namoluk, Losap, Nama, and Kuop to the south and east; with Murilo, Nomwin, East Fayu, Namonuito, Pulap, Puluwat, and Pulusuk to the north and west. All but Truk are coral atolls or single coral islands. The natives of the area speak closely related dialects and are equally closely related culturally.[1]

Truk itself is a complex atoll. It consists of a great ring of reefs and low coral islets within whose lagoon rise seventeen small, volcanic islands. Truk's name, a corruption of the native name Cuuk,[2] means literally "mountains" or "heights." The high islands within its lagoon are the only such between Ponape, 383 miles to the east; Guam, 590 miles to the northwest; Yap, 825 miles to the west; and St. Matthias Island, 600 miles to the south (Fig. 1). Truk's mountains, therefore, are a unique feature in a wide area whose only other lands are tiny coral islets.

There are about 40 islets strung along Truk's outer reef (Fig. 2). The lagoon, which ranges from 30 to 40 miles in diameter and has an area of 822 square miles, contains a number of low islands and coral heads within it in addition to the high islands. All told, there are some 98 islands in the reef and the lagoon. Table 1 lists the volcanic islands (with native names in parentheses), their areas in acres and square miles, and their maximum elevations.[3] They tend to form two distinct clusters (see Fig. 2). The eastern group (Dublon, Eten, Falo, Fefan, Moen, Param, Tarik, Tsis, and Uman) is called *Nömwunujääs* (Windy Harbor) by the natives, since it is more exposed to the northeasterly trade winds. The western group (Eot, Eiol, Falabeguets, Pata, Polle, Tol, Udot, and Ulalu or Romonum[4]) is called *Fääjicuk* (Below the Mountain) because of its domination by Truk's highest peak, Mt. *Winipwëët* (Nose Summit), on Tol.

[1] A good summary description of the area is contained in CAHB (see bibliography for full references).

[2] This name is variously rendered in the literature as Djuk, Rough, Ruck, Torakku, and Tuck. Truk is also called Ola or Holla in some sources from *Wëënë* (Puluwatese: *Weela*), the native name for Moen Island. A third name is variously rendered as Hogolu, Hogoleu, Lugulus, or Ugulut. Krämer (1932: 19–21) suggests that these forms are corruptions of *cukunuuk* (given by him as *djuk u luk*), meaning "mountains in the middle." For an explanation of the spelling of native words, see below under the heading "Linguistic Note."

[3] Data on areas are taken from Bryan (1946: 4), and on elevations from CAHB: 11.

[4] All names for Truk's high islands are given as they appear on standard maps and charts (see, for example, Bryan, 1946, Map 36) except for Ulalu. This name represents the native *Wynaany*, an island in Namonuito atoll figuring prominently in the legendary history of Uman. There is no indication that this name has ever been used for an island in Truk's lagoon, except as it appears on charts. For this reason we shall henceforth employ the more correct Romonum.

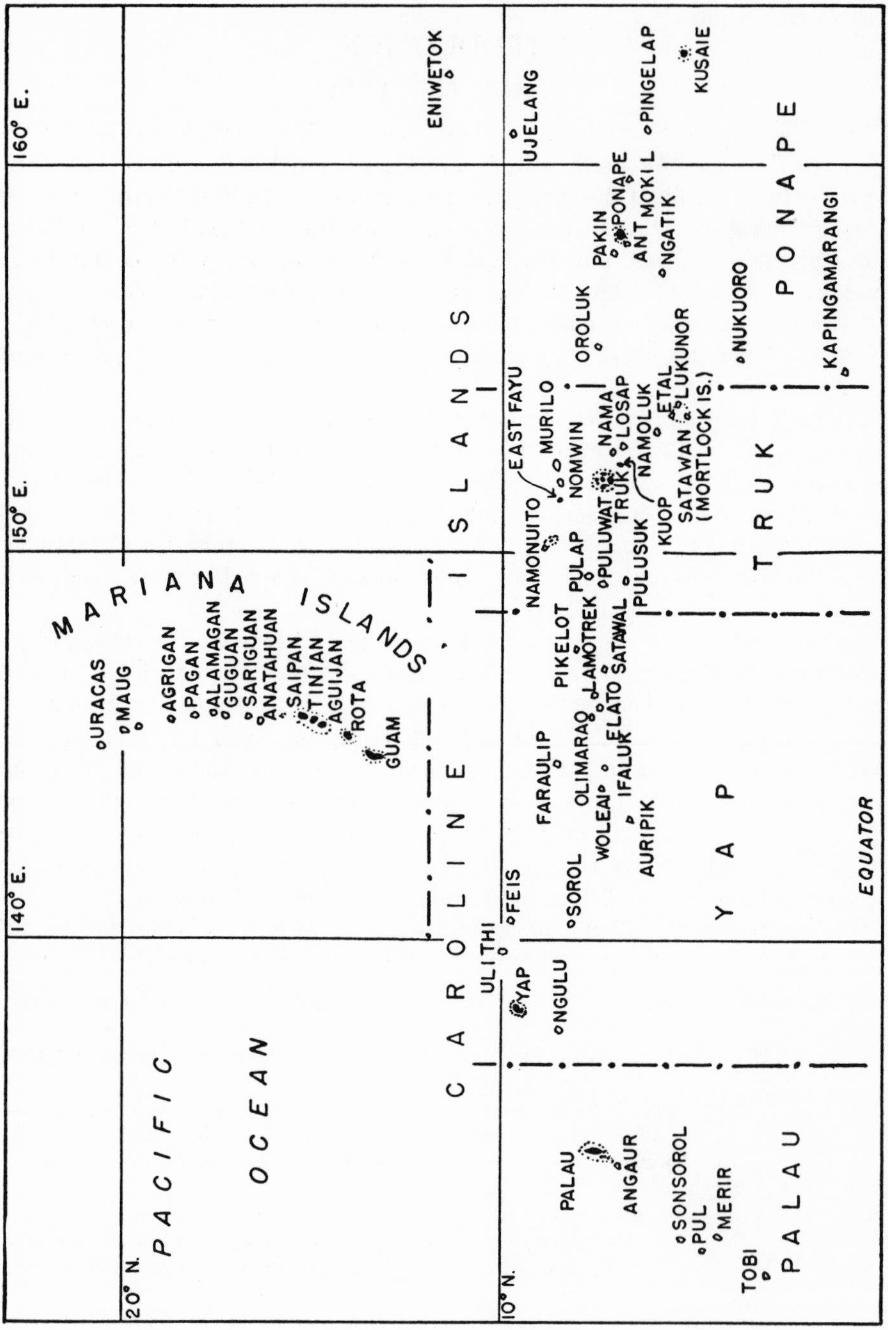

FIG. 1. Map of the Caroline and Mariana Islands.

Truk's location gives it a tropical, oceanic climate, characterized by little temperature variation[5] and a heavy annual rainfall.[6] Ordinarily, however, the skies are not
greatly overcast. During the rainiest months the sun shines a good deal of the time, rain
coming down in short, heavy showers. Humidity is high, August, September, and

TABLE 1. AREAS AND ELEVATIONS OF TRUK'S ISLANDS

Volcanic Islands	Acres	Square Miles	Elevation in Feet
Dublon (*Tonowas*)	2,160.0	3.375	1,168
Eot (*Jëët*)	119.7	0.187	200
Eiol (*Jëëjan*)	17.0	0.027	40
Eten (*Jetten*)	140.0	0.219	197
Falabeguets (*Fanapeges*)	388.0	0.606	390
Falo (*Fënö*)	82.3	0.128	200
Fefan (*Feefen*, old name *Faa*)	3,267.0	5.105	1,027
Moen (*Wëënë*)	4,670.0	7.297	1,234
Param (*Perem*)	369.0	0.576	236
Pata (*Paata*)*	832.0	1.300	646
Polle (*Pwene*)*	2,240.0	3.500	679
Tarik (*Tëëtiw*)	115.0	0.180	230
Tol (*Ton*)*	5,376.0	8.400	1,483
Tsis (*Siis*)	150.0	0.235	249
Udot (*Wytëët*)	1,217.0	1.902	797
Ulalu (*Romönum*, *Römönum*)	184.4	0.288	167
Uman (*Wuuman*, old name *Kuwopw*)	1,162.0	1.816	948
Reef Islands	1,016.1	1.588	
Other Lagoon Islands	182.6	0.285	
Total Dry Land Area		37.014	

* Tol, Pata, and Polle actually form a single land mass cut by narrow channels and mangrove
swamps into three islands. Tol is further broken up by narrow isthmuses, the natives distinguishing
four separate units: *Ton* (Tol proper), *Fëëwypë*, *Fëëwyp*, and *Wonej*.

October being most humid while January, February, and March are least so.[7] Although
the humidity is sufficient to effect rapid mildew of leather goods, it keeps soft and pliable

[5] Uchida (1930: 725) gives the highest average monthly temperature in 1927 as 28.3 degrees centigrade for October, and the lowest as 26.2 degrees centigrade for March. Similarly, in 1928 the difference
between the highest and lowest monthly average was only 1.5 degrees centigrade. Diurnal variation
considerably exceeds seasonal. Krämer (1932: 45) cites Kubary's temperature recordings from June to
October, 1887, as showing an average diurnal variation between 32 degrees centigrade in the early
afternoon and 26 degrees centigrade at night.

[6] Measurements of rainfall on Dublon Island in 1927–29 give an annual mean of 90 inches. The
annual mean for the years 1903–11 on the adjacent island of Eten was 129 inches. Monthly records on
Dublon show greatest rainfall in June (351 mm.) and lowest in March (66 mm.), with intervening
months showing a gradual increase and decrease to and from these high and low marks. The average
number of rainy days per year in 1927–29 was 227. For details, see CAHB: 5.

[7] The mean monthly humidity for 1927–29 shows a low of 80 per cent for January and a high of
86 per cent for September (CAHB: 5).

the native mats and baskets, which quickly dry out and crack when brought to the United States.

Seasons on Truk are marked by wind conditions rather than by temperature changes. The "dry" season, from November to June, is characterized by the Trade Wind, which blows steadily and evenly from the northeast and kicks up enough waves to make native navigation on the open sea hazardous. It is sufficiently strong to keep the heat

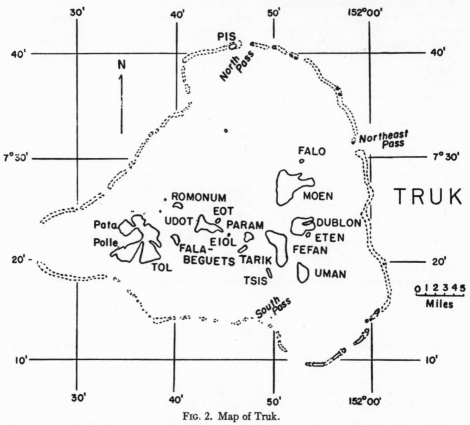

FIG. 2. Map of Truk.

and humidity from being unpleasant. The "wet" season, from July to October, is characterized by southerly and changeable winds, which are less strong. Its higher humidity and frequent calms are mildly discomforting. Truk just misses a regular monsoon season, as it lies on the eastern edge of the monsoon area. During the wet season, there are intermittent periods of two or three days each when the monsoon may touch Truk. Serious storms occur as infrequent typhoons, which do great damage, especially when accompanied by tidal waves. Since 1891 only two of the seven typhoons reported in the area actually hit Truk.[8]

[8] See CAHB: 6. During the autumn of 1947 a succession of four typhoons caused considerable dam-

Of volcanic origin, Truk's high islands are formed chiefly of basalt. They comprise either a single mountain, a mountain ridge, or a small chain of mountains.[9] Originally they must have been heavily forested. Long ago, however, the natives cleared off most of the natural vegetation, replacing it with breadfruit and coconut groves and with small garden plots of upland taro, arrowroot, and turmeric. Krämer (1932: 38) states that by 1900 only Uman, Fefan and Tol possessed real forests, and these toward the mountain tops. Although the land remains heavily wooded, it is largely by man-made growth. The vegetation can be classified into roughly four zones. The first consists of mangrove swamp stretching along large portions of shore. Next comes a sandy coastal fringe producing coconut palms, breadfruit, pandanus, and hibiscus, with taro and ivory-nut palms in fresh-water swamps. Above this, the mountain slopes are covered with groves of breadfruit, interspersed with other useful trees and gardens. Finally comes the uncut forest at the tops of the higher islands. During the war, the Japanese cleared large areas of food trees and some remaining forest in order to plant extensive fields of sweet potatoes and manioc. Much of this land has now gone into brushy second growth. Partly on their own initiative and partly because of governmental stimulation, the natives are gradually bringing it back into production, mainly of breadfruit and coconuts.

Except for fish, Truk's fauna is limited.[10] Mammals include but two genera of bats (one of them the flying fox or fruit bat), rats, one variety of native domesticated dog, a few cats of European domesticated type, and domesticated pigs and cattle. The latter are of recent introduction, few in numbers, unimportant as food, and without ceremonial associations. There are but 50 species of birds, very few of which are land varieties. Reptiles include only a half dozen species of lizards and sea turtles; there are no snakes. Insects make up in numbers what they lack in variety, and flies, mosquitoes,[11] and gnats are great pests.

Truk's small land area and limited animal resources force its inhabitants to rely for food almost exclusively on vegetable and marine resources.[12] The staple food is supplied by the breadfruit tree, which is well suited to the steep slopes, its roots preventing soil erosion. Since it provides a seasonal crop, breadfruit is stored and fermented in pits for the lean period, when the diet is further supplemented with taro, sweet potatoes,

---

age on Yap, but none of them came close to Truk. Because of its high islands, Truk has been a traditional place of refuge for the inhabitants of the low coral atolls in the East Central Carolines when typhoons made them temporarily unfit for habitation.

[9] Detailed descriptions of topographical features are given by Hall and Pelzer (1946: 1–5) and Krämer (1932, *passim*).

[10] Discussions of fauna are given by Kubary and Krause (1889: 62–3), Finsch (1893: 298), Bollig (1927: 226–7), Krämer (1932: 139), Hall and Pelzer (1946: 90–5), and Elbert (1947, "bird,","fish," and "shellfish").

[11] The anopheline mosquito is not present. While local varieties carry the rare filariasis, malaria is absent.

[12] A detailed description of the native economy has been prepared by LeBar (MS). Published accounts are presented by Kubary (1889: 46–78), Krämer (1932), Hall and Pelzer (1946), and Pelzer (1947).

and manioc.[13] These are cultivated in small gardens, which the natives abandon after the harvest, for the soil does not permit of intensive cultivation, except in the taro swamps. This is an added reason for reliance on the perennial breadfruit, which, though producing less food per acre, requires no rotation, its fall of leaves actually enriching the soil. While not unimportant, coconuts play a less prominent role in the native diet than they do on coral atolls, where vegetable resources are more limited. Bananas provide between-meal snacks, and sugar cane, which is chewed, is the chief confection. Yams, the staple food on Ponape, are not grown on Truk. Collecting breadfruit and cultivating gardens is largely in the hands of the men, who also do the heavy work connected with preparing and cooking vegetable foods. Great value is attached to fish, no meal being complete without some as a side dish. While there are a great many fishing techniques, most of which are performed by men, the main contribution to this part of the diet comes from the women, who fish in teams with hand nets in the offshore shallows and along the reefs.

Vegetable resources supply not only most of the food but also most of the raw materials in the native technology. Over 200 species of plants, most of which are used in one way or another, were collected by Clarence Wong in the autumn of 1947.[14] Those which are of greatest all-round usefulness in technology are the coconut palm (providing thatch, timber, cordage, baskets, and solid containers), breadfruit (providing timber for houses, canoes, and wooden bowls), pandanus (providing baskets and mats), and hibiscus (providing fine cordage and threads for loom weaving).

At present, Truk's native population numbers a little under 10,000. The people are of relatively short stature and well built. Obesity is rare. Skin color ranges from light to dark and hair color from brown to black. While a few natives have frizzy hair, on most it is straight or wavy. Facial features are highly variable, but headshape is predominantly dolichocephalic.[15] Despite popular opinion to the contrary, maturation appears to be slower than among Europeans, certainly not more rapid. Women do not mature physically at an early age with respect either to menarche or to breast development. On Romonum Island no girl eighteen years old or younger, married or single (and at present nearly all over fourteen are married), had yet conceived a child, despite premarital freedom, an apparent absence of contraceptives, and an assumption of sexual activities by the age of fourteen or fifteen. Youths of sixteen are still beardless. As far as senility

[13] Manioc has replaced arrowroot in recent years. Not only can it be processed as arrowroot was, namely, to make tapioca pudding; it can also be prepared in the same manner as breadfruit, a fact which has made it popular.

[14] Mr. Wong made botanical collections as a member of the CIMA expedition on Truk and Yap. His information is available in the files of the Cross-Cultural Survey (now the Human Relations Area Files) at the Institute of Human Relations in New Haven, Conn. Published discussions of Truk's flora are given by Kubary and Krause (1889: 53–4); Finsch (1893: 298, 326); Krämer (1908: 170–1; 1932: 412–24); Bollig (1927: 226); Hall and Pelzer (1946: 87–90); and Elbert (1947, "plants").

[15] No investigation of Truk's physical anthropology was undertaken by the CIMA expedition. Krämer (1932: 21–6, 400) reports the results of all measurements which have been made so far and discusses possible racial affinities.

is concerned, most men remain active until about fifty years of age, some longer. Women look older at a somewhat earlier age, but remain vigorous for about as long as do men.

A thorough discussion of population trends is given by Pelzer (Hall and Pelzer, 1946: 6–14). His conclusion that there has been a serious decline in the past century from 35,000 to about 11,000 in the year 1900 is based on a highly suspect figure from 1824 given by an anonymous source (Lesson, 1839: 197). The first reliable estimate, made by Kubary in 1887 (Kubary and Krause, 1889: 55), places the population at about 12,000. Considering the native reliance on tree crops, there appears to be little likelihood that Truk ever supported as many as 35,000, which would mean a density of nearly 1,000 per square mile. During the late war, despite the intensive modern agriculture and efficient fishing methods of the Japanese, a near famine was suffered by the

TABLE 2. DISTRIBUTION AND DENSITY OF TRUK'S POPULATION

Administrative Area	Population	Density per Square Mile*
Moen, Falo, Pis	2,033	267
Dublon	1,155	342
Fefan, Param, Tarik, Tsis	1,408	231
Uman	922	507
Udot, Eot, Falabeguets, Romonum	1,035	347
Tol, Pata, Polle	2,632	198
Total and Average	9,185	233

* The density for administrative areas is based on the areas of inhabited islands only, excluding the reef islets, which are also exploited for food. The average density for all of Truk is based on the total dry land area, including the reef islands. It should be noted that Uman also exploits Kuop atoll (0.19 square miles) to the south of Truk. This island, with the densest population, suffered most heavily during the wartime famine.

combined military and native population of 45,000 as a result of the American blockade. It would appear, then, that Truk's native population has remained fairly stable from pre-colonial days down to the present with ups and downs reflecting a measles epidemic in 1918, subsequent improved medical conditions under the Japanese, and the privations of 1944–45. Table 2, adapted from Hall and Pelzer (1946: 13) gives Truk's native population in 1946 by administrative area.

Truk came under effective foreign control only 50 years ago, when Germany acquired it from the nominal rule of Spain. Prior to this, western contacts were limited to brief visits by an occasional ship and the presence of a handful of traders and missionaries, who first appeared in the latter part of the nineteenth century.[16] The pacification of Truk was not accomplished until 1903. Its economic development under Germany was limited to a stimulation of native copra production. After the Japanese

[16] For a good summary of these early contacts, see Krämer (1932: 1–13). For an account of the Spanish-German dispute for control of Micronesia, see Yanaihara (1940: 17–28).

took over in 1914, they undertook an intensive exploitation of Truk's fisheries and later used its magnificent anchorage to base their South Pacific Fleet. Since the war, no attempts have been made to exploit Truk's few resources. Following a brief period of readjustment, the natives have settled back to maintain much of the economic self-sufficiency which they were beginning to lose under Japan.

Despite the large immigration of Okinawan fishermen under the Japanese, all of whom have been repatriated, and despite the presence of 35,000 troops and laborers during the war, the native social structure remains fundamentally unchanged from aboriginal times. This is probably due in no small part to the fact that Truk has been spared the ravages of depopulation. It has also been helped by the Japanese prohibition, continued by the United States, against purchase of land from natives by foreigners. Aside from the small area on which the administrative garrison is presently housed, the Trukese continue to use all the lands which they traditionally exploited. Every native community that existed in 1900 appears still to be intact. Despite the discontinuance of warfare, an almost complete conversion to Christianity, a high proportion of literacy, and considerable modification in technology, Trukese society is still a vigorously going concern, its pattern of organization little changed by the events of the past 50 years.

LINGUISTIC NOTE

Like other Micronesian languages, Trukese belongs to the Malayo-Polynesian linguistic stock (Dyen, 1949: 420). Closely related and mutually intelligible dialects are spoken on the Nomoi (Mortlock) Islands, Namoluk, Losap, Nama, Nomwin, Murilo, and Namonuito (Fig. 1). Also closely related but not mutually intelligible with Trukese are the dialects spoken on Puluwat, Pulap, and Pulusuk. The natives of Truk say that they can understand the former group of people but cannot understand the latter, who speak Trukese as a second language for purposes of trading. While they cannot follow Trukese, the Puluwatese say that they can with difficulty understand the people of Nomoi. Closely related dialects are spoken as far west as Ulithi (Fig. 1), but precise determination of their relationship awaits linguistic study.

Since there will be frequent occasion to use native words in the ensuing description, a brief sketch of Trukese phonemics will prove helpful to the reader.[17] The following are the symbols which will be used throughout:[18]

p   a bilabial stop, voiceless, unaspirated, articulated with the tongue forward and low. It may be slightly voiced between vowels.

pw   a bilabial stop, velarized, voiceless, unaspirated, articulated with the tongue retracted and raised. It may be slightly voiced between vowels. Dyen (1949) uses q for this phoneme.

[17] Although Bollig (1927) presents an outline of Trukese grammar, his failure to work out phonemes seriously impairs its value. Elbert (1947) made the first study of Trukese phonemics. His findings were subsequently revised by Dyen (1947, 1949).

[18] The symbols used here are as recommended by Dyen (1947: 137) in recommendations 2, 4, 5, 6, 7, 8. The phonemic system is essentially that of Elbert (1947) with the addition of the phoneme *j* and some symbol substitutions: *g* for *ng*, *c* for *ch*, *y* for *ü*, *ë* for *ö*, and *ö* for *ó* (cf. Dyen, 1949).

t	an alveolar stop, voiceless, unaspirated. It may be slightly voiced between vowels.
c	a cacuminal stop, voiceless, unaspirated, released with some rill affrication, and articulated with the tip of the tongue at the front of the palate. This retroflection of the tongue makes it sound sometimes like an English "tr," while at other times the affrication makes it sound more like an English "ch." It may be slightly voiced between vowels.
k	a velar stop, voiceless, unaspirated. It may have a rounded release following a back vowel, and may be slightly voiced between vowels.
f	a labiodental rill spirant, voiceless, like the "f" of English.
m	a bilabial nasal, voiced, articulated with tongue forward and low. It may be incompletely articulated between vowels, giving the impression of a nasalized, bilabial, voiced spirant.
mw	a bilabial nasal, velarized, voiced, articulated with tongue retracted and raised. It may be incompletely articulated between vowels, giving the impression of a nasalized, back semivowel. Dyen (1949) uses b for this phoneme.
n	an alveolar nasal, voiced. It may have flapped articulation between vowels with weak nasalization, giving the impression of a flapped "r" or an "n" spoken by a person with a bad cold. Older natives frequently use an alveolar voiced lateral in free variation with it. This "l" is not phonemic, but falls within the permitted range of phonetic variation covered by Trukese "n."[19]
g	a velar nasal, voiced, like the "ng" of English "singer." It may be incompletely articulated between vowels with weak nasalization, giving the impression of a voiced velar spirant.
s	an alveolar laminal rill spirant, voiceless. It may be slightly voiced between vowels.
r	an alveolar trill, voiced. It is always heavily trilled. In initial position it may be only slightly voiced.
j	a front unrounded semivowel, articulated slightly higher than the vowels surrounding it.
w	a (1) central unrounded semivowel when surrounded by front or central vowels, and (2) back rounded semivowel before or after a back vowel.
i	a high front unrounded vowel, like the "i" of Italian.
e	a middle front unrounded vowel, like the "e" of Italian.
ä	a low front unrounded vowel, a little higher and tenser than the "a" of English "hat."
y	a high central unrounded vowel. There is no counterpart in English.
ë	a middle central unrounded vowel, like "u" of English "but," "uncle."
a	a low central unrounded vowel, like the "a" of Italian.
u	a high back rounded vowel, like the "u" of Italian.
o	a middle back rounded vowel, like "o" of Italian.
ö	a low back rounded vowel, slightly more to the front and tenser than the "aw" of English "law."

All consonants and vowels may be either long or short, the vowels in any position, the consonants anywhere within a phrase, but not at the beginning or end of a phrase where they are always short. This difference in length is phonemic. Length will be represented by doubling the consonant or vowel, i.e., pp, ppw, tt, cc, kk, mm, mmw, nn, gg, ss, rr,

[19] In all other dialects of the Greater Truk Area *n* and *l* are phonemically distinct. Their convergence in Truk is apparently due to the weak articulation of consonants between vowels within a phrase.

ii, ää, yy, ëë, aa, uu, oo, öö.[20] The quality of vowels is not altered by length, except for "i" and "u", which are slightly higher and tenser when long. The semivowels are without length. Stress is not phonemic, a phrase being spoken evenly. An entire word may be stressed for emphasis, in which case all its syllables are equally strongly stressed in contrast with other words of the utterance. Lack of stress is sometimes confusing to the English speaker, who tends to hear length as though it were stress.

The above sketch of Trukese phonemics applies specifically to the dialect of Romonum Island. There is some minor variation in dialect from island to island and community to community within the Truk lagoon. These variations do not, however, alter the phonemic pattern for Trukese, but express themselves as vocabulary differences and by minor differences in the selection of phonemes in the same roots, e.g., compare *maaj, määj, jecep*, meaning "breadfruit" in the dialects of Moen, Romonum, and Pata respectively. The first two words show a variation in selection of phonemes, while the last shows an outright vocabulary change. The native words used hereinafter are those of the Romonum dialect, except where otherwise indicated.

[20] No confusion results from writing "ppw" and "mmw," since *p* plus *pw* is the same phonetically and phonemically as *pw* plus *pw*, whereas *pw* plus *p* is the same as *pp*, the preceding consonant being assimilated to the latter. Combinations of *m* and *mw* assimilate in a like manner.

PROPERTY

INTRODUCTION

A SYSTEMATIC presentation of Trukese social structure begins with the organization of property relationships. The conceptual framework which governs these relationships is extended by the Trukese to cover situations which involve property only indirectly. Because of this it provides a logical starting point for elucidating the fundamental elements out of which the structure of Trukese society is built up and elaborated. There are other possible points of departure, for Trukese social organization is composed of more than one structural system. The several systems of interpersonal relationships cut across each other, any one of them at times modifying, reinforcing, or conflicting with the others. It is because such important aspects of the social organization as matrilineal kin groups and territorial and political groupings are best defined in terms of the property system that we have chosen to start with it.[1]

The previous literature on Truk lacks an adequate account of the native property system. Krämer (1932) makes no attempt to discuss it seriously. Bollig (1927) misses its main features and is, therefore, unable to present a coherent account. Yanaihara (1940: 128–30) relies on Bollig, whose material he is admittedly unable to make intelligible. Hall (Hall and Pelzer, 1946: 76–9) appears to have applied preconceptions of his own about inheritance and ownership in matrilineal societies, for he erroneously concludes that land used to be owned collectively by the matrilineal sibs or name groups but has now become the private property of individuals in the European sense as a result of German and Japanese influence. Actually, the property system of aboriginal times appears to be operating today with little modification. Such innovations as money have been largely worked into the native system rather than destroying or seriously modifying it.

The main body of information that provides the basis for this account is derived from what amounts to a series of searches of title conducted on Romonum Island by Dr. G. P. Murdock and the writer. The method was to map all the named plots of land on the island and then to trace the history of their use and ownership as far back as the genealogies of the living natives would permit. A preliminary summary of the results has been published in Murdock and Goodenough (1947). The information obtained on Romonum was later checked with informants on Pata and Uman at opposite ends of the Truk lagoon. No significant differences among the three islands were found. Some brief but intensive interviewing of natives from Puluwat suggests that the property system there is fundamentally similar to that of Truk, though differing in a number of important details. To generalize freely from Truk to the surrounding islands would thus appear unwise.

Reworking the material, comparing it with the rules governing movable goods, and

---

[1] This does not imply that the property system is necessarily historically antecedent to the political and kin group organization. It is merely a logical antecedent within the present framework of Trukese society as we have analyzed it.

relating it more closely to kin-group and political organization, significantly altered the perspective from which the property system had originally been viewed. While the basic facts, of course, remain the same as those summarized by Murdock and Good-enough (1947), the new perspective necessitates a change in terminology, which will be noted below at appropriate points. It makes possible not only a more systematic presentation of the property system itself but also a closer integration between it and other aspects of social structure.

GENERAL ATTITUDES TOWARD PROPERTY

The Trukese appear to be interested in property primarily for its productive or practical potentialities rather than for social prestige or non-material rewards. For example, trees whose wood is important in the building of houses and canoes are owned, but no one cares from whose land trees good only for firewood are cut. Anything that has acquired a productive or practical value as the result of human labor is owned as property, whereas ownership is less likely with things directly consumable from nature. Thus there are fishing rights in water areas, but water itself is the property of no one, especially fresh water. The main source of drinking water on Romonum is a spring in the center of the island. The land on which it is located is owned, but the spring itself is free to all and in the old days,before the introduction of rain barrels,was used by every-one on the island. When the native storekeeper recently ran a pipe from this spring to his house some distance away, he incurred no obligations toward the people owning the land from which the water is piped. Similarly, medicinal herbs, dried coconut fronds for kindling, wild cooking herbs, and leaves for wrapping food bundles may be freely gathered by anyone, anywhere, without first speaking to the owner of the land on which they are found.

Women have equal rights with men in the ownership of property of all types, but their role is often less obvious. The dominance of brothers over sisters tends to make administration of property largely a masculine responsibility. Since cultivation is primarily a male task, husbands ordinarily work the land belonging to their wives. In land disputes, too, a male lineage mate or close relative frequently represents a woman's interests. In consequence of the division of labor by sex, moreover, certain types of property are more likely to belong to men than to women. Thus our survey of Romonum holdings revealed that women, though they own considerable real property, hold appreciably less than do men.

CORPORATIONS

Property may be owned by either an individual or a group. When a group of persons is the owner, it has the legal status of an individual as far as rights, obligations, and the various rules governing the transfer of property are concerned. Even in relation to its own members, the group functions as an individual within the property system. This fact will become clear as the types of ownership and transfer are discussed in detail. Groups that function as individuals in relation to property will hereafter be referred to as corporations.[2] Not any group of persons may hold property as a corporation. The Trukese conceive of a property-holding group as composed fundamentally of siblings.[3] Relations between the members of any Trukese corporation are patterned after the relations between siblings. In short, the corporation in Truk is an organized kin group, whose prototype is a group of own siblings.

The bonds between siblings are considered to be closer than those of any other relationship. Siblings form a basic cooperative work group. Whenever possible, sisters reside together in the same household. Siblings are expected to support each other and back each other up, regardless of the situation or its possible consequences. Anything which their collective efforts produce in the way of property belongs to all of them as a group. Any property which they inherit from their father also belongs to all of them collectively. Such property is administered by the oldest brother in the interests of the group, whose members may not put it to personal use without his permission. Called *mwääniici* ("senior man"), the eldest brother represents the group to others, can order his siblings to work as a group in their collective interest, and supervises such work. Since the division of labor by sex largely separates the activities of men from those of women, the sisters tend to operate as one work team and the brothers as another. Just as the *mwääniici* acts as "straw boss" of his brothers in their collective activities, the oldest sister plays a similar role among the women and is correspondingly called the *finniici* ("senior woman").

Younger siblings must obey and respect their older siblings of the same sex. Nor is this obedience and respect a matter of theory only. It is strictly observed in practice, and anyone failing in this is severely censured. Similarly sisters must obey and respect their brothers regardless of their relative age in years, provided only the brothers are past the age of puberty. A sister who consistently fails to do so is virtually disowned by her brothers, who no longer concern themselves about her welfare.

An important additional element in the relations between siblings is the sharing among them of property which belongs to one of them as an individual. This is largely confined to siblings who are of the same sex and is more likely if they are of nearly the same age. A young woman, for example, frequently borrows a sister's dress. Such sharing of property is on an informal loan basis. Some one person is always the actual owner. Property which is treated in this manner is not to be confused with property which siblings own as a corporation. Use of the latter requires the permission of the *mwääniici*.

These relationships between siblings pattern their organization as a corporation. Whatever differences there may be between them as individuals, as a corporation their

---

[2] This use of the term corresponds to the definition of a corporation as "any group of persons or objects treated by the law as an individual or unity having rights or liabilities, or both, distinct from those of the persons or objects composing it," as given in *Webster's New International Dictionary*, Springfield, 1923.

[3] It was a partial recognition of this which apparently led Bollig (1927) to speak of what he called the property of brothers.

unity is paramount, and to violate it is as serious a moral breach as is possible for the Trukese.

While persons other than own siblings are frequently members of the same corporation, their relations to each other as such are patterned after the sibling relationship. They even refer to each other as siblings. The usual way in which such persons become members of the same corporation is through application of a rule of matrilineal descent. Children have automatic membership in the corporation to which their mother belongs. Their relations with the older generation are those of younger to older siblings whenever common membership in a corporation provides the context for their behavior.[4] This means that an only child is not deprived of membership in a group of siblings. Not only may he reckon his maternal aunts and uncles as siblings in the same corporation, but he also includes the children of his maternal aunts. Thus the organization of the corporation as a group of siblings regularly cuts across the respective generations to which its members belong. This gives the corporation a continued existence, though its individual members come and go with each passing generation. Membership in a corporation, therefore, is commonly based on the fact that everyone in it is descended in the female line from a group of own siblings several generations back. This matrilineal kin group preserves its organization as a corporation only so long as it holds property in relation to which it must function as a unit. There are matrilineal kin groups which are not at the same time property-holding corporations, but they do not concern us here. The fact that the latter are not corporations is what largely distinguishes them in organization and function, and leaves them with little unity of action and no well-defined leadership, although their internal relationships are still patterned after those of siblings.

A corporation, as noted above, starts as a group of own siblings, who are to be defined as the children of one woman. Children of the same man by different wives are not considered own or even half siblings, but have the same relationship to each other as do the children of two brothers. The children of one woman by different husbands, however, are normally classed as own siblings.[5] Any group of siblings becomes a discrete corporation when it acquires collective title to a piece of property, whether through inheritance from a father or through cooperative effort. This may be the case even though the sibling group already has membership in a larger corporation started by its matrilineal forbears. Thus an old corporation founded several generations back commonly includes a number of younger corporations within it. Some of these will consist only of own siblings; others will include several generations in a particular line of descent. Two types of matrilineal corporation may thus be conveniently distinguished: one whose members at the same time belong to a larger corporation and one whose

---

[4] When the fact of common membership in a corporation is not relevant, and the younger and older generations are interacting solely on the basis of their relationship as blood relatives, their behavior is patterned after a different set of criteria. This will be made clear in the discussion of the kinship system.

[5] The Trukese definition of own siblings is *pwiipwi nëwyn emën cëk feefin* (siblings, children of but one woman).

members do not. Hereinafter the former type will be called a *descent line*, the latter a *lineage*. Either a lineage or descent line may consist of own siblings only or include several generations. A descent line is always a segment of a lineage; a lineage is never a segment of any larger corporation within the community. When a descent line severs itself from the lineage of which it was a part, it becomes a lineage in its own right.

There is no difference in the way in which a descent line and lineage are internally organized. The oldest man in each is its *mwääniici* and the oldest woman is its *finniici*. As a general rule, however, it may be said that just as the interests of the individual are subordinate to those of the corporation or corporations to which he belongs, so the interests of the descent line are subordinate to those of the lineage of which it is a part. When a descent line places its interests above those of its lineage, this leads to a parting of the ways and to the establishment of the descent line as an independent lineage.

A corporation, as already noted, has the same status as an individual as far as the tenure of property is concerned. Both corporation and individual are subject to the same rules of tenure and transfer. Both may create, purchase, and inherit property. A corporation on Truk even has natural heirs in precisely the same way as an individual. The natural heirs of any individual holding full title to property are his or her children. In precisely the same manner the heirs of a corporation are regarded as its "children." The notion that a corporation may have children, though alien to us, is axiomatic to the Trukese.

The children of the men of a corporation, be it a matrilineal descent line or lineage, are called its *jëfëkyr*. Analysis of the use of kinship terms on Truk reveals that the members of a lineage, for example, call its *jëfëkyr* their "children," using the same kinship term that a man or woman employs for his or her own child. The *jëfëkyr* in turn call all the members of the father's lineage "father" or "mother" regardless of how they may actually be related in a strictly genealogical sense. The *jëfëkyr* relationship may be tentatively defined as the parent-child relationship when a corporation occupies the status of parent and the offspring of its men occupy the status of children. It is this usage which gives concrete expression to the axiom that a corporation on Truk may have children.

The *jëfëkyr* relationship is important because the Trukese corporation is not perpetual in fact, despite its organization as a self-perpetuating matrilineal kin group. When a corporation dies, with the extinction of the matrilineal descendants of its founders, its surviving *jëfëkyr* are the natural heirs to its property in exactly the same way that a man's children are the heirs to any property which he owns as an individual.

FORMS OF OWNERSHIP, TRANSFER, AND PROPERTY

Two basic forms of ownership must be distinguished. One of these will be called *full ownership*, be the owner a person or a corporation. It confers on an owner what will be called a *full title*.[6] The other divides a full title asymmetrically between two parties,

[6] By *ownership* is meant a total complex of reciprocal relationships with respect to the enjoyment and use of something as property. By *title* is meant a constellation of rights, privileges, and duties devolving on one party as owner in such a complex of relationships. Cf. Murdock *et al.* (1950, "Property").

either or both of whom may be individuals òr corporations. This will be called *divided ownership*. It confers on the two owners two distinct titles respectively, each characterized by different rights and duties. One will be called a *provisonal title* and the other a *residual title*.

Differences in title result from different property transactions. These include not only the several methods for transfer of title, but also acts which bring something into existence as property or conversely extinguish its existence as such within a Trukese community. The several forms of property transaction are: (1) creation or discovery, (2) sale or exchange, (3) inheritance, (4) conquest or forceful seizure, (5) a form of gift called *kiis*, (6) a form of gift called *niffag*, (7) loss or destruction through deliberate act or through natural deterioration. Creation or discovery brings property into social existence within a community and always results in full ownership. Sale, inheritance, conquest, and *kiis* result in the transfer of possession and full title from one party to another. *Niffag* transfers possession with attendant obligations, and with some forms of property transforms full ownership into divided ownership. While not a property transaction in the sense that the parties to ownership are affected, loan temporarily delegates some of the rights of a title holder and involves clearly defined reciprocal obligations.

The several forms of ownership and transaction apply in a general way to all forms of property. The nature of the property itself, however, has a bearing on the extent to which it is likely to be subject to the various forms of transaction and on the way in which the resulting obligations are likely to be expressed. A distinction must first be made between property which is corporeal (land, movables, livestock) and that which is incorporeal (magic, skills, knowledge).[7] The latter will be treated separately after corporeal property has been clarified. In connection with *niffag* and loan some forms of corporeal property involve formalized obligations while other forms do not. Analysis reveals that the former are important as sources of food while the latter are considerably less so. It is convenient, therefore, to classify corporeal property as *productive* and *nonproductive*.

Before listing the various forms of productive property it will be necessary to consider what the Trukese allow as separable property units. They follow the rule that a person who makes improvements on property has full title to these improvements, even though he does not hold title to the property on which they are made. In a dispute between a man and a woman on Romonum, for example, it was decided that the man must vacate the woman's house in which he was then living and which stood on her land. It was recognized, however, that he could remove all the lumber which he had built into the house in repairing it, for this was his.[8]

It is in the realm of what may loosely be called real property that the regularity

---

[7] The concept of incorporeal property is used here as presented by Lowie (1920: 25–243).

[8] It appears that a person may not make improvements on property, unless he holds full or provisional title, without the title holder's consent. When consent is obtained, however, he acquires full title to the improvements. Our data are not sufficient to delineate restrictions on improvements more clearly.

with which certain improvements are made gives rise to property distinctions that are unfamiliar to us. A house or a tree may be owned separately from the land on which they stand. Land, in turn, is separable as territory and soil. Title to virgin territory is one thing; to make it into productive soil by clearing, planting, and otherwise improving it is to establish title to the portions of soil affected, productive soil being classed as an improvement of virgin territory. Similarly, title to a fish weir is separable from title to the section of lagoon in which it stands. We must distinguish, then, between territory and soil, between soil and trees or houses, and between lagoon and fish weirs. These distinctions have more than an occasional relevance, for they enter into the majority of situations where rights in real property are involved.

We can now list the standard forms of productive property as territory, soil, trees, lagoon, fish weirs, canoes, and livestock. Non-productive property covers nearly everything else which may be owned, including houses, tools, and fishing and agricultural equipment.

THE CREATION OF PROPERTY

When something comes into a community as property, the ordering of social relations with respect to its enjoyment and use must be automatic in order to avoid conflict. The Trukese solve this problem by according to the person responsible for its existence the rights of a full title holder. When property is created by the collective efforts of the members of a corporation, the corporation acquires full title. If two persons who are not actual siblings or are not members of the same corporation jointly create property, they do not form a corporation; either each owns the part for which he is responsible, or one must compensate the other, or one makes a *niffag* or *kiis* of his labor and its product to the other.

In some instances the action which produces property is formal and stereotyped. A man establishes full title to territory by going out and staking a claim to hitherto unclaimed, virgin land. As previously indicated, if he makes the territory productive in some way he creates property in the form of soil. The planter of a tree owns it. The maker of a garden has full title to it, though he may not have title to the territory or soil on which it stands.

If a man discovers goods which another has lost, he acquires full title to them, provided the loser is not a person who is known to him (i.e., a member of the same community or a kinsman from another island). The discoverer is owner because he brings the goods into existence as property within the community of persons with whom he interacts. If the former owner is known to the finder, however, their relationship to each other is presumed to have been established already with respect to the goods lost, and the finder must return them or be branded a thief. On the other hand, if the loser is a stranger from another island whose lost canoe, let us say, has drifted over to the finder's island, then the loser must buy back from the finder just as though he were making a new purchase. If the finder returns it without accepting the purchase price, he has in effect made a *niffag* to the loser, who becomes heavily obligated and can be counted on to furnish hospitality and protection when the finder visits his island.

FULL OWNERSHIP

Full title carries with it the maximum number of rights and privileges and the minimum number of obligations. Except for two restrictions, a full title holder may sell, destroy, lend, or give his property as *kiis* or *niffag* as he sees fit. Inheritance and membership in a corporation are the two considerations which restrict a full title holder in the exercise of his privileges. He may not present his property in the form of a *niffag* to someone other than his natural heirs, his children, without the latters' consent, for the recipient of the *niffag* supplants his children as heir to the full title. Should a full title holder fail to gain the consent of his children in making a *niffag*, they are empowered to confiscate the property given away. This applies mainly to property which is productive, non-productive property being less subject to this restriction, at least in practice. A junior member of a corporation may not alienate his property by sale, or presumably by *niffag* or *kiis*,[9] without approval of his *mwääniici*. The reason for this seems to be that a corporation may call upon its members for contributions of their personal property or its produce, should its interests demand it. Before alienating his property, therefore, a junior member makes sure that he will not jeopardize his corporation's interests by doing so. This restriction, again, is less likely to apply to non-productive property.

Power to destroy property resides with its full title holder and with no one else. The above-noted interests of his heirs and corporation, however, make the exercise of this power an unfriendly act. Deliberate destruction of one's property, therefore, normally occurs only in extreme anger occasioned by a slight from one's lineage mates or one's heirs and their lineage mates. It is condemned as tantrum behavior, though the owner is legally within his rights.

When a corporation is full title holder, its property cannot be alienated in any way except by the unanimous consent of its members. The *mwääniici* has the most important voice, and his veto is final. Corporate property in movables is known as *pisekin sööpw* (lineage movables) and ordinarily consists of large paddling canoes, sailing canoes, and large wooden bowls. However, anything else toward whose acquisition a corporation's members contribute their personal property or labor becomes corporate property. One of the Romonum lineages, by virtue of contributions from its members, acquired a 100-pound bag of rice for the 1947 Christmas feast. Half of this rice remained after the feast was over, and the *mwääniici* declared it would be kept as *pisekin sööpw*. It could be used only with his permission for occasions of importance to the lineage, such as the celebration of a child's birthday, the entertainment of an important guest, or the payment of some obligation incurred by the lineage as a corporation.

Although responsibility for administering its *pisekin sööpw* rests with a lineage's *mwääniici*, he does not keep such property in the house where he lives, for this is usually a dwelling belonging to his wife's and not his own lineage. A corporation's movables are entrusted to the immediate care of its *finniici* instead. It thus remains in a house belonging to the owning group in the care of its women, whose husbands would be subject to immediate divorce should they tamper with it in any way. When a corporation has a

[9] Unfortunately direct information on *niffag* and *kiis* in this connection was not obtained.

meeting house, its *pisekin sööpw* may be kept there. A lineage which owns large canoes regularly keeps them in a canoe house by the shore, which may also serve as its meeting house. According to one informant, when a *mwääniici* is about to die, he calls the older men of his lineage together and enjoins them to care for its *pisekin sööpw* and not let it get out of their lineage's hands.

When plots of soil or trees are owned by a corporation, its members exploit them on a share basis rather than as a single working team. The relationship of a share holder to his corporation is that of a provisional title holder to a residual title holder in divided ownership, the corporation, in effect, making a *niffag* of portions of its real property to its individual members. The details of this situation will be discussed below in connection with divided ownership.

NIFFAG

Broadly defined, *niffag* is a form of gift which obligates the receiver to the giver. The resulting obligations differ, depending on whether the property involved is classed as productive or non-productive. With productive property a *niffag* results in divided ownership, the donor retaining residual title to the property while the recipient acquires provisional title. When property is non-productive, the obligations are less formalized; they are expressed mainly by the feeling that the recipient must make some return gift or favor in the future, and that the giver of the *niffag* may call upon him for such a return gift or favor whenever need may arise. If a provisional title holder fails in his obligations to a residual title holder, the latter may confiscate the productive property he gave as a *niffag*. If the recipient of non-productive property fails to render his obligations, the donor does not have the power to confiscate it (or, if he does, he would apparently never exercise it). Instead, he marks the recipient as a person to whom he will refuse all help or favors in the future. When the recipient of a *niffag* of non-productive property makes a return *niffag* or favor, the obligations are presumed to be reversed, not simply canceled.[10] This type of gift, therefore, serves to reinforce cooperative relationships between individuals who belong to different corporations. Indeed, relationships in which two people are ready to help each other out when occasion arises tend to be such mutually reinforcing *niffag* relationships.

The concept of *niffag* does not apply exclusively to the giving of property. It also pertains to the giving of one's time and labor, to entertaining at a meal, and to the loan of property. In the last case again, if the loan involves productive property, the obligations of the borrower are somewhat formalized. For the moment, however, *niffag* will be discussed only in relation to the transfer of titles to property. Its application to labor as a commodity, to the relations involved in lending and borrowing, and to the rules of hospitality will be considered in subsequent sections.

Although a *niffag* represents an investment by the giver from which he expects some

[10] The situation in this respect is very much like that of letter-writing with us. While a letter in reply to another cancels the obligation to reply, it frequently obliges the writer of the first letter to answer in his turn, resulting in a chain of correspondence in which the obligation to write always devolves upon the last person to receive a letter.

sort of return, it is definitely regarded as a gift and is always ostensibly given with the intention of doing another a favor. Any return gift, therefore, must not be made on the same day, unless a request for a favor immediately accompanies the gift. To make a return on the same day under other circumstances operates to transform the gift into an exchange or sale, a trade of favors, and in Trukese opinion robs the *niffag* of its quality as a gift.[11]

The Trukese are nevertheless quite conscious of the investment quality of a *niffag*. People frequently make gifts for the express purpose of obligating the recipient and predisposing him to do a return favor. The giver then feels free to make a subsequent request of the recipient, who would be embarrassed to refuse it. Gifts made with the specific intention of coercing a favor from another person are called *jefisifis* ("accomplishers" or "clinchers"). They are made for all sorts of purpose, e.g., gaining the support of a chief, the sexual favors of a woman, or the consent of a girl's family to her marriage.

The motivation behind a *niffag* is, therefore, a dual one. A native may give to another as an expression of his liking for him or of his sense of obligation to him. He may also do so to get something out of him. The recipient's attitude toward the giver varies somewhat, depending on how he interprets the motivation. Frequently both motivations are involved at the same time. A man provides for his children, for example, because of his fondness for them, but also because he thereby obligates them to care for him in his old age.

A revealing illustration of the mixture of feelings which a *niffag* may entail was given by an informant who was discussing the taboos surrounding a magical specialist. The particular specialist has it in his power to make another person who has offended him sick by inviting the latter to share with him a meal consisting of taboo food. The victim later gathers together sufficient goods to make a handsome present to the specialist, who is also the only one who knows the cure. As our informant put it, the specialist now "likes" his victim and prepares the necessary medicine to remove the affliction. A *niffag* is thus felt to have the power to change another's attitude even when its purpose is perfectly clear.

DIVIDED OWNERSHIP

Divided ownership always involves two parties, either corporations or individuals. It results from *niffag* when the property concerned is productive, i.e., territory, soil, trees, lagoon, fish weirs, canoes, livestock. A *niffag* divides full title between giver and recipient, the former retaining residual title and the latter gaining provisional title.

---

[11] I learned this the hard way. I had asked a man and his wife if the latter would do some embroidery for me. That I was to make a return gift was understood by the woman's relatives with whom I discussed the matter and who advised me as to what would be appropriate. When I received the finished embroidery work, I immediately presented the woman with my return gift. She protested vigorously at taking it, but finally did so at my insistence. That evening her husband came and expressed the hurt which he and his wife felt, for had I not asked it of them as a favor, and had they not agreed willingly, and why was I therefore paying them as though I had hired their services? Had I made the return gift a week later when some occasion naturally presented itself, it would have been accepted as quite in order.

A provisional title holder gets physical possession and is responsible for the property's maintenance. A residual title holder is free of responsibilities, but continues to enjoy certain rights.

The duties of a provisional title holder are as follows:

1. If he sells the property, he must give the residual title holder a portion of the price received.
2. He must give the residual title holder a share in the produce of the property, just what form this produce takes depending on the specific nature of the property in question.
3. He must maintain the property in good order.

A residual title holder has the power to confiscate, regaining full title to the property, should the provisional title holder fail in any of his duties. If confiscation is impossible, due to sale or destruction of the property, the residual title holder has the right to demand and receive property of equivalent value. A provisional title holder has the following privileges and powers:

1. He may delegate as a privilege to others his right to work and enjoy the fruits of the property in the form of a temporary loan.
2. He may sell the property, subject to his duty to give the residual title holder a portion of the price received.
3. He may improve the property as he sees fit with the right to acquire full title to the improvements.

He does not have the power to make a *niffag* of the property to some one else, nor does the residual title holder. This can be done only with the consent of both parties. It amounts to a voluntary return of full title to the residual title holder, for he retains residual title after the new *niffag*, the former provisional title holder losing all rights and privileges. In practice, such a subsequent *niffag* does not take place except when the provisional title holder has made improvements of his own on the property. When these are included in the subsequent *niffag*, he retains residual title to them, while the former residual title holder keeps residual title to the property minus the improvements.

A provisional title holder is also heir to the full title, which he acquires on the death of the residual title holder. It is for this reason that a full title holder must get the permission of his children, his natural heirs, before he can make a *niffag* to someone else. By giving their permission, his children waive their rights in favor of the provisional title holder. If a provisional title holder dies first, the residual title holder regains full title to and possession of the property, less any improvements made on it. Since the provisional title holder had full title to the improvements, they are inherited by his children (see *Inheritance* below). With the residual title holder's permission, of course, the children may take their father's place as provisional title holders, but this amounts to a new *niffag*. Divided ownership, therefore, amounts to a splitting of the full title between two parties. On the death of either, the survivor acquires the rights of the other and full title to the property.

The less formal situation in relation to the *niffag* of non-productive property reflects some of the rights and duties incurred under divided ownership. If a man makes something for someone else, for example, and the latter immediately turns around and sells it, the maker is entitled to some of the proceeds of the sale. If the recipient keeps it for a while, however, he is evidently presumed to have made some return favor already, for the maker apparently does not have any right to a share in the proceeds of a later sale. Thus, while the obligations of divided ownership are reflected to some extent in the *niffag* of non-productive property, they do not endure, and in due time the recipient is felt to have gained full title to the property. With productive property, however, the various rights and duties endure for the life of the property.

Individuals rather than corporations are the usual parties to divided ownership of livestock. There are but two types of livestock of any importance in Truk: pigs and chickens.

If a man's pig has a litter, the shoats represent the products of his husbandry and he has full title to them. He ordinarily makes a *niffag* of the shoats to those of his children and lineage mates who ask for them. If he gives them to anyone else, he must first get permission from his children. The recipients of the shoats, as provisional title holders, are responsible for raising them. When a shoat has grown into a pig and is slaughtered by the provisional title holder, the residual title holder is entitled to receive a share in the meat, which is the food produced by the pig. The residual title holder may claim the price of the pig if his rights are not respected in this way. The provisional title holder, however, has full title to any of the offspring produced by the pig, for they represent the products of his own husbandry. Divided ownership covers only the particular pig which was presented as a *niffag* and does not extend to its offspring.

The case of chickens is similar. A residual title holder, however, does not get a share in the meat of a chicken when it is killed but in the eggs which it produces while alive. A provisional title holder gets full title to any chicks hatched as representing the products of his own husbandry.

A canoe is apparently the only type of movable goods (*pisek*) that is classed with productive property. The builder of a canoe has full title to it. A man who knows how, therefore, cannot make one for someone other than his children without their consent. Even a member of the builder's lineage must clear the matter first with the builder's children, unless the builder is requested to donate his services to his lineage as a corporation. If the children refuse permission, then the builder must be paid the purchase price of the canoe, and the transaction becomes a sale and not a *niffag*. When the canoe is finished, the provisional title holder may not lend it to anyone or use it for any purpose until he has first gone fishing in it and turned over the entire catch to the builder. This apparently satisfies his obligation to pay the residual title holder a portion of the produce derived from the property. The provisional title holder is then free to lend his canoe and to use it for any purpose he wishes. He is still obliged, however, to get permission from the residual title holder before giving the canoe to some one else, and if he sells it he must give the builder a portion of the price received.

The trees which a man plants belongs to him as the products of his husbandry. He may make a *niffag* of them to his children or, with their permission, to anyone else. In either case he retains residual title to the trees. The recipient must bring a share of the fruit whenever he gathers from them. As provisional title holder, he may not give the trees to someone else without permission of the residual title holder, and if he sells them, the residual title holder must get his share of the proceeds. If the provisional title holder plants new trees with the fruit or shoots from the old, he has full title to them, for they represent products of his own husbandry. The provisional title holder is heir to the full title upon the death of the residual title holder. In fact, a *niffag* of trees results in all the rights, privileges, and duties of divided ownership outlined above.

The builder of a fish weir has full title to it and to its produce. No one may use it without his permission. If he gives it to another as a *niffag* he is still entitled to receive a share of the fish caught in it whenever it is used.[12]

The parties to divided ownership of soil are frequently corporations rather than individuals. They are subject, however, to exactly the same rights, privileges, and duties as obtain between individuals in divided ownership.[13] A provisional title holder may not give the soil to someone else without permission of the residual title holder. If the soil is sold, the latter has a right to a share of the proceeds. The provisional title holder must give the residual title holder a share of the food grown on the soil. The latter has the usual power to confiscate the property should the provisional title holder fail in his duties. The provisional title holder is heir to the full title on the death of the residual title holder, who, in his turn, regains full title if the former dies first. The provisional title holder has the privilege of planting on the soil and otherwise improving the holding. He acquires full title to what he has planted or to any other improvements he has made, since they are the products of his own labor.

The Trukese speak of lagoon in the same way that they speak of soil. A provisional title holder is supposed to give the residual title holder a share in the fish caught. Just as with soil, there are recognized "plots" of lagoon. Administration of title to lagoon is vested in the *mwääniici*. Divided ownership usually results from the building of fish weirs, the owner of a weir having a provisional title to the portion of lagoon on which it stands. If a man permits his daughter to build one, he need not *niffag* to her the entire section of lagoon, retaining for himself and his corporation mates all other fishing rights.[14]

When we come to divided ownership of territory, we are dealing with political as well as property relationships. The boundaries of a territory are at the same time the boundaries of a political district. Residual title to territory carries with it chiefship of the

[12] Fish weirs seem to have been much more important in the native economy in aboriginal times. One end of Romonum Island is studded with weirs. They do not appear to be kept in repair, and there seems to be considerable freedom in their use. Should they again begin to play an important role in the economy, it is likely that property rights to them will be reasserted.

[13] Full or residual title to soil was called the "lineage fee simple" by Murdock and Goodenough (1947), while provisional title corresponds to what was there called "usufruct."

[14] Property rights to lagoon, like those to fish weirs, are not observed today, at least on Romonum Island. The natives still know who has what rights in theory, however, though ignoring them in practice. It is possible that with the renewal of aboriginal fishing techniques, following the recent removal of Okinawan fisherman from Truk, there may be a tendency to start reasserting property rights to lagoon.

district, or, to put it the other way round, the relations between a chief and the people of his district correspond closely to those between the parties in divided ownership. Because of its political aspects, discussion of territory as property will be deferred until political organization is considered in detail.

CORPORATIONS AND DIVIDED OWNERSHIP

When a corporation holds full title to soil or trees, a special situation arises in that its members do not ordinarily work such holdings as a team. Trees and soil are usually apportioned among them to work as individuals. The resulting relationship between the individual members and their corporation corresponds exactly to that between provisional and residual title holder. A corporation may be said to have full title to certain plots of soil and/or trees, but its internal organization with respect to these plots is such that the corporation occupies the status of residual title holder while its individual members occupy that of provisional title holders.[15]

As provisional title holders, a corporation's members are responsible for maintaining the property. They have the privilege of developing or improving it, and they acquire full title to the improvements. They may not sell their holdings nor give them to someone else without consent of the entire membership of their corporation. As administrator of the residual title, the *mwääniici* calls upon them to contribute food to meet the corporation's obligations, these contributions representing the share of produce to which the residual title holder has a right. In the name of his corporation, a *mwääniici* may confiscate the holdings of a member who defaults in his duties. When a member dies, his corporation, as surviving residual title holder, regains full title to the property, which it then reallocates to a junior member. Such reallocation may take place prior to the death of the former provisional title holder, who being too old to continue working the property, states that he is through with it. In practice, it is usual for a member to share his holding with a younger sibling or sister's child as the latter comes of age. When he ceases to exhibit further interest in it, his junior is tacitly confirmed as provisional title holder in the absence of any objections from his corporation mates. This process of reallocation and sharing gives the superficial impression of matrilineal inheritance. It must not be confused with inheritance, however, because the relationships resulting from it are typical of divided ownership.

When provisional title to soil or trees is held by a corporation, a similar allocation among its members may take place. The corporation again stands in the position of a residual title holder in relation to its members.[16] As has been stated, a provisional title holder may not make a *niffag* of his holdings to someone else without permission of the residual title holder. In this instance, however, a corporation holding provisional title may reallocate its property among its own members without consulting the residual title

[15] This was described as "intra-lineage usufruct tenure" by Murdock and Goodenough (1947).

[16] This situation corresponds to that with which we are familiar in our own society when a person renting an apartment sublets it to another. The person holding the sublease has much the same relationship with the regular tenant as the latter does with the legal owner.

holder, for possession of the property has not passed outside the corporation to another party. Should the corporation wish to give the property to other than one of its members, permission of the residual title holder must be obtained.

A complication in the case of divided ownership arises from the fact that a provisional title holder has the right to improve his holding and acquire full title to the improvements. If they are of a short-lived nature, such as a garden which quickly matures for harvesting, no complications result. But if the improvements are such that they will outlast the lifetime of the provisional title holder, then on his death the residual title holder regains full title to the original property, but the natural heirs of the provisional title holder, his children, get full title to the improvements on it. If the provisional title holder outlives the residual title holder and thereby acquires full title to the original property, the latter with the improvements on it become a single holding. It is in the situation where the residual title holder is a corporation and the provisional title holder an individual that a complication arises, for the lifespan of an individual is generally shorter than that of a corporation, which may extend over a number of generations. In other words, the complication results from the allocation of soil and trees by a corporation to its members. The problem is the same whether the corporation has full or provisional title to the property, for allocation among its members may occur in either event. There are two ways in which the Trukese handle this problem.

The first solution is a relatively simple one. When a plot of soil needs replanting of its trees, it may be allocated to a woman or a child in the corporation. The woman's husband or the child's father gets the responsibility for working and improving the plot. His children duly inherit full title to the improvements and continue in possession of plot as provisional title holders within their corporation. The Trukese rules that a man can demand labor from his sister's husband and that a husband must work his wife's land for her serve directly to implement this solution of the problem.[17] An illustration is provided by Simiron of Romonum. As a child, his adopted son, Pëwytaw, was allocated a large plot of soil by his descent line. Simiron planted 100 coconut trees on it for Pëwytaw. The latter, now a young man, holds provisional title to the soil from his descent line and provisional title to the trees from Simiron. As a residual title holder Simiron gets a share in the produce of the coconut trees. When Simiron dies, Pëwytaw will have full title to them and continue to enjoy provisional title to the soil on which they stand.

The other solution is for the corporation to permit a male member to make a *niffag* of his holdings to his children, who become the provisional title holders. Their father becomes residual title holder of any improvements he has made on it (to which his children in due course acquire full title), and their father's corporation retains residual title to the holding minus the improvements. The children owe their father a portion of the

---

[17] As a corollary, it is probable that when a corporation allocates a plot of soil and trees to one of its members the latter may not plant or improve on it without permission of the *mwääniici*, if the improvements are likely to be long-lived, for by doing so he might be jeopardizing the corporation's interests. Unfortunately I am without the necessary information to make this definite.

produce of the trees he planted for them and owe their father's corporation in the person of its *mwääniici* a portion of the produce from that to which it holds residual title.[18] It frequently happens, therefore, that one plot of land and trees, while held under provisional title by only one party, comprises a number of discrete holdings (based on past improvements) in which different parties have residual title.

A series of successive transfers of this kind accounts for the complicated situation on a number of the land plots of Romonum at present (see Table 14 in Appendix B). In each case the history of the plot has been approximately as described below.

With the approval of his *mwääniici* a man made a *niffag* to his children of a plot which he held under provisional title from his corporation. Receiving this collectively, his children founded a corporation holding provisional title to the soil, to which their father's corporation held residual title. As a corporation, they also held provisional title to the trees which their father had planted on it for them and to which their father held residual title. As a corporation, the children divided the holding among themselves. Thus as individuals the children were provisional title holders of their respective portions of the soil and trees in relation to the corporation which they constituted. As a corporation, they were provisional title holders in relation to their father and his corporation. When their father died, the children as a corporation acquired full title to the trees which he had planted, but continued as provisional title holders of the soil, to which their father's corporation continued to hold residual title. With the permission of both his own and his father's corporation one of the children then made a *niffag* of his portion of soil and trees to his children, and planted new trees on the soil for them. The grandchildren thus became provisional title holders of that portion of soil and trees. Their father held residual title to the trees he had planted. Their father's corporation held residual title to the trees the grandfather had planted (for it had acquired full title to them on the grandfather's death), and the grandfather's corporation continued to hold residual title to the soil. The grandchildren owed their father, their father's corporation, and their grandfather's corporation shares in the produce. If they failed in this, any of the residual title holders could confiscate that to which he or it had formerly held full title. After their father's death, the grandchildren acquired full title to the trees he had planted. Thenceforth, these trees could no longer be confiscated though the remaining property could. When the trees their grandfather had planted died, their father's corporation dropped from the picture, since there was no longer anything to which it held residual title. The grandfather's corporation continued as residual title holder of the soil. If other portions of the soil and trees were similarly disposed of, there would be several corporations, all of them *jëfëkyr* of the previous corporation, with holdings on the original plot. The soil in each case would be held under residual title by the corporation of their common grandfather. This is by no means an uncommon situation. Appendix A gives two concrete examples of the processes involved.

The division and subdivision of plots through successive *niffag*, while keeping provisional holdings fairly equitably distributed (see Appendix B for statistics), reduces

---

[18] This situation corresponds to what was called "extra-lineage usufruct tenure" by Murdock and Goodenough (1947).

the size of individual holdings with each generation. There are cases where a man's holding on a given plot may consist of one tree. This process tends to scatter holdings, too, so that a man holds provisional title to a number of widely separated bits of land. The Trukese are aware of the problem, and wherever possible try not to break up existing holdings into smaller ones. If a man makes a *niffag* of several of his holdings to his children, they try to allocate them among themselves on the basis of one sibling to a holding. This does not entirely solve the problem, however, for at one time there are always some men with many children and few holdings to give them. Another solution to which the Trukese sometimes resort is the trading of adjacent holdings so as to make one larger one instead of two separate smaller ones. Keeping holdings within a corporation by having the husbands of its women make improvements on them is also used as a preventive, especially when the corporation's holdings are few. It should be added that aboriginal warfare and feuding produced periodic reshufflings of holdings into larger blocks as a result of conquest and the seizure of title. This remedy is, of course, no longer available.

It is not surprising that after several successive transfers from fathers to their children some of the obligations are forgotten. Each corporation is careful, however, to remember those plots in which it holds residual title to the soil. Sections of soil are thus traditionally associated with certain lineages or descent lines holding residual title to them, regardless of the situation respecting the trees on them or of the number of provisional title holders.[19] As residual title holders such lineages may step in and regain possession of the soil if the corporations holding provisional title become extinct. If the lineage holding residual title becomes extinct, the provisional title holders acquire full title to their portions. Named sections of soil to which a corporation holds full or residual title are its *jejif* ("sub-sections"). The aggregate of a corporation's *jejif* constitutes its *sööpw* ("section").[20] These aggregates are in turn frequently named, their names being used to designate the corporations holding them under full or residual title.

INHERITANCE[21]

One's own or adopted children are considered one's natural heirs. The general rule of inheritance can thus be stated simply: *any property to which a man, woman, or corporation holds full title at the time of their death or extinction is inherited by their children.* In the case of a corporation, its children are its *jëfëkyr* (the offspring of its men). If the full title holder is an individual, his children inherit collectively. If the full title holder is a corporation, the *jëfëkyr* separately inherit full title to the plots which their respective fathers had held under provisional title. Actually, when a corporation has no more child-bearing women, it usually permits its remaining men to make a *niffag* of their holdings to their children. As provisional title holders, the children thus acquire full title to the *niffag* when their fathers' corporation becomes extinct.

[19] Cf. the "lineage fee simple" of Murdock and Goodenough (1947).

[20] The terms *jejif* and *sööpw* have other connotations as well. A political district is a *sööpw* of the island, and the corporations (lineages) within it are its *jejif*.

[21] By *inheritance* is meant an orderly succession to title occasioned by the death of its former holder. Cf. Hoebel (1949: 354).

Neither a provisional nor a residual title is theoretically heritable, for on the death of either party to divided ownership the survivor acquires full title. As noted above, this is the reason why a full title holder may not make a *niffag* of his property to someone other than his children without their consent, for by doing so his children are disinherited with respect to the property given away.

In actuality very little property remains to be inherited on the death of an individual or of a corporation. The practice is to make a *niffag* of most of one's property to one's children when they reach adulthood. As long as one lives, then, one has the rights of a residual title holder. As a man gets older and is no longer vigorous he continues to receive his share of the produce, while the responsibility for working and maintaining the property rests with his children. *Niffag* thus constitutes a sort of old age insurance, and gives legal sanction to the dependence of the aged on their children via the obligations of the provisional to the residual title holder. Simiron of Romonum, for example, has one adopted son. To this, his only child, he has given as *niffag* much of his former land holdings. He also has planted a great many trees on land which his son had been allocated by his own corporation. These trees, too, represent a *niffag* to his son. When his son was called away from the island to serve on the newly created Trukese native police force, Simiron was greatly disturbed as to who would now keep him supplied with food, for he was too old himself to go out and work.

Personal effects of both men and women are not ordinarily subject to inheritance. Some are buried with the deceased, and the rest are burned in a special ceremony three or four days thereafter. It is believed that the good soul[22] of the deceased ascends to heaven in the smoke of this fire.

The Trukese say that men prefer to give some of their land holdings to their own children (with the permission of their corporation) and some to their sister's children. What they have not given their children is claimed by their sister's children. This was interpreted by Murdock and Goodenough (1947: 337) as meaning that land is inherited matrilineally unless previously given to the children with the permission of the matrilineal heirs. Actually, neither of these transfers, either to the children or the sister's children, is a matter of inheritance. That to which a man has full title as an individual is inherited by his children. However, a man does not ordinarily have full title to his land holdings. He holds them under provisional title from his corporation. In accordance with the rules governing divided ownership he cannot give these lands to his children without the permission of the residual title holders, i.e., at least his own corporation and possibly another as well. If he dies without having so transferred them to his children, full title reverts to his corporation, which reallocates the land to a junior member, who is, of course, frequently a younger sibling or sister's child of the deceased.

---

[22] Everyone is believed to have both a good soul, *gynyjëëc*, and a bad soul, *gynyggaw*. The good soul goes to heaven with the gods and may by possessing mediums act as intermediary between gods. and men. The bad soul remains on earth as a ghost who is malevolent and to be feared. It is possible that the gifts which are placed in a grave by relatives of the deceased and which are always of a type especially attractive to spirits and gods (e.g., perfume) represent a *niffag* which will obligate the good soul to be well disposed towards his surviving relatives and help them by possessing one of them, who will thereafter serve as his medium.

What at first appeared to be a matter of inheritance thus turns out to be subject to the rules of *niffag* and to accord with the rights, privileges, powers, and obligations of the parties in divided ownership.

GUARDIANSHIP

A *mwääniici*'s relationship to his siblings, both as administrator of their corporate holdings and as their representative and leader, provides a ready-made solution to the problem of selecting a guardian who will administer a child's property holdings until he reaches an age when he can take them over himself. A man's children are usually very young when, with the permission of his corporation, he gives them those of his holdings which he has in mind for them. This clears the way for him to plant on them and otherwise improve them without establishing title to trees on property which his corporation does not wish to alienate. In the latter event his children would inherit the trees while his corporation kept everything else, and serious conflict might break out between them over the property. By clearing this up when his children are as yet infants, a man can feel assured of future good relations between his corporation and his children. Although the father is now residual title holder, he continues to work and improve the property for his child. The child's interests as provisional title holder, however, must be handled by someone outside the father's corporation. Thus, if the father dies while his child is still young, the latter is not liable to be done out of his rights by his father's corporation. The person who fills this guardian role and who administers the child's rights is either the *mwääniici* of the lineage or descent line into which the child is born or the *mwääniici* of his particular generation in his descent line or lineage. In either case the guardian plays the role of older sibling to the child. The closer they are to being actual siblings, the better it is considered to be.

Once a guardian has been brought in on the property, he has the right to exercise the role of provisional title holder with its various rights, duties, and privileges. If a father dies before his child has come of age, the guardian exercises the role of full title holder, where full title is held, on behalf of his younger sibling. When the child comes of age, the guardian does not cease his connection with it. They hold it together as siblings, and it is their corporate property. Guardianship is not separable, therefore, from the sibling relationship and its corporate aspects.

While guardianship is usually exercised by the *mwääniici*, if there is no older "brother" it may be exercised by an older "sister." For example, a descent line in one of the lineages on Romonum is composed of one woman as *finniici* and her mother's sister's children, three women and a small boy. The boy has a different father from that of his sisters and holds provisional title to some land from him. The oldest of his sisters, however, exercises the guardianship over this land. A house has been built on it for the women of his descent line. There is an older "brother" in the lineage, but he is in a separate descent line and not so closely related by blood. Consequently the sister has stepped in as guardian instead. This may represent a special case, for the sister is an exceptionally forceful woman who has taken over the masculine responsibilities in her descent line since the death of its men during the war. One informant, shaking his head, remarked that she is "just like a man" in the way she goes at things. All other cases of guardianship noted on Romonum involved an older "brother."

SALE

Sale involves the transfer of full title from one party to another. In Trukese thinking this is equivalent to a trade. The seller and buyer each give the other property of value equivalent to that received. The Trukese word for such a transaction, *jekkisiwin*, means literally an "exchange." A full title holder is free to sell his property as he wishes so long as the corporation to which he belongs, and which with his permission has enjoyed the use of the property in its cooperative undertakings, will not suffer from the transaction. Unless a seller is himself *mwääniici* of his corporation, therefore, he clears the transaction with his *mwääniici* first. The latter may veto the sale, not because he has any rights himself to the property, but because his younger sibling is bound to obey him in any matters possibly affecting the welfare of their corporation, and because the solidarity of a corporation takes priority over the interests of any one of its members. If a corporation is the seller, the unanimous consent of its adult members is required before the transaction can be effected. In theory a seller does not need to clear the matter with his natural heirs because they suffer no loss from the sale, standing to inherit the property received in exchange, which is presumably of equivalent value. In practice, the natural heirs, being the seller's children, are aware of the impending sale and will voice their objections if they have any. Since a father cannot persist in refusing the request of any of his children who are over puberty, they can in effect veto a sale. Neither an heir's nor a corporation's veto, however, stems from property rules but from rules governing the parent-child relationship and the relationship of a *mwääniici* to his younger siblings. Since a sale of perishable goods is not likely to impair corporate interests, the seller may not take the trouble to clear such a transation with anyone, provided he has full title.

There is a correct procedure for making a sale. As one informant put it, the seller is embarrassed to name a price. It is the buyer who first names a price. If it is satisfactory, the seller agrees readily. If, however, he thinks it is too low, he is embarrassed to say so directly. He says instead: "It's up to you entirely." From this the buyer perceives he has made a poor offer and says: "Well, this is what I will give you now; later, when I can, I will bring the remainder of the exchange value of the property." He then takes his purchase away and thinks of how another day he may make amends for his poor offer, the transaction having taken on some of the aspects of *niffag*. The Trukese do not haggle or bargain in such an approach to sale as this. Usually a sale is initiated by the buyer, not the seller. The former offers to purchase something he wants, when it would be awkward to ask for it as a *niffag*. If the other refuses to sell, but makes a *niffag* of it to him anyway, the would-be purchaser is said to be extremely embarrassed and to feel heavily obligated. He considers what he can do in return to relieve his embarrassment. If the transaction goes through smoothly as a sale, however, there is no embarrassment and all obligations are considered closed. The books, as it were, are balanced.

It is quite possible for a man to sell trees to which he has full title and not sell the soil on which they stand. It is also possible for a man to sell his rights as a provisional title holder to another, provided the residual title holder is agreeable. At least there are a number of instances on Romonum where a provisional title holder of soil has sold his trees to someone else. The purchaser exercises the rights of full title holder to the trees and of provisional title holder to the soil, which is still said to belong to some lineage as residual title holder. There are other instances where the purchaser of trees has no rights to the soil as a provisional title holder. He may pick from his trees, but he may not plant any new ones on the soil.

It is rare for a corporation to agree to the sale of any soil to which it holds residual title. Only two instances were encountered in which the purchaser claimed to have bought the soil as well as what stood on it. One of these was on Uman Island, where a man claimed that an old woman for whom he had cared during the war had sold him the soil of certain lands just before she died. He had no witnesses to the sale, and her lineage mates were contesting his claim. The other case was on Romonum Island, where a Chinese trader had settled during the German administration and had acquired considerable land in payment of debts to his store. His son, the present holder, claims he holds full title to the soil. He is sufficiently powerful so that no one on the island openly contests his claim, but some maintain in private that the soil is properly the property under residual title of the lineages which had previously controlled it. Which claim has greater merit, of course, depends upon the facts in the transactions in question. The trader's son apparently does not render any of the obligations of a provisional title holder, so he is the *de facto* if not the *de jure* owner of the soil.

KIIS

So far this discussion has said little about the form of gift which the Trukese call *kiis*. We have seen that *niffag* results basically in a situation where the recipient is in some way obligated to the donor. Depending on the type of property, a recipient is obligated to make a return *niffag* or to render the obligations of a provisional title holder to the donor, who retains residual title. *Kiis* may be defined as that form of gift in which the giver retains no rights to the property given and in which the recipient assumes no obligation. It amounts to a voluntary transfer of full title without a compensatory payment of any kind.

Kiis plays an important role in the relations between brothers-in-law. In fact, informants almost always defined it as a gift from a man to his wife's brother. The word appears in other contexts, however, when emphasis is placed on the gratuitous nature of a gift.[23] Use of the word is usually accompanied by a wave of the hand such as we would use to express the notion of "total loss" or "written off the books."

A Trukese husband must render obedience and respect to his wife's brothers. This is a strictly one-sided relationship. Any land or trees held by a woman are worked by her husband, and in this activity he is responsible to her brothers, who are her guardians and the protectors of her interests. A husband must also help render his wife's obligations to her corporation for her. This means that her brothers may call upon him to donate

---

[23] E.g., the accusing words of the love song: *nupwen gaag meji toori neenijomw, kaa kiisegeni pwyny-womw ne manawej*, "When I was down at your place, you made a *kiis* of my life to your husband."

his labor and goods toward the creation or purchase of property by his wife's corporation. He is not a member of that corporation, however, and has no rights to the property so created or purchased. Nor is his wife's corporation obligated to him in any way in return for his donation. If a man made a *niffag* of his labor or goods to his wife's corporation, the latter would be obligated to him and hence not in so good a position to hold him to his responsibilities to his wife. Any gift, therefore, which a man makes to his wife's brothers is in the form of a *kiis* rather than a *niffag*, and carries no reciprocal obligation. It is for this reason, apparently, that *kiis* is identified in Trukese thinking with the brother-in-law relationship. It is also apparent why *kiis* as a form of transfer appears to be largely confined to this relationship.[24]

In practice, *kiis* works as follows. If a wife's brother expresses a need or liking for something which his sister's husband owns, the latter is expected to make a *kiis* of it to him. When a wife's brother borrows something from his sister's husband, which he may with only his sister's permission, he is expected to offer to return it. His sister's husband, however, must refuse to take it back, telling him to keep it. The wife's brother then brings something in return. The return gift, too, must be refused by the sister's husband. For him to accept it would make a *niffag* or trade of the transaction and would stigmatize him as a "bad" husband. The wife's brother is under obligation, according to one informant, to offer a return gift, but the husband is under obligation to refuse to accept it. By this refusal he makes it clear that the wife's brother is under no obligation to him for the original gift. It is this fact which confirms it as a *kiis*.

No cases were encountered in which property in soil or trees had been subject to *kiis*. This transaction seems to apply to movable goods only.

LOAN

Loan [25] on Truk is a temporary transfer of possession or the right to use property. A provisional title holder is free to lend his property in the same way as a full title holder. Property is always loaned for a specific purpose, which the borrower states when asking for the loan. When he has accomplished his purpose, he is expected to return what he has borrowed.

If the owner does not wish to lend his property, he does not say so in so many words. Instead, he claims that he is going to use it himself or that it is in disrepair and needs mending, or he makes up some other excuse.

If the borrower wishes to increase the likelihood of his getting the loan, he makes a *niffag* of some sort to the owner. On return of the loan, the borrower does not request a return of the *niffag*, so that it is not a security for the loan but a gift to predispose the owner to make the loan in the first place.

When a borrower fails to return a borrowed object promptly, the owner tells his wife or child to go to the borrower's house and inquire if he has finished using it, saying

[24] That it is not completely confined to this relationship is evidenced by an informant who made a *kiis* of his canoe to his father-in-law.

[25] There is no single word in Trukese indicating loan. The notion of use without ownership is expressed by a grammatical process rather than a lexical form, see below, p. 63.

that the lender will need it on the following day. The borrower then returns the borrowed article. If he refuses to do so, the owner feels obligated to the borrower, for only if he were heavily obligated to the borrower could the latter presumably make free with his property. He therefore drops the subject entirely and does not again request the return of the object. The loan has been transformed, as it were, into a *kiis*. At the same time, the true owner is angry. He will not again lend anything to the recalcitrant borrower nor do him any favors.

In returning non-productive property, a borrower does not make any kind of a gift to the owner. The loan is treated as a favor, which means that at some future date the borrower will, when occasion arises, grant the lender a return favor of a similar kind. In this sense a loan is treated like the *niffag* of non-productive property, but one requiring a lesser return favor.

The loan of productive property, however, does call for a return gift to the lender in the form of a share of the produce. If a person borrows a canoe, for example, the return will consist of a share in the fish caught with its help. If the canoe is borrowed to go to another island in search of food, some of the food brought back is given to the canoe's owner. This gift is called the *woseniwa* (lack of the canoe).

Another instance where a loan of productive property is fairly common has to do with land. It not infrequently happens that someone may request the provisional title holder of a plot of soil to give him permission to grow a garden on some portion of it. Once this is prepared, the borrower of the land has full title to the garden as a product of his labor. After the food has been harvested, however, the garden ceases to exist as property. The lender of the land may then indicate that he needs it and ask for the return of the garden site. Should he wish to take it back before the garden has been harvested, he must reimburse the borrower for the loss of the as yet unharvested produce.[26] A borrower, of course, always gives the lender a portion of the produce harvested from borrowed land.

The relations between borrower and lender are manifestly similar to those between provisional and residual title holder in divided ownership. They differ in that a lender is free to terminate a loan and take back his property at will, whereas a residual title holder can claim property back only for cause, namely the failure of the provisional title holder to fulfill his obligations. A provisional title holder, too, acquires full title on the death of the residual title holder. On the death of a lender, however, his heirs may claim back whatever has been loaned. A borrower gets no title on the lender's death.

CONQUEST AND SEIZURE

The transfer of full title by forceful seizure is well attested in the history of certain of the land plots on Romonum. In some cases this resulted from interlineage feuds in

[26] With the owner's permission an informant on Uman Island had made a garden on another man's land. The owner decided to take the land back and destroyed the as yet unharvested garden without speaking to the borrower about it. The borrower claimed that the lender had a perfect right to take his land back once the garden was harvested, but was seeking damages for the garden which had been destroyed and to which he, the borrower, had title.

which the defeated lineage was driven off the island. The lands which it had held under full title were thereupon taken over by the victorious lineage, while the provisional title holders took over those holdings to which the losers had held residual title. There are also cases where a strong lineage took possession of a desirable plot held by a weak lineage which could not contest the action. In one such instance the weak lineage held only provisional title; here the residual title holder also lost his rights, the seizing lineage acquiring full title. The appropriator was in several instances a lineage, in others a descent line, and in one instance a powerful individual. In each of these cases the seizing party acquired full title through failure of the legal residual title holders to assert their rights.

One case is reported where full title to a plot of land was transferred from one lineage to another as a sort of wergild to avert a feud following a murder. This was reported as an exceptional case, and it is to be noted that the feud shortly broke out again despite it.

The Trukese seem to feel that acquisition of title by conquest is a legitimate form of transfer. Cases of seizure from weak groups by strong ones when there is otherwise no quarrel between them, however, do not meet with their approval.

INCORPOREAL PROPERTY

Incorporeal property on Truk consists of all types of magic and medicine, lore of land and people, and the more difficult technological skills. Indeed, all knowledge is susceptible of being treated as property. This is especially likely if it is not widely known or is difficult to learn and has some practical or prestige value.

The Trukese pay little attention to formal property rules in making, using, and giving away objects that are easily replaced and whose manufacture requires only those skills which are known to everybody. Similarly, ordinary knowledge and skills are freely handed around without paying much attention to the formal rules governing incorporeal property. It appears, however, that even those skills which everyone must know in order to live are taught mainly within the framework of two overlapping social groups, the nuclear family and the lineage. A father and mother have the primary responsibility for the education of their children. When a person begins to function as a member of a cooperative sibling group, such as his descent line and lineage, its personnel also come to play an important educative role. It is, then, to his father, older brothers, and mother's brothers that a youth looks for training, while a girl looks to her mother, her maternal aunts, and her older sisters. It is from these relatives also that a person learns those technical skills and esoteric types of knowledge which are more carefully guarded as private property.

Functionally we may distinguish between two types of knowledge and skill. Application of the first results in the creation of corporeal property, while application of the second does not. The first type includes, for example, such magic and skills as are necessary in canoe making.

To ask a person to make a canoe is to ask him to make a *niffag* of a canoe to which he, as maker, has full title. Unless the maker's children permit the *niffag*, the canoe must be paid for just as if a finished canoe were being purchased. In Trukese thinking, to hire a man to build a canoe is the same thing as buying one he has already made for himself. If I ask a man to teach me how to make a canoe, I am in effect requesting from him a gift of the future canoes which I may make with this knowledge. The Trukese complete the analogy by requiring me to get the permission of the craftsman's natural heirs before he can teach me. If they refuse permission, I must buy the knowledge.

It is also important for the lineage to control such property in knowledge. Without it, the members must ask others for *niffag* of the products of their knowledge, or must hire others to make things for them. It is of great importance that the cooperative work group, the lineage, be capable of creating as much of its corporeal property as possible. For this reason a man may not withhold his knowledge from his lineage mates if it is to their interest as a corporation to possess it. This is analogous to the power of the corporation to veto a man's disposal of his personally owned property and to demand contributions from him toward the purchase of other property. A man's junior corporation mates are thus considered to have a right to learn what he knows, so that there will always be some member in possession of his knowledge.

There are, then, two sets of claimants to a man's knowledge, his children (who are in other respects his natural heirs) and his lineage mates (e.g., his sister's children).

The above considerations are extended by analogy to knowledge and skills which do not in their application directly create corporeal property, such, for example, as the magical and medicinal formulae used to cure illness. Knowledge of this kind is freely applied to the curing of a lineage mate or other close relative as a personal favor. Any one else, however, must pay in advance. The patient brings goods to the specialist and requests his aid. When cured, he is further obligated to the practioner and makes him a present. Such knowledge, then, not only has practical social value, but through its application can provide other forms of wealth for the specialist. To this knowledge, too, the specialist's children and lineage mates have a claim. Without their permission, he may not teach it to another unless he receives compensation for it. For if the specialist teaches someone else, he dissipates the monopoly his heirs will someday enjoy and lowers their future earning power.

The Trukese treat lore and fighting skills in the same way. The history of an island, the nature of the world, genealogies, mythology, all that the Trukese would classifv as facts or the explanation of facts are called by them *wuruwo*, best translated as "lore." To have a monopoly of such knowledge gives one an edge over his fellows when it comes to a land dispute or being listened to in district meetings. People are willing to pay for such information, if only for the prestige it may bring.[27]

Fighting skills in aboriginal times included knowledge of the manufacture as well

[27] Much of the information on which this report is based is considered *wuruwo* by the Trukese. For the writer to trade such information with informants helped overcome their reluctance to teach him what they knew. The native attitude toward *wuruwo* is well illustrated by an incident in which the writer was telling three informants how the earth turned on its axis to make night and day. When he finished they agreed among themselves not to tell others this important *wuruwo* so that they could be in exclusive possession of it. A great deal of the more technical information gathered by the ethnographic team on Truk was acquired only after the ethnographers had been sworn to secrecy as far as telling another Trukese was concerned.

as of the use of the various weapons: the club, spear, sling, knuckle-duster, and in more recent time the knife and rifle. Of great importance, too, was a knowledge of the various holds in a system of hand-to-hand encounter remotely reminiscent of Japanese jiu-jitsu.[28] To acquire these skills required considerable practice. In aboriginal times the various lineages used to hold periodic month-long training courses in their respective meeting houses. Although each political district fought engagements as a united military group, training was given independently by the various lineages. Those present were the men of the lineage, the husbands of its women, and the sons of its men, in con-formance with the pattern of confining the transmission of knowledge to one's children and one's lineage mates. It is said that by no means everyone knew all of the various weapons nor all of the tricks of hand-to-hand fighting. Knowledge of the proper magic was required in the manufacture of the several weapons and also to increase the effec-tiveness of their use thereafter. It is not surprising, therefore, that fighting skills were treated in the same way as other types of incorporeal property.

The teaching of magic (*roog*), medicines (*säfeej*), and lore (*wuruwo*) usually involves the same persons as attend the military training sessions. Instruction is carried on in the house where the women of the lineage or descent line reside together. Also present are their husbands, the men of the lineage or descent line, and the children of the latter. If someone else comes around, all instruction stops until the visitor departs, lest any secrets be let out.

Instruction is by no means confined, however, to such formal situations. Much of the teaching of magic and skills is limited to occasions when the teacher is called upon to apply his knowledge. When Kekin of Romonum, for example, was asked to build a canoe, he took this occasion to encourage his son, Renipu, to come out with him and get started on the long road to becoming a master builder, a *sineenap* (main knower). Renipu was but seventeen years old, and his interest was slight. As he grows older he will accompany his father more and more in such activities and slowly acquire the knowledge. Since the number of canoes a man builds is limited—there are no full-time specialists on Truk—it takes several years for him to transmit his knowledge, all of which must be committed to memory, to his sons or junior lineage mates. For this reason the more complicated specialized forms of knowledge are concentrated in the hands of older people. Romonum Island, with a population of 240 souls, for example, has but three recognized master canoe builders. All three have only a few active years ahead of them, and each now has adult children. There is also one man about 40 years of age who is a skillful adzeman and has made a couple of small canoes on his own. He is not considered the equal of the other three, however, and drops in on them when they are at work to see what additional pointers he can pick up. The younger people are just starting seriously to try their hands at such work. Several middle-aged men were attempting their first canoes when our field work was being conducted. These attempts were modest, and the builders were usually so related to the master builders

---

[28] This system, known as *jëëmmwënëëw*, is highly developed, including ways to disarm opponents equipped with various weapons, ways of knocking them overboard in canoe fighting, etc. It appears to be completely native in origin.

that they could call them for advice and help, and even to perform for them some of the more critical operations such as laying out the right measurements.

The monopoly of the older people over magic and skills has been somewhat augmented by the fact that in recent years some of it has fallen into disuse. Nevertheless, informants insisted that the situation today is much the same as in aboriginal times in this respect. They pointed out that the practice of most important skills requires sexual continence of a craftsman over long periods, too great a privation for younger men successfully to observe. Younger people have the attitude that such things are for oldsters, and that they are not supposed to know or care about them until they get older. A fundamental factor appears to be the length of time it takes to learn in the informal, intermittent training situation. Most important, however, is the fact that a person must learn from his father or an older lineage mate. Until the death of an established craftsman, his pupil is not likely to be called upon to exercise his skills and knowledge for others or to have the chance to reap the attendant rewards. Only as some of the older experts die off do those a little younger begin to get recognized as experts themselves, since they serve much the same clientele of kinsmen and neighbors as their predecessors did. In line with this is the expert's tendency to transmit his knowledge piecemeal, withholding some portion of it until he is too old to exercise his skill. This may be likened to the situation in which a giver of productive corporeal property retains a residual title to it, full title being acquired by the recipient only on the donor's death. Here again the teaching of knowledge is analogous to the *niffag* of corporeal property. It is quite probable, too, that a pupil has definite obligations to his teacher in connection with the application of his knowledge and that these obligations terminate only on the teacher's death.[29] The Trukese commonly enquire respecting a craftsman, *mësëwen ijë?* ("whose pupil?").

Incorporeal property tends to be associated with one sex or the other depending on the degree to which it is related to activities performed exclusively by one sex. Otherwise there is no difference between men and women with respect to the possession of incorporeal property. It frequently happens, indeed, that a woman knows the magical formulae associated with men's work, and vice versa. While such a woman will not practice the skill herself, she is in a position to teach what she knows to a son, who will exercise this knowledge.

All religious practitioners as well as craftsmen and magicians are owners of the knowledge necessary to exercise their specialties. The Trukese make no distinction between them and other skilled personnel. There is one important exception to this rule, the spirit medium (*wäätawa* or *wään ëny*). His (or her) position is not based on knowledge so much as on having been possessed by a spirit. This spirit is in no way classed as the medium's property, nor can it be inherited automatically by a son or lineage mate. The position of a spirit medium, therefore, is different from that of a property holder, except as he uses his abilities to diagnose illness.

There are systems of knowledge which are subject to special rules of their own.

[29]Since the writer had not gained this perspective on the subject before leaving the field, it did not occur to him to inquire into this aspect of the problem.

For example, to learn knot divination a pupil must pay the diviner (*sowupwe*) even if the latter is his own father or mother's brother. An *jitag* (a sort of lawyer, general, diplomat and orator all rolled into one, who occupies the most prestigeful position in Trukese society) is alleged never to teach his own children as much as he teaches his sister's children. This contention does not, however, appear to be supported by the genealogical connections of the past *jitag* of Romonum Island. Despite special rules governing specific forms of incorporeal property, their over-all organization is analogous to that of corporeal property and does not require a new conceptual framework to make them intelligible.

LABOR AS A COMMODITY

The automatic acquisition of full title to the products of one's husbandry makes of labor a commodity similar to other types of property.[30] Just as a corporation may call upon its members to donate their corporeal and incorporeal property, so it may call on them to donate their labor and the products thereof. It is this which enables the corporation to function as a cooperative work group and to meet its collective obligations.

If a man helps another to do some work, the latter is obligated to him just as if he had received a *niffag* or loan and considers how he may make a return favor in the future. The Trukese speak of making a *niffag* of their labor. If a man works for wages, as occurs nowadays, he is viewed as selling his labor and its products to his employer. This is comparable to a trade and leaves no obligations on either side except to fulfill the bargain as agreed. As with corporeal property, a man may be called upon to make a *kiis* of his labor and its products to his wife's brothers.

Labor, then, is treated by the Trukese in much the same way as non-productive, corporeal property. It is intelligible within the same conceptual framework as being subject to sale, *kiis*, and *niffag*.

MONEY

Money has been introduced into Truk only within the past 50 years. There was no aboriginal money such as occurs elsewhere in the Carolines, notably on Palau and Yap. Purchases were paid for in goods (*pisek*). Since a fairly lively trade was carried on with Puluwat to the west and the Mortlock Islands to the southeast, there was a system of standardized equivalents of value. A canoe was equal to so many lavalavas (woven on a loom from hibiscus and banana fiber), so many pieces of processed turmeric (important aboriginally as a cosmetic), so many belts of shell beads, etc. The chief imports from Puluwat were *sään* (heavy rope), *nyyn* (light rope), *kijeki* (sleeping mats plaited from pandanus leaves), *kiin* (shell-bead belts), and *menijuk* (sailing canoes). Truk's chief exports were *cëëjityr* (woven lavalavas), *jakkacawar* (woven loin-cloths), *tejuk* (turmeric), *nëë* (perfume), and *suupwa* (tobacco).[31] One informant gives the following table of equivalents.

[30] The native word for labor is *jagaag*, which seems to be the doubled form of the same root as appears in *jageej* (take hold of something).

[31] These goods and the technical processes by which they were manufactured are described by Krämer (1932) and LeBar (MS).

1 *cëëjityr* equals 1 hundred-fathom coil of *sään*, or 1 sleeping mat, or 2 sticks of turmeric.
1 coil of *nyyn* equals 1 large bottle of tobacco.
1 *menijuk* equals up to 20 lavalavas and loin-cloths plus possibly 10 sticks of turmeric.

Perhaps the closest thing to a standard medium of exchange was processed turmeric. Turmeric was usually grown by a corporation as a cooperative undertaking, and when processed became corporate property under the *mwääniici*'s control.[32] Individuals presumably were allotted shares for personal use.

As a result of the German, Japanese, and American administrations, the natives have become thoroughly aware of the value of money in relation to specific situations. It is needed to pay taxes and is required for the purchase of goods from local retail outlets. Money is in fairly wide use in native transactions, though barter continues as the more practical form of exchange. Two informants, for example, had no trouble in estimating the cash price of a coconut tree (if not old) at $2.00 and that of a breadfruit tree at $5.00, a big one fetching perhaps as much as $10.00. Sales of trees are, however, fairly rare. If they should become more common, one might predict that the price would rise to accord with their economic importance. As the present prices suggest, money plays no part in the domestic food economy. It is needed to purchase food by only a handful of natives. Except for them, money is treated simply as an important sort of movable property (*pisek*). One may make a *niffag* of money, trade it for goods or for labor, and have it appropriated by one's wife's brothers as a *kiis*.

Payment of taxes is considered a lineage (i.e., a corporation) matter. A native who earns money donates it to his corporation for the payment of its members' head tax. The Trukese claim that during the Japanese administration it was necessary for every lineage to have someone working for wages with the Japanese or with the Okinawan fishermen or earning cash through copra production in order to pay taxes. Even now, when the annual $2.00 head tax on able-bodied men comes due, there is a stimulus to copra production in order to raise the necessary cash. For these reasons, while money is the private property of the person who earns it, he is not always free to spend it as he wishes. His corporation has too strong a stake in the cash and, as with other types of property, may call on him to donate money to its treasury.

The writer found himself party to an episode involving money which illustrates the legalistic approach of the Trukese toward property disputes as well as the position of money in the property system. The Protestant congregation on Romonum decided to hold what the natives call a "food war" in connection with the 1947 Christmas feast. For this purpose two lineages of the Pwereka sib and the three lineages of the Jacaw sib organized themselves into opposing teams. The aim was to see which side could present the other with the greater variety and quantity of food at the feast.[33] It became known by the Jacaw team that the Pwereka side had obtained some rice. Jacaw had none and immediately tried pulling all the wires it could to obtain some to match that of Pwereka. As a participant member of the Protestant congregation and the adopted

---

[32] Turmeric is now grown only by a few persons specifically for the Puluwat trade, since it has dropped out of local use with the introduction of European clothing.

[33] Competitive feasts of this kind appear to be a well established institution. See the account by Bollig (1927: 182-184).

brother of a husband of one of the Jacaw women, the writer duly reported for work to help the Jacaw side. The particular lineage with which he was identified had only two able-bodied men, the old head of the lineage, Simiron, and his sister's son, Jakiwo. It happened that Jakiwo was married to a sister of the local storekeeper, whose younger brother, Puruuta, the island policeman, was in turn married to a sister of Jakiwo. Jakiwo knew that the storekeeper had a bag of rice and asked to purchase some of it. The storekeeper, being on the authoritative end of the brother-in-law relationship, refused on the ground that he needed it himself for his own household. After all other efforts failed, Simiron gave the writer money his lineage had raised and asked if he could purchase rice from the Navy commissary, to which the natives did not have access. The writer agreed, but found that he was two dollars short of the necessary price and out of cash himself. Puruuta had just received his policeman's pay and was able to supply the necessary money. When the writer went to pay it back later in the day, Puruuta refused to accept it, saying that he was embarrassed at not having helped his wife's lineage in its preparations for the food war and asking the writer to make it clear to Simiron and Jakiwo that he had contributed two dollars towards the purchase of the rice in fulfillment of his obligations. Simiron and Jakiwo were pleased with Puruuta's *kiis*.

After the feast was over, half of the rice remained. Simiron and Jakiwo decided to keep it as the corporate property of their lineage to be used only for special occasions, rice being considered a luxury food. Meantime, the storekeeper had run out of rice and was himself unable to acquire any more.[34] He therefore sent his sister to Simiron to purchase 50 cents' worth of the Jacaw rice. Since she was Simiron's niece by marriage and therefore a "daughter" (see discussion of the kinship system), Simiron could not under the rules of kinship behavior deny her a request, let alone refuse to sell her something. He was forced, therefore, to give her a *niffag* of rice, even though he was well aware of the fact that the storekeeper was behind it. When Jakiwo heard of this he was outraged that the storekeeper should have refused him rice before but now was getting free donations of it from him and his lineage. When informed of Jakiwo's anger, the storekeeper felt under obligation to return the rice. In retaliation, however, he demanded repayment of the $2.00 which his younger brother had contributed towards the purchase of the rice on the ground that he, as *mwääniici* of his corporation, had never given Puruuta permission to give the money away.

This episode reflects the fact that money has not as yet become fully distinguished in the property system as something which a junior member of a corporation may give to someone else without preliminary clearance with his *mwääniici*. Puruuta acted as though no permission were necessary. When it was convenient, however, his older brother could allege that money was the sort of property where permission is necessary.

There is similar uncertainty about the power of a wife's brothers to appropriate money as in the case of other sorts of movable goods. Simiron regularly turned over to his wife the weekly three dollars he earned as an informant. His wife gave a dollar of it

---

[34] The storekeeper's standard of living was sufficiently above that of most natives so that rice was a standard article in his diet.

to her brother as *kiis* from Simiron, another dollar as *niffag* to her son, and kept a dollar for herself and Simiron. Simiron did not like to see his money disappearing in this manner, but felt there was nothing he could do about it. On the other hand, the local school teacher, who had little time to work the land and prepare food for his family and who was largely dependent for food on what he could buy from his small salary, refused to make a *kiis* of any of his earnings to his wife's brothers. He explained that they could take his other movables of the kind traditionally given as *kiis*, but not his money since this was his source of food. His case is rather unique because few Trukese depend on money for the acquisition of other than luxury foods. Should money become important to any large number of natives for the purchase of the food necessary for daily life, it is possible that resistance will develop to its being classed as the sort of movable goods with which one's wife's brothers can make free, and that money will come to be regarded as productive property.

Except for these areas where native opinion is as yet in conflict, money appears to be fairly well integrated into the native property system. Even where conflict exists, it is not between a native and an alien set of attitudes, but is rather a matter of just how the native conceptual system is to apply to money.

SANCTIONS

There are three main ways in which the property rights of others may be infringed on Truk. The first is theft or the deliberate destruction of another's property. The second is trespass. The third is default in one's obligations as a provisional title holder or as the recipient of a loan or *niffag*. To refuse a *kiis* to a wife's brother is more a breach of marital than of property relations.

The possibility of stealing seems to arouse considerable anxiety in the Trukese today as well as formerly, and this despite the fact that they scrupulously respect each other's rights when in anyone else's company. They seem always ready to attribute the worst of motives to their fellows.

In aboriginal times no formal action was taken by the community against a thief. It was up to the individual and his corporation (lineage) to collect damages or kill the offender, the latter action frequently leading to a feud with the offender's lineage. If the identity of a thief was unknown, divination was resorted to in order to discover it. The injured party demanded restitution or payment. If the thief refused, a fight resulted. District chiefs did not interfere directly in such matters. Informants indicated that for them to do so would have been to court the enmity of the entire community. On the other hand, a chief used to preach to his people about the evils of stealing and exhort them to respect each other's rights in order to hold down dissension within his district.

Trespass applies to two types of situation. The first has to do with entering another's house without permission. Such action is construed as motivated by a desire to steal something, to leave an object which will sorcerize its occupants, or, if at night, to commit adultery. Its occurence is bound to precipitate, if not a fight, at least bad relations with the occupants of the house.

The other type of trespass consists of entering a section of lagoon or a plot of land on which a "no trespass" sign has been placed. Such a sign is made by tying a young coconut leaflet on a stake in the water or around the trunks of trees. This is called *röög* (not to be confused with *roog*, magic). A man may put a *röög* sign on his property if he is going to be away from his district on a protracted visit. It is (or at least used to be) customary when someone dies for his relatives to put a *röög* sign on his coconut trees and fishing areas. It may be that this action provides a "cooling off" period before settlement of his holdings. In any case, it serves notice on members of the community that trespass will be construed as an insult to the memory of the dead and will be done at the risk of one's life. After a few months such a *röög* is lifted ceremonially, and the property is taken over by the proper heirs. Informants denied that the violator of such a taboo sign on property incurs any penalties of supernatural origin. Violation involves only the risk of having open season declared on one's life by the property holder and/or his lineage mates.

One might assume that dependence on private sanctions for breaches of this kind would provide a situation in which powerful persons and lineages could take advantage of weaker ones. While this has happened, the entire community is likely to unite against a too frequent offender. The property system does not depend, however, on the threat of direct retribution alone. Trouble makers tend to be socially isolated. Even their own lineage mates may eventually withdraw support if their activities too frequently put the lineage in embarrassing situations. These less formal sanctions are usually effective, and a person or group is not likely to violate another's property rights deliberately and openly except with the definite purpose of precipitating a show-down.

Similar considerations apply to the failure to fulfill one's obligations as the recipient of a *niffag* or loan, or as a provisional title holder. Where *niffag* of non-productive property is concerned, sanctions are expressed informally by the culprit's getting a bad name and being talked about. When a provisional title holder fails in his obligations, the residual title holder must rely on the power of his lineage to confiscate the property, the situation resembling that where a theft has occurred. In addition to the threat of open conflict and social ostracism, however, there is an important moral factor, which we may call a sense of obligation. This is thoroughly inculcated in early life, and the natives appear to be uncomfortable if they are suspected of having failed in their obligations.

Obligation or indebtedness is called *kinissow* by the Trukese. The sense of obligation has a wide application to many situations, a number of which at first glance seem strange to us. A native is *kinissow* to anyone who has done him a favor and to anyone who has suffered or been deprived because of his actions. As a matter of formal courtesy, he says *kinissow* where we would say both "thank you" and "excuse me," or "much obliged" and "I beg your pardon." The recipient of a *niffag* or loan is *kinissow* to the giver, a provisional title holder to the residual title holder, a visitor to his host. People are *kinissow* to the good chief, to their gods and benevolent spirits,[35] to anyone who by

[35] This has been directly transferred as the basis for one's relationship with the Christian divinities.

his behavior expresses his good will towards them. At the same time a discovered thief is *kinissow* to his victims; an adulterer to the injured spouse; a defaulting provisional title holder to the residual title holder. The way to diminish one's sense of *kinnisow* is to make amends, to do something for the other person to compensate his loss, deprivation, or injury. To be heavily *kinissow* is an uncomfortable state of affairs requiring positive action. The sense of this term is perhaps best rendered by our somewhat obsolete word "beholden."

Since *kinissow* enters into many situations of both major and minor import in everyday life, indeed whenever anyone does another a favor, it is thoroughly ingrained as a part of what we may call the native conscience. It therefore provides a strong motivation to operate within the property rules. It is apparently this inner sanction, appreciably more than the threat of external sanctions, which keeps the Trukese operating within their various behavioral codes.

SOME METHODOLOGICAL CONSIDERATIONS

Two fundamentally different approaches are possible in the analysis of property relationships. The first is to seek to isolate specific configurations of rights, privileges, and powers (and their counterparts: duties, lack of rights, and liabilities) and to classify types of ownership and title accordingly. The second is to start with linguistic forms, both lexical and grammatical, having to do with the relations of persons to objects of ownership and to isolate semantic criteria on which their usage is predicated, deriving types of possessive relationships therefrom. Our analysis has been based primarily on the first approach, though we have used the second to get helpful clues as we went along.

An analysis based exclusively on the linguistic approach has been published by Capell (1949), who in discussing ownership throughout the Pacific area draws certain conclusions about its expression on Truk. Briefly he classifies ownership on Truk as follows:[36]

1. Simple ownership, expressed by suffixing a possessive pronoun to the word for the object possessed, e.g., *waa* (canoe), *wääj* (my canoe); *wuuf* (clothes), *wufej* (my clothes); *fëny* (land), *fënywej* (my land); *saam* (father), *semej* (my father).

2. Ownership from the standpoint of the object owned, expressed by suffixing a possessive pronoun to a classifying word which is then followed by the word for the object owned. Capell makes two subdivisions here: (*a*) by the use to which an object will be put, e.g., *jenej määj* (my-cooked-portion-to-eat breadfruit), *wocaj wuuc* (my-uncooked-portion-to-eat banana), *wynymej nyy* (my-drink coconut); (*b*) by class of object owned without reference to use, e.g., *waaj citosa* (my-canoe automobile), *wufej sëëc* (my-clothes shirt), *semej sömwoon* (my-father chief), *neji najif* (my-child knife), *jääj rawyses* (my-general-object trousers).

While it is not our purpose here critically to evaluate Capell's classification, there are good grounds for suspecting its validity as far as Trukese grammar is concerned.

[36]It will be noted that Capell does not distinguish between the legal concepts of "possession" and "ownership." Cf. Cook (1933).

Distinction between simple and classificatory modes of possession becomes unnecessary when we consider that in any expression involving a possessive, the pronoun is always suffixed to the word denoting the class of object possessed. It is entirely optional as to whether or not this is followed by a modifier. The expressions *neji mwään* (my-child adult-male, i.e., my adult son), *neji najif* (my-child knife, i.e., my knife), and *neji kykkyn* (my-child little, i.e., my little child) are syntactically identical. If the context were clear, one could simply say *neji* (my child object) of all of these without a following modifier. Similarly one can say *wääj* (my canoe object) for either a canoe or an automobile, or one can differentiate them by saying *wääj waa* (my-canoe canoe) and *wääj citosa* (my-canoe automobile). In short, where we distinguish between nouns and adjectives, Trukese distinguishes between forms which may be inflected by suffixed possessives and those which may not, but either type may function as a modifier of the first. There is by this interpretation but one system of possessive formation in Trukese, namely by suffixation of pronominal forms to classifying forms, and not two as suggested by Capell.

His analysis, however, remains highly suggestive, for by his reasoning when a Trukese speaks of an object as *neji* (my child) he means that he possesses it in a different way from that when he speaks of it as *wääj* (my canoe) or *jääj* (my general class of object). This is certainly reflected in the contrast between *neji mwään* (my adult son) and *jääj mwään* (my older brother), or between *jenej määj* (my portion of cooked breadfruit for me to eat) and *jääj määj* (my breadfruit for other than eating purposes). Unquestionably the possessor signifies a different kind of relationship between himself and an object according as he classifies it. The fact that the same object may be differently classified, with a difference in meaning accordingly, is proof of it.

How does this relate to concepts of ownership within the framework of property relationships? Very little, if at all. We have seen that Trukese behavior differs depending on whether the property concerned is productive or non-productive of food. The use of classifying forms in their language, however, cuts right across this distinction. One says *neji piik* (my-child pig) and *neji najif* (my-child knife), but pigs are classed with productive and knives with non-productive property. One also says *neji mwään* (my adult son), but persons are not objects of ownership in the way that animals and material things are. A father cannot subject his son to any transaction nor enjoy the rights, priviliges, and powers of full, residual, or provisional title with respect to him. We obtain similar results when we seek to correlate other possessive classifiers with differences in property relationships. While linguistic classification unquestionably reflects differences in the ways in which the subject and object of a possessive pronoun are related to one another, the criteria on which these differences are based fall outside the realm of ownership in a property sense.

The question remains as to how Trukese concepts of ownership are reflected in their language, now that examination of their use of possessive formations gives negative results. Of immediate importance to a Trukese are holdings from which he gets his food. Such a holding is called an *jäpär* (*jäpäri*, my land holding). This word would never be used for something to which one held only residual title; it indicates actual possession

63

or control for purposes of food exploitation, whether one is full or provisional title holder. In speaking of property in land, another frequent expression is *fënywej* (my land, my home island, depending on context). As "my land," it means simply that a person has some kind of interest in the plot in question, either as full, residual, or provisional title holder, or as member of a corporation holding any of these titles. A third expression is "my land with (or from) So-and-so," as in *fënywej me Kinöwus* (my land from Kinöwus, or Kinöwus' and my land). It means that the speaker holds the land under provisional title from Kinöwus, who is residual title holder, or that the speaker and Kinöwus hold the land jointly as a minor corporation in which Kinöwus is *mwääniici*. It may also mean that the speaker owns a garden on soil which he exploits on loan from Kinöwus. This expression is regularly used as the polite way of speaking about a holding in the presence of its residual title holder. As far as the writer knows, these are the standard ways of expressing "ownership" of land. It is important to note that none of them indicates the precise nature of legal ownership, and that there are no Trukese words which can be translated by what we have called full ownership, divided ownership, full title, residual title, or provisional title. Neither are there any grammatical forms functioning in this way.

To acquire property as a result of sale, inheritance, *kiis*, or *niffag* is expressed by suffixing the form *-ni* to the word denoting the class of object acquired, e.g., *wufeni* (acquire clothes, *wuuf*), *wääni* (acquire a canoe, *waa*), *newyni* (acquire a child-object, as of a knife), *jääni* (acquire something not otherwise classified, *jaa-*). Use, under loan or otherwise, is expressed by doubling the word denoting the class of object borrowed, e.g., *wufowuf* (use or wear clothes), *waawa* (use or ride in a canoe), *newynew* (use a child-object, such as a knife), *jaaja* (use something otherwise not classified). Elbert (1947: 85) gives the following sentence showing the difference between acquisition under some form of title and simple use: *wywa fëffëny jeej fëny gë wyse wesewesen fënyweni* (I'm using this land but I-have-not really acquired-title-to-it).[37] This difference in meaning applies, however, only to objects which can be owned within the framework of the property system. When parents get a child they also *newyni* (acquire) it, just as they *newyni* a knife. When they behave as parents to a child, they also *newynew* it, just as when they behave in ways appropriate to the use of a knife. But as we said before, a parent does not acquire title to a child in the same way that he acquires title to a knife, nor does he have the same rights, powers, and privileges with respect to it. In its broader sense, *-ni* simply means that one has entered into a relationship with an object or person such that one enjoys certain rights in that relationship which are denied to others, without any implication as to the nature of these rights or their alienability, except as may be inferred from the total context.

Linguistic forms which proved most helpful in our analysis of property were those denoting transactions. Analysis of their use provided an initial opening for isolating the different configurations of rights, privileges, and powers to which objects other than persons are subject on Truk. Our primary aim, however, was to get at the latter by

---

[37] It will be noted that the forms to which *-ni* can be suffixed and the forms which may be doubled to indicate use are the same ones that can take a suffixed possessive pronoun.

whatever means possible, so that our analysis is not based on the words for transactions alone.

Our aim was that the conceptual framework finally arrived at for describing property relations should account fully for all of our data, leaving as few exceptions to any rule as possible. Wherever exceptions were encountered, our framework was modified accordingly. The extent to which such modifications were necessary can be seen by comparing the present formulation with that presented in an earlier publication (Murdock and Goodenough, 1947). In this connection, the criterion of economy has been consistently employed. No more forms of ownership have been established than proved necessary to account for the different configurations of rights and privileges presented by our data. To this end we have found the linguistic criterion of "complementary distribution" (Bloch and Trager, 1942: 42–5) exceedingly helpful, though applied to non-linguistic data. This can be illustrated in connection with *niffag*.

It will be recalled that what the Trukese call *niffag* can result in radically different relationships between the parties concerned. With one *niffag* a recipient has permanent and formalized obligations to the giver, with another his obligations are informal and impermanent. Within the first there is additional variation in the form which a recipient's obligations take, as reflected in the different kinds of food he gives a residual title holder in connection with canoes, pigs, chickens, and land. Does this mean that we have to distinguish two or more distinct transactions, all called *niffag* in Trukese, or that we are dealing with different aspects of a single transaction, analogous to the allophones of a phoneme or the forms of a verb in language? It was found that of the various configurations of obligations resulting from *niffag* only one could occur with any one form of property and that it occurred with this one consistently. The forms of obligation resulting from *niffag* were thus in complementary distribution with respect to forms of property, and could be classed as different expressions of a single type of transaction. Contrariwise, the occurences of *kiis* and *niffag* were applicable in part, at least, to the same forms of property. Since they contrasted with each other, it was necessary to consider *kiis* and *niffag* as distinct transactions.

MATRILINEAL KIN GROUPS

INTRODUCTION

WE HAVE seen that the Trukese are organized into corporations in which membership is based on matrilineal descent. Tracing descent through the female line also serves to affiliate persons into groups which have no corporate functions. The use of matrilineal descent does not mean that the natives do not count their fathers and relatives on their fathers' side as kinsmen; they do. There is also a well defined kin group composed of near relatives on both the father's and mother's side. Its functions, however, are distinct from those of the several types of matrilineal kin group.

In all, there are five distinct types or levels of matrilineal groups. Two of them, the descent line and lineage, have already been encountered in connection with corporations. Not all of the five types are readily discernible to the casual observer. In specific instances two or more may coincide. Nor do the natives have a terminology consistent with them, since they frequently rely on context and circumlocution to indicate the particular type to which they are referring.[1] Exogamy and an internal organization based on the sibling relationship are about all that the five groups have in common. Native law does not approve marriage between fellow members in any of them.

There are five criteria by which these groups are severally to be defined: (1) common name, (2) common ancestry, (3) common residence in the same political district, (4) common membership in a major corporation, i.e., one whose members belong to no larger corporation, and (5) common membership in a minor corporation, i.e., one which is included in a larger corporation. The first criterion defines the most extensive and loosely knit of the five kin groups. Successive addition of each of the remaining criteria reduces the size of the group and increases the tightness of its organization and the closeness of the bonds between its members. The five kin groups are:

1. The sib. A group of people who share a common name. An individual always takes the name of his mother's sib. Members of a sib may be located on more than one island or in more than one political district, and may have membership in more than one major corporation. The bonds between members are weak, since for practical purposes they consider themselves related in name only, though recognizing that in theory their common name presumes some ultimate common ancestry in the female line.

2. The subsib. The members of a sib who share a definite tradition of common ancestry in the female line, though it is not traceable genealogically. Members of a subsib may be located on more than one island or in more than one political district, and may have membership in more than one major corporation. The bonds between members are strong, since they consider themselves to be actually related.

---

[1] It is this fact which apparently led such previous reporters as Krämer (1932), Bollig (1927), and Hall and Pelzer (1946) to mention only one of the five types and to ascribe to it in various ways the functions of the others.

3. The ramage.[2] The members of a subsib who have residence in the same political district, but who are organized into more than one major corporation.

4. The lineage. The members of a subsib who are organized into a single major corporation. The bonds between members are very strong, and they can often trace common descent genealogically from a remembered ancestress.

5. The descent line. The members of a lineage who are organized into a minor corporation. The bonds between members are very strong, and they can always trace common descent genealogically from a remembered ancestress, who may be a mother, grandmother, or great grandmother.

The lineage, which is functionally the most important of the kin groups on Truk, will be considered first. As a major corporation its outlines are clearer than are those of the descent line, so that its delineation will facilitate description of the latter as well as of the non-corporate kin groups, the sib, subsib, and ramage.

THE LINEAGE

NAME AND PHYSICAL ARRANGEMENT

The lineage has been defined as a major corporation, one whose members belong to no larger corporation, though they may belong to different minor corporations (descent lines) within it. The members of a lineage can usually trace actual genealogical relationship with each other through the female line, though this is not necessarily the case. While the genealogies are not known to all members of a lineage, they are normally known to the older members, who pass them on as younger members grow into positions of greater responsibility. Genealogical knowledge is important because of its usefulness in tracing back the history of property held under various forms of title by the lineage as a corporation. The genealogies of the various lineages on Romonum Island show that often the name of an ancestress in the female line is no longer remembered while the name of her husband is, if it was through him that the lineage acquired an important part of its land holdings. The genealogies can usually be traced back four or five generations from that of the oldest living member.

There is no Trukese word which means "lineage" in the strict sense in which it has been defined above. A lineage may be referred to as a *tetten* (line) of a sib, subsib, or ramage. The terms most frequently used in aboriginal times were *jetereges* or *cöö*, the latter apparently meaning "people." These terms are also applied to the subsib, but within one district they ordinarily refer to a lineage. Since the coming of missionaries in the latter part of the nineteenth century, the Trukese have taken over the English word "family" as *faameni*, which is similarly used to mean both subsib and lineage. It is now in regular use on Romonum, the older terms being rarely heard.[3] Another common way of referring to a lineage is by the sib name of its members. This ordinarily creates little confusion, since in the majority of cases, Romonum being an exception, a

---

[2]This term is borrowed from Firth (1936: 371), who introduced it to designate the branching but related lineages of Tikopia.

[3]It should be pointed out that the term *faameni* never has the English meaning of "family" but always refers to a matrilineal kin group.

sib is represented by only one lineage in a given district. It is apparently this fact which has led previous reporters to fail to distinguish the lineage from the sib.

As a corporation a lineage holds certain plots of land. Its members, of course, must have provisional title to plots of soil in order to support themselves. An old and long established lineage in any district has a series of plots to whose soil it holds either full or residual title. The corporate property of newer lineages may consist only of provisional titles to soil. The plots of soil held by a lineage under full or residual title, regardless of who has provisional title to them, collectively constitute its territory or estate. Plots in the territory of an older lineage in a political district are more likely to be contiguous than are those of newer lineages. A lineage territory is known as a *söpwun faameni* (lineage section, from *sööpw,* section).[4] Such a territory is frequently named and a lineage may be referred to by this territorial name as the "people of such and such a place." In fact, a lineage, as a social group, is frequently referred to as the people of one *sööpw.* In Trukese thinking, therefore, each lineage has a locality, even though its holdings may in reality be widely scattered.

In aboriginal times there used to be associated with most lineages a dwelling house, *jiimw.*[5] This house varied in size depending on the number of its inhabitants. Since married men normally went to live in the *jiimw* of their wives' lineages, the occupants of an *jiimw* were the women of a lineage and their husbands. The only males of the lineage who resided there were boys below puberty. A large *jiimw* was usually partitioned off into sleeping compartments along its side walls under the eaves, one for each married woman and her husband with their small children, and a separate one for the unmarried girls past puberty. The house had a sand floor spread over with coconut fronds. Its occupants slept and sat on mats plaited from pandanus leaves. The central part of the house formed a sort of living room in which minor cooking was done over an open fire, where ordinary meals were taken, and where the members of the household whiled away the time before going to bed.[6]

Not all houses were of this type, for some were much smaller, without partitions, and were occupied by only one or two couples. Such houses were used when a lineage had only a few women, or when a man brought his wife to live on his own land instead of going to live in her lineage household. In the latter case it was customary to build a separate house for the man and wife, since it is normally taboo for a man to sleep in the same house with his sisters. A small house might also be built alongside the main one if the latter became too crowded.

The old, large lineage house is in little use today. The Trukese now live in smaller houses of the old type or in new-style houses, raised on posts and built of planks with corrugated iron roofs. These smaller houses are still occupied by the women of a lineage, either singly or in pairs, and are clustered together either by lineage or by descent line.

[4]This is not to be confused with the *söpwun fëny* (section of the land or island) which is the territory of a political district.

[5]It is called *jimwejicëën* on Uman.

[6]The details of housing, house construction, furnishings, etc., are fully discussed by F.M. LeBar (MS). See also Krämer (1932).

Thus the old pattern of organization is still maintained even though the physical arrangement has been somewhat modified.

An *jiimw* is the corporate property of the lineage or descent line whose women live in it, but it is normally built by their husbands. The lineage, as represented by the children of these men, duly inherits full title to the house as its corporate property. A lineage's *jiimw* is regarded as the true "home" of its men as well as its women, and gives physical expression to its unity as a lineage. Although men live in their wives' houses, they keep their valuables in their own lineage house in the care of their sisters.

A large and important lineage might have a meeting house, *wuut*.[7] In some districts only the chief's lineage has one; in others only the well established lineages. At one time or another every lineage on Romonum has had its own *wuut*. When a man's lineage is without a meeting house, he attends that of his father's or his wife's lineage.

Under aboriginal conditions a lineage's *wuut* was not necessarily located near its *jiimw*. It frequently stood by the shore, where it served as a canoe house (*wutten waa*) as well as a meeting house (*wutten mwiic*). A meeting house was not in itself taboo to women, although normally they did not enter it if men other than their husbands were present. Both men and women, however, could be present together at such feasts and dances as did not exclude one sex and were held in the meeting house. During certain ceremonies, men kept away from the meeting house and it was used exclusively by women. The women of a lineage could hold meetings of their own in its *wuut*.

Its *wuut* was the place where the unmarried young men of a lineage slept. Its older men, and at times the husbands of its women, also slept there whenever they were observing important sexual taboos.[8] A meeting house was the lounging place for men during the evening, where they visited and told stories. In it visitors from other islands and districts were received, entertained, and put up for the night.

All the old lineage meeting houses of Romonum are gone today. All over Truk, however, every district still maintains at least one meeting house. Women enter them more freely now than they used to, because the unmarried men no longer sleep there. The latter now go to sleep in the houses of non-taboo relatives. Several unmarried men may together occupy a small hut for sleeping purposes, the hut being built in the style of an *jiimw* rather than of an *wuut*. The district meeting house is still the place where the men sleep before a ball game or track meet. Guests are still entertained there, and it still is the place for feasts and district meetings. All local governmental functions are carried on in the district *wuut*.

Each lineage of normal complement used to have, and still has, a *fanag*, which may

[7]The term "meeting house" will be used in preference to the more usual "men's house," because it more accurately describes the function of this building on Truk. It corresponds to the so-called men's house among other Oceanic peoples, but on Truk its use is not restricted to men only.

[8]Taboos on sexual intercourse are observed in connection with a great many activities, e.g., warfare, canoe-building, various aboriginal religious rites, many types of fishing, learning magic, processing turmeric, preparing for long voyages, and nowadays prior to important baseball games or other sports events.

be translated as "hearth" (lit. "ashes"). It is the site of a lineage's earth ovens (*wuumw*).[9] It may or may not be covered by an open-sided, thatch-roofed hut. The *fanag* is the work place for the members of the lineage. Whenever, as a corporation, a lineage must prepare food in quantity to present to the district chief or to pay off obligations to the residual title holders of land to which it holds provisional title, its men assemble and work at the *fanag*. A small lineage may have no *fanag* of its own, its men using that of their fathers' lineage and joining forces with their fathers' lineage in the preparation of food for feasts and ceremonies involving the entire district. In aboriginal times the *fanag* was not necessarily located in the vicinity of the *jiimw*, but it frequently was.

Now that the women of a lineage live in smaller adjacent houses, there is usually a cook house (*jimwenikkuk*) associated with each dwelling. Household cooking is done in the cook house, especially where the plank floors of the new-style *jiimw* make cooking within it impossible. On Romonum, a lineage's *fanag* is today usually and ideally at the cook house attached to the house in which its senior woman resides.

Each *jiimw* used to have associated with it a menstrual hut (*jimwerä*). It was built in the same manner as a small *jiimw*, but on a very small scale. Here women of the lineage were isolated during their first menstruation, and here they prepared and ate their meals apart during subsequent menstruations. At childbirth, an expectant mother retired to the *jimwerä* at the onset of labor pains and remained there until after delivery. Menstrual huts are no longer built or used.

All lineage buildings normally stand on land to whose soil the lineage, or some member of it, holds provisional or full title. If this is not feasible, the *jiimw* may be built by the husbands of the lineage women on land held by one of them. In such a case his children acquire provisional title to the house and land on which it stands, receiving them as a *niffag* from their father. With the *mwääniici* of their lineage acting as guardian, the house and its site became a part of the property of the lineage whose women live there. Dwelling sites used to be shifted about once in a generation's time, if the lineage had sufficient lands at its disposal. The purpose was to keep its house near breadfruit trees which were bearing well, so that a good supply of this staple food would always be near at hand.[10] In the old days an *jiimw* was sometimes surrounded by a stone wall for defensive purposes.

Each *wuut*, *jiimw*, and *fanag* was named. It might be given the name already applied to the plot of land on which it stood, or it might receive a new name which in turn could come to be applied to the plot of land. Such a plot would continue to keep the name thus acquired after the building had been torn down and a new one erected elsewhere. This custom still prevails and has resulted in a proliferation of place names

[9]Cooking in aboriginal times was done in earth ovens, especially when food was to be prepared in quantity. The oven consists of a hollow in the ground which is filled with stones. Cooking is done by building a fire on the stones, then lining the hollow with the hot stones, placing the food wrapped in green leaves on them, and covering the whole over with earth. The moisture from the leaves and green grass on the stones steams the food.

[10]Dwellings believed to be haunted by an evil spirit causing illness among the inmates, were also abandoned for a new house site.

within the various districts. A lineage may be referred to by the name for its past or present house or meeting house as well as by its territorial name.

The island of Romonum has a population of roughly 240 people of all ages. At the present time this population is organized into 13 functioning lineages distributed between 2 political districts. The average number of persons per lineage is 18. They range in size from 3 persons in the smallest to 34 in the largest, excluding members by birth who are permanently resident on other islands. Some of these lineages are new. Others which at one time flourished on the island are now extinct or no longer function independently, their few survivors having been taken in as clients of other lineages.

The various lineages of Romonum will be referred to by their sib names. Where a sib is represented by more than one lineage, they will be distinguished by a number, thus: Jacaw 1, Jacaw 2, etc., Jacaw being the sib name in this case. All of Romonum's past and present lineages are listed in Table 3, together with their present population and their associated place names, if there are any, by which the natives also refer to them. Complete genealogies of Romonum's lineages are given in Charts 3-22.

The nucleus of each lineage, and often its entire membership, is composed of the matrilineal descendents of a group of real or classificatory siblings who founded it as a major corporation. It is evident from Table 3, however, that a lineage may include other persons as well. This may come about in several ways, resulting in two types of membership: membership by adoption and what will be called client membership.

Persons adopted when they are still infants become full-fledged members of the adopting parent's lineage. In such cases it is desirable that a child be kept ignorant of the fact of adoption. In consequence, he loses membership in the matrilineal kin group into which he was born and has no obligations to its members. When children are adopted at a somewhat later age, however, they retain membership in their lineage of birth while at the same time acquiring membership in their lineage of adoption. This results in a double set of allegiances and obligations.[11] A child may be adopted by either a man or a woman. In the latter case he takes the lineage of his adopting mother, in the former that of his adopting father, regardless of the affiliations of the spouse of the adopting parent.

Lineages may also count as members people who were neither born into them nor adopted as children, and whom we may call client members. Lineages acquire client members for several reasons. When there are only one or two surviving members of a lineage they become associated with their father's lineage. An example of this is provided by the two surviving men of the Söör 1 lineage on Romonum. They have affiliated themselves with Pwereka 2, of which the father of one and stepfather of the other had been a member.[12] The head of the Pwereka 2 lineage exercises the same kind of authority

[11] Rooke of Romonum is such a case. Born into the Pwereka 3 lineage and adopted into the Pwereka 1 lineage by Taapen, its old chief, he is called upon to render services to both groups.

[12] The latter had been an illegitimate child. When his mother married, her husband assumed the responsibilities of fatherhood towards him. This is a normal procedure in the case of illegitimacy.

and control over these two men as he does over those who were born into the group Since they have some property of their own, these young men constitute a minor corporation within the Pwereka 2 lineage. Their property, like that of any other descent line within the lineage, may be used for the benefit of the entire lineage.

A woman who marries patrilocally from another island, and who is, therefore, without lineage membership in her husband's district, is often taken into her husband's lineage

TABLE 3. ROMONUM'S LINEAGES

Lineage	Population	Associated Place Name
Jacaw 1	20	Wunuugëwyg (*sööpw* name)
Jacaw 2	21*	Nuukan (*sööpw* name)
Jacaw 3	5	Wiiton former *jimw* name)
(Jeffeg)	Extinct	Jeffeg (*sööpw* name)
(Jimwö)	Extinct	?
Pwereka 1	10*	Mwej (former *jimw* name)
Pwereka 2	11*	Neepiiköw (former *wuut* name)
Pwereka 3	32	Näämärew or Winisi (former *jimw* and *wuut* names)
(Pwëën)	3	
Pwukos	17	
(Söör 1)	2	
Söör 2	25	Pwowunög (*sööpw* name)
Wiitëë 1	12*	Jinyykywu (*sööpw* name)
Wiitëë 2	34	
(Wiitëë 3)	Extinct	Söönnuuk (*sööpw* name)
(Wiitëë 4)	12	
Wuwäänyw 1	17*	
Wuwäänyw 2	15*	Wukupw (former *jimw* name)
Wuwäänyw 3	25	
(Wuwäänyw 4)	9	Jinipw (*sööpw* name)
(Wuwäänyw 5)	4	

* Figures include members of lineages given in parentheses. Thus Jacaw 2 includes one Pwëën man; Pwereka 1 includes Wuwäänyw 5; Pwereka 2 includes Söör 1; Wiitëë 1 includes two Pwëën women; Wuwäänyw 1 includes Wuwäänyw 4; and Wuwäänyw 2 includes Wiitëë 4. The lineages in parentheses no longer function separately or are extinct. Wiitëë 4 has never functioned as a separate lineage but has always been a client of Wuwäänyw 2. It is given separate listing only because of its different sib affiliation. Lineages with *sööpw* names are the oldest on Romonum. In one case, that of Jeffeg, the *sööpw* name became the sib name, replacing the earlier sib name of Sowupwonowöt. Except for Jimwö, of which little is remembered, the lineages without associated place names are relatively new.

as a client member. Her husband's lineage takes responsibility for her, and in return she gives it the services which are obligatory to regular members. Such a woman's children may remain resident in their father's district, acquiring land from their father under provisional title. They will continue to be associated with their father's lineage as client members unless they are sufficiently numerous and have acquired sufficient holdings to set themselves up as an independent lineage.

72

The Wiitëë 4 group on Romonum provides a good illustration. A member of the Wuwäänyw 2 lineage married a Wiitëë woman from Moen Island about 50 years ago. When he became chief of his lineage he brought his wife and her brother to Romonum, where they became affiliated with Wiitëë 1 as client members because of their common sib membership. The woman lived patrilocally with her husband, however, and their children were counted client members of Wuwäänyw 2, their father's lineage. This lineage was getting very small by this time, so that these children acquired considerable land from their father under provisional title from his lineage. The daughters continued to reside with the women of their father's lineage after marriage, as do their daughters today. Thus Wiitëë 4 became established as a distinct descent line with client membership in Wuwäänyw 2. It is sufficiently identified with Wuwäänyw 2 so that Piin (Wiitëë 4) married Raany (Wiitëë 2), a man of her own sib, without arousing much comment. The Wuwäänyw 2 lineage will soon be extinct, having no women of childbearing age or younger. Therefore, as its *jëfëkyr*, the Wiitëë 4 line will fall heir to its corporate holdings. The younger people of Romonum are not aware of the original Wiitëë affiliation of this group but think of it as Wuwäänyw. It is possible that Wiitëë 4 may lose its Wiitëë affiliation entirely in another generation and be considered a full-fledged member of the Wuwäänyw sib. If it does not, it will emerge as an independent Wiitëë lineage with the former Wuwäänyw 2 holdings as its corporate property.

In recent time a man of Jacaw 1 married a Maasanë woman from Dublon Island. He has brought her with her mother and baby brother to Romonum in patrilocal residence. His wife, mother-in-law, and baby brother-in-law are now classed as client members of the Jacaw 1 lineage.

Inter-island or inter-district marriages are not the only cases in which an immigrant acquires client membership in a local lineage. For both economic and physical security it is imperative that everyone belong to some lineage in the locality of his residence. Thus every immigrant from another island is taken into a local lineage as a client member. Otherwise he must leave. There are no people on Romonum, now or in the past, who are completely without local lineage affiliation of some sort.[13] Individual clients who have no bond of kinship to reinforce their client status in a lineage must be scrupulous in the rendering of their obligations, for laxity in these may result in loss of client membership and acquisition of a reputation which will make another lineage reluctant to take them in.[14]

[13] Pwuna of the Maasanë sib from Moen is counted a member of the Pwukos lineage on Romonum, with which he has a remote blood relationship through his father's father. The native Protestant preacher from Tol and his wife from Falabeguets with their two small children function as members of the Pwereka 1 lineage, which is the chiefly lineage of the district of Corog from which the mission holds its lands.

[14] The school teacher on Romonum, who is from the Mortlock Islands, was taken into the Wuwäänyw 1 lineage on the basis of common sib membership. Later expelled for stealing the wife of one of its members, he is now affiliated with Pwereka 3, the chiefly lineage of Winisi district in whose meeting house the school is located. His affiliation with this group is marginal, because of his earlier difficulties and his own rather individualistic personality. Economically, his position is more precarious than is that of most persons. Without his Pwereka 3 affiliation, however, he would have no house site on which to live and would be forced to leave the island. For food he relies mainly on his salary as school teacher.

Whenever possible, client relationships are established on the basis of some preexisting tie of kinship, common sib membership, or affinal relationship. When a recognized relationship already exists with its requirements of mutual cooperation, a client can be more readily integrated into the lineage with which he is affiliated. Otherwise the client relationship must be established on the basis of mutual good will, mutual need, and the services which the client can render as a member of the lineage he joins. The writer has the impression, but cannot verify it, that a client does not normally become head of a lineage so long as he is clearly in a client status. Informants describe certain clients in the past as occupying a position akin to that of domestic employees, being granted certain economic privileges in return for the labor they could perform under the direction of the lineage head.

INTERNAL ORGANIZATION

As noted in our discussion of corporations, the organization of a lineage is based on that of a group of own siblings. In a corporate sense, therefore, all the members of a lineage are regarded as siblings. The kinship terms for siblings are used to designate the membership collectively when comparing its activities and responsibilities with those of such non-members as the fathers or spouses of the lineage personnel. This is true whether or not a lineage is composed of several important descent lines and whether or not it includes client members. On the other hand, since a lineage perpetuates itself by the successive addition of new generations in the female line, its members recognize differences in generation and interact accordingly in their kin relationships. The interaction of individual members of a lineage is thus based on two different kinds of relationship. One of these disregards generation differences while the other recognizes them. In reference to the first, for example, a mother's brother is called an "older brother," while in reference to the second he is called a "father." The latter relationship obtains when lineage mates interact simply as kinsmen apart from the context of common lineage membership, while the former obtains when they interact as members of the same cooperative and corporate group with its lines of recognized authority and responsibility. Their relations as kinsmen will be considered in connection with the kinship system. Since authority and responsibility are expressed in the sibling relationship, it is this bond which is relevant to the internal organization of the lineage and descent line as matrilineal corporations.

Internally, each lineage is separately organized into its men as one group and its women as another. The fact that its women ordinarily reside together in one household, while its men reside in the lineage households of their wives, separates the sexes physically. The division of labor by sex further contributes to the separate organization of a lineage's men and women. Its women not only function independently of its men in connection with household affairs but also operate as a separately organized work team even when their activities are oriented towards the same joint objective for which the men are working.

Our discussion of corporations included a brief sketch of the separate organization of "brothers" and of "sisters," with the oldest brother, the *mwääniici*, directing the activities of the men and the oldest sister, the *finniici*, directing the women. The *mwää-*

74

niici was also noted as the leader of the entire sibling group. It was further indicated that brothers are considered the guardians of their sisters and have authority over them, while older siblings stand in the same relationship to their younger siblings of the same sex. All this characterizes lineage organization.

As "oldest brother" in the corporation, the eldest living man in a lineage is its head, its *mwääniici,* barring mental deficiency or complete lack of interest, in which case the next oldest assumes his responsibilities. In the same way, any descent line or minor corporation within a lineage has as its *mwääniici* its oldest male member. To distinguish the *mwääniici* of a lineage from that of a descent line or group of own siblings, the Trukese refer to a lineage head as the *mwääniici nöön faameni* (senior male in the lineage) or the *sömwoonun faameni* (chief of the lineage).[15] The same considerations apply to the "oldest sister" as female head of a lineage. She is called *finniici nöön faameni* (senior woman in the lineage) or *finesömwoonun faameni* (chief woman of the lineage). The younger brothers of the *mwääniici,* i.e., the younger men in his lineage, are his *mwääniinyk* (adjacent men). In the singular, a *mwääniinyk* is the next senior man in his lineage, and will succeed the *mwääniici* as its head. The same term may be used to designate the younger sisters or younger women of a lineage in relation to its *finniici.* A younger brother refers to an older brother as *jääj mwään* (lit. "my man"), as does a younger to an older sister.[16] The youngest of a group of sibling or lineage mates, regardless of sex, is the *setipwitur.*

The men and women of a lineage are thus ranked strictly in terms of seniority as defined by relative birth order. Authority and responsibility follow this seniority line. It is the *setipwitur,* in this case the youngest adult present, who is the errand boy for his seniors, and to whom such tasks as collecting firewood, cooking snacks, and fetching water regularly fall. These chores are performed by the youngest "sister" around the house and by the youngest "brother" when the men are off working as a group.[17] If the *mwääniici* is not present, the next in the seniority line automatically acts as *mwääniici* in his place. This automatic application of the seniority rule means that the same person may be *mwääniici, mwääniinyk,* or *setipwitur,* depending on which of his siblings he is working with at any particular time. The result is that any aggregation of any part of a lineage's membership has an implicit organization as a social group, with a recognized leadership and clearly defined roles for every member. Because of this, when a member of the lineage dies or is temporarily absent, no disorganization results. Ordinarily, there

[15]The use of the term *sömwon* (chief) for the lineage head may be a recent development and restricted to Romonum Island. The term *mwääniici* is however universally understood in relation to this office.

[16]Only the terms *mwääniici* and *finniici* distinguish the sex of the person referred to. Otherwise lines of authority among sisters are expressed by using the masculine terms. There is confusion in this respect even in the use of *mwääniici* and *finniici.* I have heard both terms used to indicate oldest brother and oldest sister indiscriminately.

[17]A descent line of the Jacaw 2 lineage had a household of its own composed of three "sisters" and an "aunt" of theirs, together with their husbands and children. Since I was "brother" to one of the husbands, I used to spend a good deal of time visiting with this group. It never failed that the two older of the three sisters would call out to Namako, the youngest, to run every errand required.

is no jockeying for position or power. The addition of new members by birth or adoption similarly has no disorganizing effects on the group.

As head of his corporation, the *mwääniici* of a lineage administers its corporate property. He allocates shares in its real property to the junior members, who hold them under provisional title from the lineage. A *mwääniici* must be consulted by his juniors before they take any action which might affect the welfare of their group, such as getting married or selling or giving away important personal property. It is the *mwääniici* who calls meetings of the lineage membership in the lineage *wuut*. He outlines the cooperative work of his lineage, and either directs it himself or leaves it to the *mwääninyk* (the next oldest) or the *mwääniici* of the next lower generation to direct. He represents his lineage to the district chief. He can veto proposed marriages of his junior lineage mates. He can order his lineage mates to pick from their lands (whether they are part of the property of the major corporation or not), to bring this produce to the lineage *fanag*, and to prepare it as food for presentation to the district chief or for the payment of any other lineage obligations, such as those to the residual title holders of lands held by the lineage under provisional title. A lineage head initiates and leads the work of storing breadfruit for preservation in the pits belonging to the individual members. If there is a big land-clearing project to be undertaken by a lineage, it is its *mwääniici* who organizes it. This was especially the case in aboriginal times in preparing land for planting turmeric.[18] Any undertaking in which the members of a lineage, or its men, must cooperate is organized and directed by its *mwääniici* or his recognized substitute.[19]

The *finniici* of a lineage plays a comparable role in the activities of its women. She supervises the management of the household in which they live together. She directs and organizes their cooperative work, such as reef fishing. She keeps track of the food supply and informs the lineage head as to the state of affairs in the household, reporting to him any behavior of the women's husbands which is out of order. In line with her role as household head she has an important voice in all lineage affairs. Like the *mwääniici* she has veto powers over the marriage of a junior member of either sex.

All of the above responsibilities and powers still rest with the *mwääniici* and *finniici* today. If a quota of laborers is called for by government officials, it is prorated by the district chief among the various lineages under his control according to their size. The lineage heads then select those members who can best be spared to fill the quota. Modifications of lineage organization are minor. The widespread absence of lineage meeting houses may make lineage meetings today a little less formal and probably less frequent. The breakdown of the single lineage house into several adjacent houses has made the senior woman in each house more an independent household head and less subject to direct supervision by the *finniici* of her lineage.

Succession to the position of lineage head, as already intimated, is based upon age.

[18] Turmeric was processed into a cosmetic in the old days for body painting purposes. Since it could be grown only on the high islands of Truk, it was an important item of trade to the coral islanders in the Greater Truk Area. The processed pieces of turmeric were the closest thing to a recognized medium of exchange in the native economy. Its production was a function of the lineage.

[19] I am indebted to F. M. LeBar for much of my information on the role of the lineage head in economic activities.

In theory, the oldest man of the oldest generation is head, then the next oldest, and so on until the generation is exhausted. Succession then descends to the oldest man of the next lower generation. If, however, the oldest man in a younger generation is considerably older than the youngest of a higher generation, actual age takes precedence over generation,[20] but if two men are of roughly equal age, position in the higher generation tends to predominate. By the time of succession, however, it is fairly evident to the lineage membership who will take over the leadership, so that even in borderline cases there is little conflict.[21]

It is important to note that succession within a lineage is not strictly matrilineal in the sense that headship stays within a single matrilineal descent line, passing to an own younger brother and thence to the eldest own sister's oldest son, as it does, for example, on Puluwat. Many of Romonum's lineages have two or more distinct descent lines going back several generations. In no such case is headship confined to one of them as a senior line. Each descent line has its own *mwääniici,* and whichever of them is senior in birth order is *mwääniici* of the lineage. Succession is based exclusively on a rule of seniority not on nearness of kinship.[22]

So far we have spoken of the organization of the lineage as a single group. It will be recalled that any group of own siblings may be organized as a corporation in its own right with respect to properties, either created by their collective efforts or inherited from their father. Because of this fact a lineage may contain within it a number of smaller corporations or descent lines. The fact that each generation of siblings is likely to acquire property from its father and hold it apart from the holdings of the larger corporation gives the younger generation a degree of autonomy within the lineage. Like any individual member of the larger corporation, these smaller corporations cannot freely dispose of their properties without the consent of the lineage *mwääniici,* but must subordinate their interests to those of the major corporation to which they belong. The autonomy of each successive generation, however, is recognized in lineage organization. Each generation is thought of as a distinct unit within the larger group. It is likely to be a cooperative working unit because of the relative nearness of age of its members. Each generation has an additional solidarity as a group of siblings within the framework of the kinship system as well as by virtue of common membership in a lineage. The *mwääniici* and *finniici* of the younger adult generation within a lineage, therefore, exercise a more direct control over the other members of their generation than do the *mwääniici* and *finniici* of the larger group, who ordinarily belong to a higher generation and, being older, are frequently unable to perform hard work. The lineage heads, therefore, generally include the heads of the younger generation in their deliberations, all of them

[20]Analysis of the genealogical position of lineage heads who succeeded one another in the past makes this quite clear.

[21]Conflict may arise between descent lines, however, when it comes to succession to the headship of a lineage which traditionally supplies the district chief, especially if the heads of its descent lines are of about the same age.

[22]This is true even in the case of succession to district chiefship, which is held as the property not of an individual but of a matrilineal corporation, a lineage. The *mwääniici* of this lineage, as executor of its property, is automatically district chief.

forming a lineage council. If a lineage consists of several important descent lines, the heads of these are also included and have considerable voice.

THE DESCENT LINE: A POTENTIAL LINEAGE

As a minor corporation, a descent line differs in no way from a lineage as far as its internal organization is concerned. It has its own *mwääniici*, for example, who is its oldest male member. Although the descent line has been defined in corporate terms, the Trukese think of it in terms of its genealogical features. Their name for it is *tetten*, whose meaning corresponds closely to English "line," "rank," "row," "file." The natives speak of the *tetten* of a marching formation, for example. They also use the term to indicate the generations of a lineage as well as its descent lines. When designating a descent line, *tetten* implies a genealogical group. The natives talk of the members of a descent line as "the children of one mother," though by this they may actually mean the descendants of one great grandmother. The word *tetten* is also used to denote a lineage, as in speaking of the *tetten* of a sib or ramage. Ordinarily a specific descent line is referred to as so-and-so's *tetten*, naming its *mwääniici* or some other known member.

The question may legitimately be raised as to why we have defined the descent line (and, for that matter, the lineage) in corporate rather than genealogical terms if the Trukese think of it genealogically. The fact is that genealogical lines do not always coincide with corporation membership. A descent line may include collateral relatives who are not direct matrilineal descendants of its founders. These collateral relatives belong to the descent line of their fellow corporation members and not that of their closer genealogical kin. Nor does the fission of lineages always follow strict genealogical lines. When the genealogical factor is in conflict with the corporate factor, it is the latter which determines membership, not the former. Closeness of genealogical relationship can be assumed from common corporate membership (except in the case of client members), but not the reverse.[23]

Because the descent line is by definition a part of a lineage, it does not often play a role that is readily apparent to the outside observer. It is fundamentally important as a potential lineage. It provides a basis for the fission of a lineage into separate lineages which may form the constituent elements of a ramage and subsib. As its lineage potential increases, a descent line becomes more obvious as a clearly defined social group. If its lineage potential is weak, it remains submerged in the lineage. The strength of a descent line's lineage potential is to be measured by the amount of real property which it controls as a corporation as well as by the number of its members.

Within a lineage, any two sisters who bear children are potential founders of new descent lines. If the children receive no new properties from the husbands of the two sisters, i.e., from their fathers, they do not have the means to organize themselves into

---

[23]The Trukese definition of the descent line in purely genealogical terms illustrates the "rule of thumb" nature of a society's formulation of its own structure. To rely on statements by informants without at the same time collecting objective data in the form of direct observations, censuses, genealogies, etc., is to run the risk of describing social structure in terms of native rules of thumb, rather than to portray it as it actually operates.

separate minor corporations. They continue as a single descent line. It is the acquisition of property, either from a father or by conquest, which starts those who acquire it as a descent line. As long as a descent line does not branch out into collateral lines, the successive acquisition of property from fathers in each generation gradually increases its lineage potential. It acquires greater autonomy within the lineage as its corporate holdings increase. Usually an important descent line gets started not so much by the successive acquisition of small amounts of property over several generations as by the acquisition from one father of a large amount of property. This can come about in two ways. If the father is *mwääniici* of his lineage, it is easy for him to give his children provisional title to large portions of his lineage's corporate land holdings. If he is the last survivor of a lineage which has extensive holdings, then at his death his children inherit them as *jëfëkyr* of the extinct lineage.

A descent line of strong lineage potential becomes clearly discernible when its women establish themselves in a household separate from that of the remaining members of their lineage. This physical separation further increases the descent line's lineage potential, and adds to its autonomy in property an autonomy in economic and household affairs. Establishment of a separate *jimw*, however, does not in itself formally separate a descent line from the lineage to which it has belonged. A new lineage emerges only with a formal division of the corporate holdings of an old lineage among its constituent descent lines. This establishes the descent line as a new lineage in its own right. If a descent line has considerable property of its own, it may refrain from dividing the original corporate holdings, leaving these to the parent lineage and establishing its independence on the basis of its own more recently acquired holdings. In this case the new lineage simply renounces all rights to the original corporate holdings. When a division of holdings is made, it is done in such a way that the former descent line acquires as its lineage property those lands which its members previously held under provisional title from the parent lineage and whose exploitation has always been associated with the descent line which is now becoming independent. Formal separation is established when the two groups agree that the *mwääniici* of the one shall no longer have jurisdiction over the personnel of the other or its property.

When a descent line severs its membership in the lineage to which it has belonged, its relations with the latter may remain close or not, depending on the nature of the events which precipitated the final separation. These relations will be discussed in connection with the ramage and the subsib.

In any event, as a descent line increases its lineage potential, new generations within it have, in the meantime, been acquiring property from their fathers and forming infant minor corporations of low lineage potential. A factor inhibiting the proliferation of new minor corporations is the relative stability of the population. This results in a high mortality among minor corporations of low lineage potential. Such a minor corporation may, for example, consist of two or three brothers, without a sister whose children could carry on its membership. Under these circumstances the brothers may take in a member of a collateral descent line within their lineage. This is especially likely if the brothers are without children of their own to whom to transmit their holdings under provisional title. In this way the holdings of two minor corporations within a lineage become the property of one. Members of two infant minor corporations in a lineage, moreover, may pool their holdings rather than keep them distinct, the *mwääniici* of each allocating shares under provisional title to members of the other. This mixing of their property obscures their identity as distinct minor corporations. Guardianship gives an older lineage brother from another descent line an interest in holdings which a child has gotten from his father. This process of passing shares in a holding back and forth between members of different descent lines in a lineage, which is going on all the time, makes determination of the distinct holdings o f most minor corporations somewhat difficult, and keeps them subordinated to the lineage or descent line of higher lineage potential. It is this process, moreover, which makes the exact delineation of descent lines in purely genealogical terms impossible.

The history of the Jacaw 2 and Jacaw 3 lineages of Romonum serves to illustrate the way in which the separation of a lineage into two distinct descent lines of high lineage potential may come about. Jacaw 2 and 3 were originally a single lineage. This fact is even traced genealogically, as the two lineages share the same remembered ancestry. A woman of the parent lineage married the head of the Wuwäänyw 4 lineage, who personally controlled a considerable portion of its corporate property. There were six children by this marriage, three sons and three daughters. When the three daughters married, their father built a house for them on Wuwäänyw 4 lands under his control, giving these lands to his children under provisional title from him and his lineage. Since his wife was dead, the next oldest woman to the *finniici* in the Jacaw lineage moved over to this house to supervise the younger women for whom it had been built. Though this older woman and her children were from a collateral line in the lineage, their association with the new household made them and their descendants a part of the newly established descent line. This descent line continued to share the same meeting house with the other members of the lineage and to work in the same *fanag*. Lineage chiefship rotated back and forth between the two groups in the lineage, going always to the older of the *mwääniici*. This division of the lineage into two distinct descent lines, each with its own household, continued until recently. During the war they even went back for a period to a single household. After the war, the two *mwääniici* agreed to a formal separation into two distinct lineages. The newer descent line, Jacaw 3, acquired as its *sööpw* those lands which had last been held under provisional title by a member of its line. Jacaw 2 continued to keep the plots which had last been held under provisional title by members of its genealogical line, which happened to include most of the older holdings of the original lineage. Jacaw 3 thus emerged as a distinct lineage with its own *sööpw*, i.e., lands to whose soil it holds full or residual title, plus the former Wuwäänyw 4 lands which theoretically it still holds under provisional title from Wuwäänyw 4. Practically, however, these are considered a part of its *sööpw* lands because the near extinction of Wuwäänwy 4 has produced a situation in which its surviving young members are unaware of the history of these lands and of their corporation's claim to the residual title to them. Jacaw 2 and Jacaw 3 now cooperate closely as a ramage.

There are indications that their formal separation may be abandoned and that

Jacaw 3 with its one old man and two women still resident on Romonum will merge with Jacaw 2 again. The writer was told that plans were afoot for having the Jacaw 3 women move their residence to the site where Jacaw 2 is now located. This appears to be a somewhat exceptional procedure. Ordinarily once a descent line establishes separate residence in a household of its own, its members do not go back into a single household with the rest of the lineage. If the number of women in such a descent line becomes too few to support a separate household, the surviving women move to land belonging to their individual husbands and function as members of the households made up of the women of their husbands' respective lineages.

In summary, a descent line is important as a potential lineage. It subdivides a lineage into lesser corporations with respect to certain properties acquired independently of the lineage and distinct from the corporate holdings which unite the entire lineage. If circumstances favor the acquisition by a descent line of a sizable amount of property in land and trees, and if the personnel of the descent line is sufficient in number to enable it to operate independently, its lineage potential is thereby sufficiently strong so that it may set itself up as an independent major corporation and lineage. The mere fact that a descent line is in a position to do this does not, however, automatically lead to its becoming a separate lineage. Several factors enter into consideration. If it happens that two such descent lines of a lineage give support to opposite sides in a feud between two other lineages to which each descent line happens to be closely related by kinship connections in the male line, this may precipitate their final, complete separation. Personal relations between the *mwääniici* of the two descent lines may be such as to produce the same result. It is the descent line with its lineage potential, however, which provides the mechanism whereby such a division may take place without disturbing the over-all tenure situation, regardless of what the immediate factor precipitating the break may be.

THE SIB[24]

The sibs or *jejinag*[25] are the largest of the various kin groups on Truk. Phratries and moieties are unknown. As previously indicated, sibs are primarily exogamous name groups whose members have a weak sense of kinship, their common matrilineally inherited name being the only indicator of blood relationship. Each sib is usually represented on a number of different islands in Truk. In fact the same sib names appear throughout the Greater Truk Area. The Söör sib, for example, is the highest ranking one on Lukunor in the Mortlock Islands, is widely represented on Truk, and also has mem-

[24] In the previous literature on Truk, this kin group is called a "clan." Because of ambiguities associated with the term "clan" in ethnographic literature, the term "sib" as proposed by Lowie (1925: 105) will be used throughout this report. This usage has the added advantage that it does not conflict with new proposals in terminology advanced by Murdock (1949).

[25] Etymologically the Trukese word *jejinag* corresponds with the Tikopian word *kainaŋa* (Firth, 1936: 361-2), denoting an aggregate of patrilineally related lineages, each bearing the name of its chief's lineage. Tikopians permit marriage between members of different lineages in the same *kainaŋa*. It is noteworthy that what is etymologically the same word denotes on Tikopia a patrilineal and on Truk a matrilineal sib.

TABLE 4. THE SIBS OF TRUK

Sib Name	Remarks
Cëëcija	Meaning: "Mangrove Leaf." Given as Poitia by Bollig.
Cëwykkyk	A local name for Sowuwefeg on Tol.
Fäänaw	Meaning: "Under the Banyan."
Fäänimej	Meaning: "Under the Breadfruit Tree."
Fesinim	Called Pesinim locally on Tol.
Fiitaw	
Jacaw	Meaning: "Cliffs," the place name of a legendary island from which its members presumably migrated, associated with Kusaie.
Jenegeejitaw	
Jeffeg	Derived from a place name on Romonum, where it is the local name for Sowupwonowöt.
Jimwö	
Jinääniföt	
Jipeges	
Keteman	
Maasanë	
Mwögunufac	Possible meaning: "Pandanus Leaf" The correct spelling may be Mogunufac.
Mwööc	Meaning: "Reef Passage." Also the name of an island in the Mortlocks.
Neefëw	Meaning: "Stone Place" or "Stony Place."
Neewow	A place name.
Nipwe	A local name for Pwee on Tol.
Nuukan	Meaning: "Its Center." A common place name.
Patan	
Pwee	
Pwereka	Meaning: "Wild Yam."
Pwëën	Meaning: "Swamp."
Pwukos	
Rääk	Possibly connected with the Mortlockese word rääk, "harvest season," whose Trukese equivalent is rääs.
Rogowu	Also called Rowoow.
Säpenö	A place name.
Sowufa	Meaning: "Proprietor of Fa." The name Fa is currently associated with Fefan Island.
Sowufär	Meaning: "Proprietor of Fär."
Sowupwonowöt	Meaning: "Proprietor of Puluwat." Represented on Truk only by Jeffeg.
Sowuwefeg	Meaning: "Sea Eel."
Sööpwu	
Söör	
Söpworeenög	Meaning: "Reenög District." Reenög (Puluwatese: Reelög) is the name of a district on Puluwat.
Söpwunupi	Possible meaning: "Grove district."
Tinik	A local name for Nippwe or Pwee on Tol.
Wiisuusu	A place name.
Wiitëë	Meaning: "On the Coral Islet." Cf. the atoll Namonuito (Nömwun Wiitëë, "Wiitëë Archipelago").

82

TABLE 4. THE SIBS OF TRUK (CONTINUED)

Sib Name	Remarks
Wuun	Meaning obscure. Cf. *wunu-*, meaning "breadfruit" in compound names for different varieties. Cf. also *wuun*, "testicle," which may be derived from "breadfruit" and which also appears as the name for the star Aldebaran and the constellation Hyades.
Wuwäänikkar	Meaning: "Fruit of the *Kkar*."
Wuääwnyw	Meaning: "Fruit of the *Barringtonia Asiatica*."

Note. Krämer, Bollig, and Kubary give the following additional names which the writer was unable to identify on Truk: Djoba (probably a misrendering of Cëëcija); Ipejatj; Leaureng (Neejöreg, a place name on Udot); Leoap; Nukfelu (Nuukenfëny, a place name on Romonum); Obudin (perhaps a misrendering of *wupwutiw*, "birth"); Pelior (Penijör, a place name on Dublon); Pommo; Sauanei or Souelei (not found on Truk today, but represented on Puluwat); Sausat (perhaps *sowuset*, "master fisherman"); Towo (Toowon, a place name); Uila or Vila (Wiina, unknown to informants, but plays a prominent role in myths reported by Krämer, who gives it a wide distribution); Ubueil; Upen.

bers on Puluwat, where it is called Höör in the local dialect. The same sib names do not extend outside the Greater Truk Area, predominantly new ones being encountered on Ifalik and Woleai in the west and on Ponape in the east.[26] The common system of *jejinag* is an important factor helping to bind the people of the Greater Truk Area into what might loosely be called the Trukese Nation.

Unlike the other kin groups of Truk, each sib has a name. A full list is given by Krämer (1932: 258-66), as collected by himself and Kubary. Our list, given in Table 4, agrees essentially with his.[27]

Sib membership in Truk averages about 250 persons. There is a wide range, some sibs numbering many fewer and some many more than the average. The Jeffeg sib, now extinct, was formerly represented by only one lineage, while the Jacaw sib is populous and widely distributed.

Taken by itself, a sib has few functions of immediate importance in daily life. It has no chief and no unity of action, controls no land, and holds no ceremonies or meetings.[28]

[26]Only one of the sib names reported by Lessa (1950: 48) on Ulithi, for example, corresponds with those on Truk today, namely, Mongolfach (Trukese: Mwögunufac). I am indebted to E. G. Burrows, S. Riesenberg, and B. Tolerton for information concerning the sibs of Ifalik, Ponape, and Lukunor respectively.

[27] This list was obtained from Simiron of Romonum, an elderly informant whose training in such matters made it possible for him to recognize most of the sibs given by Krämer. To the names which he gave me, I have added a few more which I encountered on other islands. Field work on all the islands would probably have revealed a few more minor sibs or variant names.

[28]Truk's sibs contrast in this respect with those of the Mortlock Islands, where Tolerton (personal communication) reports that the Soor sib owns certain lands as a sib, to which all its members, wherever located, have rights. Confusion of other kin groups with the sib by earlier reporters has led to much misunderstanding of its functions on Truk. Hall and Pelzer (1946) ascribe land ownership to the sib, their "clan"; Krämer (1932) gives lists of men who are supposed to be sib chiefs and interprets literally the mythical accounts that sibs fought wars against each other as units, wars which were probably fought on a local scale, involving lineages and ramages, or at the most subsibs.

Trukese sibs are not, properly speaking, to be classed as "groups" at all, for they have no organization as such. They are simply social divisions, marked off by matrilineally inherited names.

Sib membership is important, however, in the regulation of marriage. In theory, at least, no man and woman belonging to the same sib may marry each other. In practice this prohibition is not strictly observed. The genealogies for Romonum record 397 marriages in which the sib affiliation of both spouses is known. Four of these were between persons with the same sib membership. While the recorded marriages cover a time span of 150 years, all four of the endogamous marriages noted took place subsequent to the beginning of the Japanese administration. In fact all four couples are still living. This would give the impression that such marriages have begun to take place only recently and in response to outside influences. Krämer (1932: 255, footnote), however, quotes Kubary as saying:

The other sibs look with scornful aversion on the division of Sorr [Söör] into two sub-sibs, the Soyan and the Sor apila, and the fact that members of one are allowed to marry members of the other (Bollig mentions three branches but nothing of this situation). There are other liberties in some cases: for example the Iwo sib [Jimwö] on Toloas [Dublon] is made up of several *eyfs* [*jejif*, used here in the sense of district], which are independent of each other. The members of any one of these groups do not intermarry, but those from two different places may, and thus incest within the sib is permitted. Similarly on the island of Param marriages occur between the members of Ipue [Pwe]. The other sibs, however, adhere strictly to the original custom.

Since Kubary was in Truk prior to any extensive outside contacts, exceptions to the rule of sib exogamy must be explained by something other than acculturation. Informants say that if the spouse comes from a different island and is from a different subsib, it is nothing to get overly excited about if the couple belong to the same sib. Three of the four exceptions on Romonum aroused little comment. All three involved persons from different subsibs, and in each case one of the marriage partners was operating as a client member of a lineage indentified with a different sib. The fourth endogamous marriage, however, precipitated a crisis. It involved members of two lineages which belonged to the same subsib and which had formerly been united in a ramage. Only threats of suicide by the couple finally forced the chief and the respective lineage heads reluctantly to give their consent, which they rationalized by pointing out that the fathers of the pair, at least, were in no way related. Kubary's information, when put together with these examples, indicates that the subsib, which provides a definite feeling of blood relationship, is the strictly exogamous unit. It should be emphasized, however, that even the three marriages which evoked relatively little comment were not considered altogether proper. The reaction of informants was not unlike that of Americans to marriages between first cousins.[29] In short, though marriage between sibmates is not definitely forbidden, it is strongly disapproved.

While common subsib membership is a guarantee of hospitality, the same cannot be said of common sib membership. Actual blood relationship through either the father or

[29]Tolerton (personal communication) reports much the same situation in the Mortlocks.

the mother, or a genuine community of interest or close friendship, provides greater claims on mutual assistance and hospitality than does common sib membership alone. The latter is useful, however, as a last resort on visits to another island where one has no closer connections on which to call, when it serves as an opening wedge for the establishment of closer artificial ties.

Informants from Puluwat stated that in case of warfare between two districts, members of the same sib would not and did not fight against each other. This was true in Truk only of the subsib. An Jacaw man on Romonum could expect little mercy from the unrelated Jacaw men of Falabeguets in the old days. If their chief ordered them to kill him, they would obey. Kubary as cited by Krämer (1932: 255, footnote) confirms this: "Hostilities between members of the same sib may occur if they live in different *eyfs* 'districts'."

THE PROBLEM OF TOTEMISM

Both Krämer and Bollig try to make a case for totemism in connection with the Trukese sibs. For each sib Krämer (1932: 258) gives a list of totems in the form of plants or fish, which he states are taboos of the sibs. He admits that those given by Bollig differ from his. The taboo objects given by Krämer, however, must be ruled out as evidence of totemism.

It will be recalled from the discussion of incorporeal property that in any one district a knowledge of certain magics (*roog*) may be associated with the members of a lineage, and thus locally a sib. The taboos connected with these *roog* are sometimes said to be taboos of that lineage or sib. By this the natives mean that knowledge of the magic is at present largely concentrated in a certain lineage. These taboos are associated with the knowledge of the magic and have no place in sib history or origins. As already indicated, knowledge of *roog* may be transmitted to people who are not members of one's own lineage or sib. In fact, such knowledge is regularly transmitted by a father to his children. They in turn teach their lineage mates, so that in a generation's time a *roog* and its associated taboos may be the property of a different lineage or sib within the same district. The particular taboo plants and fish given by Krämer are specifically those associated with *roog*. This explains his finding that not all members of a sib knew its *roog* or observed the taboo, and his noting that Bollig had the same *roog* associated with different sibs. This is what we would expect if Bollig gathered his data in different districts or at a different time.

Bollig (1927: 79) states: "Very ancient myths tell of men who descended from plants and animals, which might be reducible to totemism. But there are only fragments of the ancient totemism left on the Truk islands." He goes on to say that they call this totemic ancestor mother, do not eat it, and mourn when someone kills it. In his list of sibs he is able to give the ancestors of only a few. They are: Jacaw from the whale (its father); Wiitëë from the *soopeepwec* ("white ghost," the name of a bird), whose flesh they do not eat and whose feathers they formerly wore in their hair; Pwe from the bat; Pwereka from the wild yam, *pwereka;* Cëëcija from the mangrove leaf, *cëën cija;* Söör from the turtle; Wiina from the boil in Sowufär's leg; Mwögunufac from the pandanus, *faac;* Fiitaw from the vine, *fitaw;* Pacaw from the shark, *pacaw;* Mwööc from the sea pike; and Fäänimej from a little crayfish. Bollig further states that the Sowufär people used to wear *söp* (white heron) feathers, but gives no indication that they reckoned descent from this bird. It is not apparent from his reporting whether all these cases were derived from information given him by informants or whether some of it is based purely on inferences he has himself drawn from the supposed meanings of the sib names, e.g., Pwereka, Fiitaw, Cëëcija, Mwögunufac, Pacaw.

When the writer asked about the coincidence of *pwereka* as the name of both a sib and a plant, informants said that it was just a coincidence, that the plant was not a totem or taboo of the Pwereka sib. Fiitaw and *fitaw*, while they look alike, are entirely different structurally. Cëëcija and Mwögunufac are typical of place names (cf. Cëë-sinifë, "hibiscus leaf," a place name on Romonum), and it has already been noted in our list of sib names that many of them are place names. There is no Pacaw sib, given by Bollig as Patau; but there is a sib called Patan. Apparently by miswriting Patan (easy enough with German script) Bollig thought this was a "shark" (*pacaw*) sib, since he regularly symbolized both "t" and "c" with a "t." This possibly reveals what Bollig has done. On the basis of similarities in name, real or fancied, he has jumped to unwarranted conclusions about the totemic ancestry of those sibs whose names lent themselves to this end. His entire list must, therefore, be considered suspect. Moreover, native interest in reconstructions of the past on the basis of popular etymologies may well have helped to mislead Bollig along these lines. The legends collected by Krämer (1932) reveal only too clearly the freedom with which native historians used word associations in their attempts to explain sib origins and the meanings of their names.

There remains, however, certain other evidence which is not so easily dismissed. According to their own myths, the Pwëën people and the Jacaw people were carried in their migrations on the back of a barracuda and a whale respectively. They do not eat their flesh, and Bollig (1927: 89) says that the Jacaw people used to make offerings to the whale whenever they saw one. According to all informants, however, neither sib is descended from the creatures in question, though Bollig claims that the whale was called "father" by the Jacaw people. One branch of the Wuwäänyw sib has the tradition that it came to Truk in a *wuwäänyw* (fruit of the *Barringtonia asiatica*.) Informants explicitly stated, however, that the *wuwäänyw* was not a taboo of this sib, but merely explained its name. It may be that some of the other sibs have similar associations. If so, the argument might be advanced that we have here a few survivals of a former widespread totemism. One may hazard the alternative suggestion that these transportation legends refer to the names of ancient double canoes in which migrations were made, these names having passed over into legend and in a few instances led to the development of associated ritual and eating taboos. In such cases, we would be dealing with an incipient rather than a residual totemism. Answer to the totemic question must await the systematic collection of legends not only on Truk but on such adjacent atolls as the Mortlocks, Hall, and Puluwat. In any case, the sibs of Truk cannot be considered totemic today.

THE SUBSIB

A subsib on Truk consists of the members of a sib who share a traditional common ancestry. The question arises as to how this differs from a sib, whose members presume some ultimate relationship on the basis of their common sib name. It is true that there are sibs which consist of but one subsib. The tradition of common ancestry in a subsib, however, is based on remembered historical facts having to do with the origins of various lineages. For example, the lineages of the Jacaw sib on Romonum have the tradition that they were founded by women who came from Pata in patrilocal marriages with Romonum men. When these women first came to Romonum, they belonged to lineages of the Jacaw sib located in the Jepin district of Pata. Their children acquired land from their Romonum fathers and formed new lineages local to Romonum, but whenever they went back to Jepin to visit their kinsmen there, they had automatic membership in their mothers' lineages. The maintenance of these ties generation after generation, though the genealogical connections can no longer be traced, has preserved the feeling that the Jacaw people of Romonum and Jepin are still one *faameni* or *jetereges*, which are terms used to designate a lineage.[30] The Jacaw people of Romonum have similar ties with the Jacaw people in the districts of Fëëwyp and Wonej on Tol and in the district of Jiräs on Moen, for it is remembered that the Jacaw people of Wonej came from Fëëwyp, that those of Jepin came from Wonej, that those of Romonum came from Jepin, and that those of Jiräs came from Romonum.

An Jacaw man from Jepin coming to Romonum automatically has membership in one of the Jacaw lineages there. If the Jacaw people of Romonum are short of food, they go to their subsib mates on Fëëwyp (who have many trees bearing out of season) and get breadfruit from them. When a man goes to another island where there is a lineage of his subsib, he has a place to stay, people who will feed and protect him, and in all probability the sexual hospitality accorded to a brother.[31] Our data suggest that in aboriginal times two districts on different islands customarily considered themselves allies in war and went to one another's help, if important segments of their populations were united by subsib ties. None of these services can be claimed on the basis of common sib membership alone.

A subsib is best seen, then, as a large lineage whose constituent descent lines have their corporate holdings in different districts and on different islands where they function locally as independent lineages while retaining absentee membership in their parent lineage. Since its membership is scattered, a subsib lacks the unity of action found in a lineage or ramage. It has no over-all *mwääniici*, nor are there any occasions on which all of its members get together for ritual or other purposes. It is held together by bonds of kinship and by the feeling that somehow its members are a sort of super-lineage. It is the most important social unit for the maintenance of friendly inter-community relations.

[30] Subsibs are not called by any special term to distinguish them from other types of matrilineal kin group. Depending on context, they are referred to as lineages (*jetereges, cö, faameni*) or as sibs (*jejinag*).

[31] Informants said that a native man might let his wife sleep with a visiting subsib mate in the old days. They tended to disclaim the practice today, but there is evidence that it is by no means entirely a thing of the past.

THE RAMAGE

It is not uncommon for a subsib to have more than one of its constituent lineages within a single district. A group of subsib mates who are organized into more than one major corporation but who are members of the same political district [32] is herewith called a *ramage*. Since the members of a ramage live near each other, it is possible for them to cooperate in various undertakings which are too great for one lineage to accomplish. There are two important features differentiating ramages from subsibs: ramages are always local to a particular district or community, whereas subsibs never are; and ramages have a recognized leadership and unity as a group, features which subsibs lack.

If a sib represented by only one lineage were to split into two lineages confined to the same district, the members of one of these lineages would not enjoy absentee membership in the other. The two lineages could not be classed, therefore, as a subsib. If, because of their common origin, they continue to cooperate for certain purposes the resulting group is what we mean by a ramage. While a subsib results from the migration of some members of a lineage to another district, a ramage results from the fission of a lineage within a district. The constituent lineages of a ramage may, of course, have the same subsib membership in that they both enjoy absentee membership in a common set of lineages outside their district, but within their district they remain distinct lineages.

A ramage has a recognized leader who is the oldest among the *mwääniici* of its severeal lineages. A ramage chief carried the title *sömwoonun ejinag* (chief of the sib).[33] This chief has authority only with respect to activities which the related lineages agree to undertake as a group. He has no control over the property of the various lineages, other than his own, in the ramage. The activities which he leads are usually restricted to large fish drives and preparations for feasts. Here his authority stops.

While each lineage in a ramage has its own lineage house, the various lineages together may share a single meeting house located on land controlled by the lineage of the ramage chief. This was the rule among the ramages of Romonum in aboriginal times. This raises a question as to how a ramage differs from a lineage which has two important descent lines each with its own house, but sharing a single meeting house. The difference is simply that the several descent lines of a lineage jointly own certain properties as a larger collectivity, whereas the lineages in a ramage do not. One lineage with several important descent lines may, of course, include more people than a ramage in the same district.

A ramage may result when a lineage splits into two major corporations, or when persons from another island or district become established as a lineage in a district where subsib mates of theirs are already organized as a separate lineage. According to Romonum traditions, the Jacaw sib, which was introduced there from Jepin on Pata, started as a single lineage. Subsequently another woman from Jepin came to Romonum,

---

[32]It is possible that common community rather than common district affiliation is what is relevant here. Our data are not sufficient to determine which.

[33]There is no special term for a ramage. The term *jejinag* (sib) is generally used to indicate a ramage when referring to the kin groups within a particular district. The terms for a lineage, while applied to a subsib, are not used in reference to a ramage.

and another Jacaw lineage was started by her children on the basis of lands they received from their father. These two Jacaw lineages kept but one meeting house and recognized the senior of the two *mwääniici* as ramage chief. Their main joint activity was fishing, when many people were needed to get a good catch. Later they became allied with different sides in a feud on Romonum, after which they ceased to function regularly as a ramage. Recently one of these lineages, already organized into two distinct descent lines, split into two major corporations which now constitute a ramage. The latter two lineages cooperate extensively today, but only sporadically with the third. During preparations for the 1947 Christmas Feast, for example, the two lineages of the present ramage operated a single *fanag* where the men prepared food, while the third lineage had a separate *fanag* of its own. The women of all three lineages, however, fished together under the leadership of the senior *finniici* in preparing for this same feast. On this occasion all three Jacaw lineages were aligned against two lineages of the Pwereka sib, which also operated as a ramage. Because of their small numbers, the two Pwereka lineages had a single *fanag* in connection with this feast under the leadership of the senior *mwääniici*, who was also district chief.

A ramage may also serve as a basis for the merging of two lineages. The Wuwäänyw 1 and Wuwäänyw 4 lineages of Romonum were at one time a single lineage, according to tradition. They then split into two lineages but continued to work together as a ramage. For a short period, as a result of feuds, they dropped their ramage organization, but subsequently resumed it. About fifteen years ago the last man of the Wuwäänyw 4 lineage took in the *mwääniici* of the Wuwäänyw 1 lineage as a fellow sibling on some of his land holdings. He also made him guardian of the Wuwäänyw 4 holdings which he had allocated to his sister's young son. By these acts he united the personnel of the two lineages in a new major corporation. Wuwäänyw 1 and Wuwäänyw 4 are now classed as descent lines of one lineage, and are regarded as one *faameni* comparable to the other lineages on Romonum. That overlapping ownership of property is what distinguishes a lineage from a ramage is apparent here, for it required a change in the property relations of the two lineages to unite them as one.

A single district may contain lineages whose members belong to the same sib but have no tradition of common origin or common subsib membership. The present Wiitëë 1 and Wiitëë 2 lineages on Romonum, and Wuwäänyw 3 as against Wuwäänyw 1 and Wuwäänyw 4 are in this relationship. A similar situation prevails on Pata in the district of Söpwötä, where there are two unrelated lineages of the Maasanë sib. These unrelated lineages do not work together as a ramage. Informants indicated that they might just as well belong to different sibs as far as the existence of any basis for collaboration was concerned. This makes it clear that common origin as well as common district membership is prerequisite to ramage organization.

The internal organization of a ramage follows that of a lineage in being patterned after the relations between own siblings. Authority follows the line of seniority. These relationships are invoked, however, only when the ramage is acting as a group in some cooperative undertaking. Otherwise its members behave toward one another according to the patterns appropriate to kinsmen as distinct from corporation mates. Members of the same subsib or sib also say that they are siblings in the sense that they belong to the same group. If sib-mates wish to invoke their common sib membership to establish stronger ties they do so as siblings. A subsib mate from another island who is visiting a local lineage fits in as a sibling when he participates in its group activities.

KIN GROUP FORMATION

Implicit in our descriptions of the Trukese kin groups is the fact that new ones are constantly becoming established as old ones die out. The processes by which this happens can now be summarized.

Logically, any matrilineal kin group has its beginnings when a set of own siblings inherits land from a father or acquires provisional title to land through a *niffag*. As a corporation holding these lands, the group of siblings perpetuates itself by including the children of its women. This gives rise to a descent line if the group already has membership in an established lineage, or to a new lineage if it does not already belong to one, as when the parents of the children are living in virilocal residence. By establishing itself in separate residence and by the acquisition of sufficient properties, the descent line's lineage potential increases to the point where it may become an independent lineage joined in a ramage with the lineage of which it was formerly a part.

A virilocal marriage by a woman with a man of another island or district leads to the establishment of her children as a new lineage there on lands they acquire from her husband. The siblings composing this new lineage, by retaining absentee membership in the lineage from which their mother came, have a subsib affiliation with the latter. The geographic expansion of a subsib in this manner may continue until somewhere one of the connections is forgotten. Then two distinct subsibs emerge carrying the same sib name.

The question remains as to how a new sib name gets started. The Jeffeg sib on Romonum illustrates at least one of perhaps several possible methods by which this can come about. The Jeffeg people originally belonged to the Sowupwonowöt sib, which is well represented on Puluwat, the traditional place of origin of the Jeffeg ancestress. The descendants of this woman acquired full title to portions of soil on Romonum which had the *sööpw* name of Jeffeg. Since it is customary to refer to the membership of a lineage as the people of such and such a *sööpw*, the Sowupwonowöt people on Romonum came to be called the Jeffeg people. In time their Sowupwonowöt affiliation was forgotten, since there were no other representatives of this sib in Truk with whom they could maintain subsib ties. One elderly informant on Romonum just happened to recall hearing as a boy that Jeffeg was really Sowupwonowöt. This illustrates how a place name may come to designate a sib. The processes by which subsibs become established could in time have spread Jeffeg people all over Truk, had their descendants in the female line multiplied. As it happened, however, the one lineage representing it has become extinct within the past twenty years.

Examination of the list of sib names on Truk reveals that many of them are typical of place names.[34] This strongly suggests that what happened in the case of the Jeffeg sib is by no means a unique occurrence, and that many sibs doubtless owe their origins as distinct name groups to similar factors. In this connection, there is a legend that the Sapeno and Sopwunupi sibs were once one. Their members lived together as a lineage in the district of Meccitiw on Moen, where they had one *wuut* and one *jiimw*. Because of incest regulations, the men were unable to find wives. Therefore the *mwääniici* divided the group into two *sööpw* (lineages), Sapeno and Sopwunupi (both place names), and declared that henceforth the men of one could marry the women of the other.[35]

The apparent meanings of other sib names on Truk suggest that immigration from other islands may lead to the establishment of new sib names. Immigrants who have no local sib affiliation may be called by the name of the land of their origin, which in time becomes established as their sib name. This may account for such sib names as those beginning with Sowu, such as Sowupwonowöt, Sowufär, and Sowufa (Proprietor or Man of Puluwat, Proprietor or Man of Fär, Proprietor or Man of Fa). It might also account for the name Jacaw, which means "cliffs" and is alleged to be an old name for the island of Kusaie, whose legendary chief was Sowukacaw (Proprietor or Man of Kacaw or Jacaw).

The fact that on various islands there are local variant names for sibs suggests that in time some of these might become established as separate sib names.[36] This could easily happen if a woman of such a group married virilocally on an atoll outside of Truk, as women occasionally do. Her descendants would be known by the variant sib name which she bore, especially if there were no representatives of the sib already located there. The other name would be lost in time, and a virilocal marriage back into Truk a few generations later would introduce the once variant name as that of an independent sib.[37]

It is clear, then, that while kin group organization has a definite pattern, there is

[34] Compare the sib name Cëëcija (Mangrove Leaf) with Cëësinifë (Hibiscus Leaf), the name of a plot of land on Romonum; the sib names Fäänaw (Under or Below the Banyan) and Fäänimej (Under or Below the Breadfruit Tree) with Fäänifac (Under or Below the Pandanus), the name of a land plot on Romonum; the sib name Mwööc (Reef Passage) with the same name for an island in the Mortlocks; the sib name Neefëw (Stony Place) with the land plot on Romonum called by the same name; the sib name Nuukan (Its Center) with the same lineage *sööpw* name for Jacaw 2 on Romonum and with the district of the same name on Uman; the sib name Wiitëë (On the Coral Islet) with Wiicuk (On the Mountain), a plot of land on Romonum.

[35] Their tradition of common origin has no organizational implications today, for sibs are not linked into phratries or moieties.

[36]E.g., Cëwykkyk, the local name for Sowuwefeg on Tol; Rowoow as a local variant of Rogowu; Tinik and Nipwe as local names for Pwee on Tol.

[37] Sib traditions give ample evidence that such marriages into outlying islands occur not infrequently. For example the Söör sib in the Mortlocks derives itself from Truk, while Söör people on Truk derive themselves from the Mortlocks. Such marriages back and forth have unquestionably served also to break subsib connections, reintroductions into Truk of the same sib name making for situations in which the older carriers of the name constitute one subsib while the immigrants and their descendants form another.

nothing static or permanent about the groups that result from this pattern. While everybody belongs to a major corporation or lineage, and to a name group or sib, he may or may not belong to a minor corporation within his lineage, to a ramage, or to a subsib. Moreover, the lineage and sib to which he belongs may coincide, as in the case of the Jeffeg sib, with its one lineage. All the lineages of one sib may likewise have subsib affiliations with each other. The limits of a sib's membership may not extend beyond the limits of a single ramage. The presence of a ramage as distinct from a subsib or sib, or of a subsib as distinct from a sib is a function of the history of the particular groups in question, though the social results of the historical events conform to the over-all pattern of the native social structure.

With the name group or sib and the major corporation or lineage as the two kinds of groups to which everyone belongs, it is clear why the Trukese distinguish only these in their terminology, the terms *faameni, jetereges*, and *cö* referring primarily to the lineage, and the term *jejinag* to the sib. *Tetten* (line) is a convenient relative term, enabling one to distinguish various groups as lines of larger ones. If a sib contains more than one subsib, one can refer to one of its subsibs as a *faameni*. Within the confines of a particular district one can refer to a ramage as an *jejinag*, thereby distinguishing it clearly from its constituent *faameni* (lineages). Except where ambiguity might result, a native uses the terms for sib and lineage, those which have universal application to all persons, whenever possible. In trying to place someone socially, therefore, one asks for his sib and district affiliation, thus learning his name group and the locality of his lineage.

While the *jejinag* has few functions as distinct from the subsib, ramage, and lineage, it is thought of as having a number of functions insofar as it coincides with, or is mentioned in reference to, any one of these smaller groups. This, together with its universal applicability and its resulting usefulness in placing other persons in relation to oneself both generally and locally, gives the sib a prominent place in the social system.

KINSHIP

INTRODUCTION

THE internal organization of corporations and matrilineal kin groups is based, as we have seen, on the sibling relationship. This is but one of several types of kin relationship which the Trukese recognize. It has been indicated, for example, that a mother's brother is classed as an "older brother" in his position as a senior member of one's corporation, but that as an individual kinsman he is classed as a "father." Kinship on Truk involves considerations other than common membership in a corporation, which is based on an extension of but one of several recognized relationships between blood kinsmen. Kin relationships, cutting as they do across various matrilineal kin groups, are important in binding the members of a native community together as a social unit.

The study of kinship, like property, can be approached from two different directions: analysis of kinship nomenclature and its application, and analysis of the different configurations of rights, privileges, and powers, together with the forms of their behavioral manifestation, which obtain between individuals who are classed as kin. In this chapter we shall deal primarily with the first approach, reserving the second for the chapter to follow.

The Trukese kinship system consists of a set of relationship categories, designated by appropriate terms, and the rules by which membership in each category is determined.[1] Since knowledge of the various types of kin groups—the descent line, lineage, subsib, ramage, and sib—is necessary to an understanding of these rules, analysis of the former has been a necessary precondition to a discussion of kinship.

The *jëfëkyr,* as previously noted, are the children of the men of a matrilineal corporation, and as such are considered the children of the corporation itself. In a broader sense this applies to the non-corporate matrilineal kin groups as well. Thus one may speak of the *jëfëkyr* of a sib as well as of a lineage, meaning the children of its men. Perhaps the best translation of the term *jëfëkyr* is "heir." It will be recalled that when a corporation's membership becomes extinct, it is the *jëfëkyr,* the children, of the corporation who are its natural heirs. Thus when a person says he is an Jacaw man and an *jëfëkyr* of Pwereka, he not only says that his mother was Jacaw and his father was Pwereka, but indicates that he is a member of an Jacaw corporation and an heir to a Pwereka corporation should the latter's membership die out. Similarly the son of a district chief is *jëfëkyren sömwoon* (*jëfëkyr* of the chief) because he is the heir to the chiefship, which is the corporate property of his father's lineage, and will succeed to the chiefship if his father's lineage can supply no adult male to administer it. The native conception that an entire matrilineal kin group counts as its *jëfëkyr* the children of all of its men, gives a sharp twist to the kinship system.

---

[1] For reasons which will become clear in this chapter and the next, we are departing from the more usual definition of a kinship system (see, for example, Murdock, 1949: 91-2) by excluding behavioral obligations from its content, treating it strictly as a terminological system.

CLASSIFICATION OF KIN[2]

CONSANGUINEAL RELATIVES

Kinship terms are used, in reference only, never in addressing a relative directly. Personal names are always used in address, even by children to their parents, although in recent times the borrowed terms *maama* and *paapa* have come to be used by some children in addressing parents. Adults, however, use these words only as terms of reference, and rarely then. Even in reference one does not ordinarily refer to a kinsman by the appropriate kinship term. It is assumed that the members of the community know the ways in which they are related to one another. Kinship terms, therefore, are used principally to explain to strangers the reasons for certain types of behavior, to orient a visiting relative from another community, to justify a course of action that someone has questioned, to instruct the young in their obligations to others, and to criticize the behavior of others in gossip. Kinship terms are also generally used in referring to someone who has died, especially fairly recently, in preference to using the deceased's personal name. In fact, kinship terms are regularly used when one wishes to avoid mentioning someone by name. Occasionally, too, certain terms are used as a means of coercing a person to do something.[3] In summary, kinship terms are employed (1) when the question of kinship is relevant to the context of a conversation, (2) when one wishes to avoid using a personal name, and (3) in order to coerce behavior under exceptional circumstances.

The kinship system will first be considered as it applies to consanguineal relatives. For such relatives there are only six basic terms which apply to all consanguineal kinsmen. In addition, there are a few special terms and a host of descriptive words and

[2] The kinship system of Truk is briefly described in Murdock and Goodenough (1947). The fuller presentation given here departs from the previous manner of description in order to state as systematically as possible not only the nature of the social categories which the kinship system defines but also the limits and manner of their extension. Previous descriptions by Krämer (1932: 266–7), Bollig (1927: 103–4), and Hall (Hall and Pelzer, 1947: 17) are inaccurate and incomplete. Their failure to understand lineage organization and the *jëfëkyr* relationship made it almost impossible for them to get an accurate picture of kinship. Only Bollig gives the correct terms, but even he misstates the rules for their application, particularly to cousins. The writer was fortunately in a position where scarcely a day went by without kinship terms playing some part in his conversation with native informants. Toward the end of his period in the field he was adopted as a brother by one informant on Romonum and became thereby subject to some of the requirements and obligations of kinship. As worked out here, therefore, the system is based on several kinds of data and experience. First, the use of kinship terms was checked against the genealogies with two male informants independently. One of them gave the reasons why he applied the terms as he did to his relatives, such as "father, because the father of my wife." The other indicated every person on Romonum as a relative or non-relative and the appropriate term. The exact relationships were then checked in the genealogies and inconsistences were investigated and explained. This information was verified subsequently by spot checks on other islands, especially Pata, Tol, and Uman, as well as through the writer's attempts to behave in accordance with kinship requirements.

[3] For example, if a woman is reluctant to give me something I want, I may say: *"mwäänumw, mwäänumw* (by your brother, by your brother), give it to me." She would then bring sickness or death on her brother if she failed to grant the request. This use of kinship terms is in effect a conditional curse and is strongly disapproved of as such by the Trukese.

phrases which can be used to distinguish sub-categories of kin or specific relatives. These will be discussed later.

Consanguineal relatives are differentiated on the basis of (1) generation, (2) sex of the relative referred to, and (3) sex of the speaker. Finer distinctions are made by using descriptive words and phrases. The terms derive their basic meaning from their use for primary relatives.[4] The generation factor divides them into three groups: (1) those in generations higher than one's own, (2) those in one's own generation, and (3) those in generations lower than one's own. In higher generations one distinguishes by the sex of the person referred to without reference to the sex of the speaker. In one's own generation one distinguishes both by the sex of the person referred to and by the sex of the speaker. In lower generations no distinction other than that of generation is made. Thus the terms as applied to primary and secondary relatives are:[5]

1. Higher generations.

jinej: "my mother"; applied to any woman of a higher generation, i.e., mother, mother's sister, father's sister, grandmother.

semej: "my father"; applied to any man of a higher generation, i.e., father, father's brother, mother's brother, grandfather.

2. Own generation.

pwiij: "my sibling of the same sex"; applied by a man to his brothers, by a woman to her sisters.

feefinej: "my sister"; applied by a man to his sisters.

mwääni:[6] "my brother"; applied by a woman to her brothers.

3. Lower generations.

neji: "my child"; applied to anyone of a lower generation, i.e., son, daughter, sister's child, brother's child, and grandchild.

All members of my matrilineal descent line[7] are classed as kinsmen. Those of a generation higher than mine in my descent line are my parents: *jinej* and *semej*. All those of my own generation are my siblings: *pwiij, feefinej, mwääni*. Those of generations lower than my own are my children: *neji*. These terms are similarly extended to the members of all other matrilineal kin groups to which I belong: my lineage, my ramage, my subsib, and my sib.

On my father's side the *jëfëkyr* relationship redefines what are higher and lower

[4] Primary relatives are one's own father, mother, siblings, and children. Secondary relatives are the primary relatives of these, i.e., one's grandparents, parents' siblings, siblings' children, and children's children (Murdock, 1949: 94–5).

[5] All these terms are given in the first person possessive form. Since they are used in reference only, they are nearly always accompanied by a possessive modifier. In some cases, too, the roots without possessives, or in apposition to other roots with possessives, have different meanings. Compare, for example: *feefinej* (my sister), *feefin* (woman), *neji feefin* (my adult daughter); and *mwääni* (my brother), *mwään* (man), *jääj mwään* (my older sibling of same sex), *neji mwään* (my adult son).

[6] This is the term on Romonum. On Moen and Uman *mwogejej* is used instead. All other terms appear to be the same throughout Truk.

[7] It should be recalled that the size of what is considered a descent line varies depending on the major genealogical divisions in a lineage. It may include no collateral relatives or may include distant cousins related in the female line.

generations. Since I am an *jëfëkyr* of my father's descent line, I am a child of his descent line as a whole. All the members of his descent line therefore stand in a parental and thus higher generation to me. Hence all the men of my father's descent line (e.g., father's mother's brother, father's brother, father's sister's son) are my fathers: *semej*. All the women (e.g., father's mother, father's sister, father's sister's daughter) are my mothers: *jinej*. The parent terms are extended to members of other matrilineal kin groups to which my father belongs, including his lineage, ramage, and subsib, but not including his sib.

The same considerations apply optionally to the lineage and subsib of my mother's father, since I am the child of their *jëfëkyr*.[8] Even more remotely one can extend this to the members of one's father's father's lineage, but in practice this is not done.

Since all the children of all the men of my descent line (e.g., mother's mother's brother's child, mother's brother's child, brother's child, sister's son's child) are in turn my *jëfëkyr*, including of course my own children if I am a man, they are regarded as of a lower generation and are hence my children: *neji*. This usage is extended to include the *jëfëkyr* of my lineage, ramage, and subsib, but does not include the *jëfëkyr* of my sib. The children of my *jëfëkyr* are in turn of an even lower generation and hence are also *neji*.[9]

Since all the *jëfëkyr* of my father's descent line (e.g., father's mother's brother's children, father's brother's children, father's sister's son's children, and father's children by another marriage) stand in the same generational relationship to my father's descent line that I do and are, like me, "heirs" of that descent line, I consider them to be in my generation and hence call them siblings: *pwiij, feefinej, mwääni*. This usage is extended to the *jëfëkyr* of my father's lineage, possibly his ramage, but not to those of his subsib or sib. The Trukese say: "He is *pwiij* because we are *jëfëkyr* of the same *sööpw* (lineage)." Since the *jëfëkyr* of my father's descent line and lineage are my siblings, their children are of a lower generation and are hence my children: *neji*.

It is apparent that the Trukese kinship system is fundamentally or originally of the so-called Hawaiian or generation type, in which parental terms are extended to all relatives of one's parents' generation, sibling terms to all relatives of one's own generation, and child terms to all relatives of one's children's generation, regardless of how they are actually related.[10] The Trukese notion that the people of a lineage stand in a

[8] Jamiwo of Romonum included them as parents in his kin to the extent of one descent line in the Jacaw 2 lineage (his mother's father had been a member of the closely related Jacaw 3 lineage), but this was by mutual agreement between himself and the members of this group. Jejiwe of Romonum did not recognize as kin the members of his mother's father's lineage.

[9] A person is in a position to recognize this relationship with the children of his *jëfëkyr* much more readily than they are to reciprocate. While a man lives, his lineage mates recognize kinship with his grandchildren, but he usually dies before his grandchildren have reached puberty or adulthood and are fully aware of the connection and prepared to act accordingly. This is more likely in the case of a man's son's children than in the case of his daughter's children, since the latter are more likely to have provisional title to property held under residual title by their maternal grandfather's lineage.

[10] That the Hawaiian type of kinship system was ancestral not only to the system now found in Truk but to those found throughout Micronesia has been demonstrated by Murdock (1948).

parental relationship to the children of its men, its *jëfëkyr*, has redefined what constitutes a higher and lower generation, thereby altering the framework of the Hawaiian type of kinship system. This redefinition is a logical outgrowth of the organization of lineages and descent lines as corporations whose members are regarded as siblings. It is possible that at one time a person stood in a dual relationship to his mother's brother's son just as he now does to his mother's brother, calling this cousin a sibling when they interacted simply as kinsmen but calling him a child when behaving as a member of a corporation toward one of its *jëfëkyr*. One might predict that if the same trend continues, reference to the mother's brother as "father" will give way to calling him "older brother" in all contexts, as appears now to be the case on Puluwat.

TABLE 5. THE KINSHIP SYSTEM

Generation*	Children of Jëfëkyr of Father's Lineage	Jëfëkyr of Father's Lineage	Members of Father's Lineage	Members of Own Lineage	Jëfëkyr of Own Lineage	Children of Jëfëkyr of Own Lineage
Higher	neji	pwiij mwääni feefinej	semej jinej	semej jinej	neji	neji
Ego's	neji	pwiij mwääni feefinej	semej jinej	pwiij mwääni feefinej	neji	neji
Lower	neji	pwiij mwääni feefinej	semej jinej	neji	neji	neji

* Generations are here given in the conventional or genealogical sense to show how they differ from the definition which the *jëfëkyr* relationship gives to them.

The result of the present usage on Truk is that one's father's sisters' children are classed as parents and one's mother's brothers' children as children. The redefinition of generations by other than strictly genealogical criteria converts the Trukese cousin terminology from the Hawaiian to the so-called Crow type.[11] This is illustrated in the schematic representation of the kinship system in Table 5.

AFFINAL RELATIVES

A native's affinal relatives are of two major types: those who are connected with him by only one marital tie, the other intervening connections being consanguineal, and those who are connected with him by two intervening marital ties. The first type includes persons married to one's consanguineal relatives on the one hand and consanguineal relatives of the person to whom one is married on the other. With this type we

[11] For a discussion of different types of kinship systems, including the Hawaiian, and for a description of the Crow system, see Lowie (1948: 60–75). See also Murdock (1949: 91–183) for a full discussion of kinship typology.

encounter some new kinship terms. The second type of affinal kin includes persons who are married to the consanguineal relatives of one's spouse. Consanguineal relationship terms are extended to relations of this type. With both types the generation of the affinal relative in relation to one's own is determined by equating the generations of husband and wife.

The most important affinal relatives of the first type are the spouses of one's primary and secondary kin and the primary and secondary kinsmen of one's spouse. For these the terms are:

1. Higher generations.

jinej: "my mother"; applied to any one my spouse calls *jinej* and to the wife of any-one I call *semej*; e.g., spouse's mother, spouse's grandmother, spouse's mother's sister, spouse's father's sister; and father's brother's wife, mother's brother's wife, grandfather's wife, father's wife (stepmother or father's other wife in a polygynous marriage).

semej: "my father"; applied to anyone my spouse calls *semej* and to the husband of anyone I call *jinej*; e.g., spouse's grandfather, spouse's father, spouse's father's brother, spouse's mother's brother; and grandmother's husband, father's sister's husband, mother's sister's husband, mother's husband (stepfather).

2. Own or spouse's generation.

pwynywej: "my spouse"; applied to my own spouse, to anyone whom my spouse calls *pwiij*, and to the spouse of anyone I call *pwiij*; e.g., husband, wife, wife's sister, hus-band's brother; brother's wife (man speaking), sister's husband (woman speak-ing).

jëësej: "my sibling-in-law of the same sex"; applied to anyone whom my spouse calls *mwääni* or *feefinej*, and to the spouse of anyone whom I call *mwääni* or *feefinej*; e.g., wife's brother, husband's sister; brother's wife (woman speaking), sister's husband (man speaking).

3. Lower generations.

neji: "my child"; applied to anyone whom my spouse calls *neji* and the spouse of any-one whom I call *neji*; e.g., spouse's child (stepchild), spouse's sister's child, spouse's brother's child, spouse's grandchild, spouse of a brother's or sister's child, son-in-law, daughter-in-law.

These terms are extended to the spouses of all the persons whom one recognizes as blood kin except the spouses of sibmates, who are not included among one's affinal kin. The terms are likewise extended to all the consanguineal relatives of one's spouse, similarly excluding those who are merely his or her sibmates.

Affinal relatives of the second major type are called by the same terms as those used for blood relatives. The most important relatives of this kind are the persons mar-ried to members of one's wife's or husband's descent line. They are the other persons who have married into the same descent line as oneself. This relationship is functionally more important for men than for women, for with matrilocal residence the men who have married into the same descent line and lineage must live and work together as members of the same household. The terms *jinej* and *semej* are applied to affinal rela-tives of this type who are associated with a higher generation (including spouse's mother's sister's spouse, spouse's mother's brother's spouse). The term *pwiij* is applied to the husbands or wives of those people whom one calls *pwynywej,* but there is no corresponding term for the spouses of those whom one calls *jëësej.*[12] The spouses of those whom one's spouse calls *neji* are likewise called *neji.* Affinal relatives of this type ordinarily include only those persons who are married to the members of one's spouse's lineage or possibly to its *jëfëkyr.* Kinship terms are not extended to persons married to members of one's spouse's subsib or sib, though they may include persons who have married into the spouse's ramage.

The use of all affinal terms is immediately dropped, along with the relationships which they express, when the marriage which instituted their use is terminated either by death or divorce. The only exception to this is the continued use of parent terms for a stepfather and the members of his lineage when he continues to act as a father to his stepchildren after the death of their mother (his wife).[13]

The kinship system as it applies to affinal relatives may be summarized as follows. Affinal kin of all types are classed as belonging to a higher, the same, or a lower generation than one's own. For those in higher and lower generations one uses the same terms as are used for consanguineal relatives. In one's own generation the spouses of siblings and the siblings of spouses are distinguished from one's own siblings, but their spouses are classed as siblings.

SPECIAL TERMS AND FINER DISTINCTIONS

Analysis of the kinship system has revealed seven basic categories of persons: fathers, mothers, siblings of same sex, siblings of opposite sex (two reciprocal terms), spouses, siblings-in-law of same sex, and children. The assignment of relatives to the appropriate categories has been found to be regular and systematic. Finer distinctions, however, may be made on the basis of sex, age, and manner of relationship.

It is quite possible for anyone to indicate the relationship between two people more exactly by describing it, as we do in English. For example, just as we say "mother's brother" in order to specify the kind of "uncle" we mean, the Trukese likewise says *mwäänin inej* (brother of my mother) to distinguish the kind of "father" he means. One may distinguish a son from a daughter by using the age grade terms for each sex: *neji jäät* (my boy child), *neji mwään* (my man child), *neji neggin* (my girl child), or *neji feefin* (my woman child).[14]

[12] While there is no term for these relatives, they are none the less considered important and are shown respect. Thus Jejiwe of Romonum is very circumspect in his behavior towards his wife's brother's wife, though she is not covered by the kinship terminology.

[13] Jejiwe of Romonum calls his wife's stepfather *semej* because the latter has continued to live with his son and stepdaughters, has not remarried, and considers his step-daughters his own children equally with his son, their half-brother.

[14] It was apparently this descriptive aspect of the Trukese terminolgy which led Hall (Hall and Pelzer, 1946: 17) to the erroneous conclusion that "until recently there were 81 terms covering relatives on both sides of the family, for four generations up and three down as well as affinals for two generations up and down. Kinship includes special terms for mother's side and father's side, as well as cross and parallel cousins, which have reciprocal terms." To ask a Trukese informant through an interpreter how you say "father's mother's brother's daughter's husband" is to invite the literal translation *pwynywen nëwyn mwäänin inen semej.*

In addition to combining the basic terms to indicate more exact relationship, the Trukese use certain special terms. Among these are distinctive terms for own father and own mother: *semenapej* (my main father) and *jinenapej* (my main mother). It is possible that they may also be applied to own grandparents. These terms apply not only to one's biological parents, but to whoever is acting in the role of true parent, such as a step-father. There are no other special terms whose use is restricted to primary relatives alone.[15]

Another special term is *jääj mwään* (literally: "my general-object-man") which is used to refer to an older sibling of same sex regardless of whether the speaker is a man or a woman. When the authoritative aspects of the relationship between older and younger siblings as members of the same corporation provide the context, the speaker refers to such an older sibling by this term. This term is used for any older *pwiij* in one's descent line, lineage, subsib, ramage, or even sib. It appears not to be applicable to those of one's *pwiij* who belong to different matrilineal kin groups from one's own, such as a father's brother's children. It is definitely not applicable to those of one's *pwiij* who are affinal relatives, such as a wife's sister's husband. The limitation in its usage to members of the same corporation (or members of the matrilineal kin groups derived from corporations) is further exemplified by the fact that a mother's brother may also be referred to as *jääj mwään*, but a father's brother may not. This term is regularly used for any older man of one's own lineage at times when property transactions and other matters pertaining to corporate organization provide the context of the relationship. The writer heard *jääj mwään* used only under these conditions and once to designate a much older sibmate of another and unrelated lineage of whose generation in relation to his own the speaker was uncertain. The reciprocal of *jääj mwään* is *mwääninyki* (literally: "my adjacent man"). It is applied in similar contexts to a younger brother or to a younger lineage mate.

A special descriptive term distinguishing a father's sister or woman of one's father's lineage from matrilineally related "mothers" is the compound *jinejisemej*.[16] The writer heard it only a few times and then only when the obligations of a father's sister to her brother's son in particular, or of a woman to the *jëfëkyr* of her lineage in general, provided the context.

Relatives classed as siblings are subdivided into three types: (1) *pwiipwii cëk* (siblings only), those in one's own descent line or lineage; (2) *pwiipwi winisam* (siblings by

[15] An own sibling, for example, can be referred to only as *pwiij emën cëk ineem* (my-sibling-of-same-sex one only our-mother). One may say *jääm pwiipwii cëk* (we-are just brothers), but this expression is ambiguous since it is applicable to lineage siblings as well. For own children one may say *wesewesen neji* or *jennetin neji* (my real or true child).

[16] This term means literally "mother of my father." There are instances in which the term *jinej* is used in the sense of older sister (man speaking). On Puluwat it is regularly used for any older woman of one's own lineage or subsib. On Truk, when speaking of behavior, a man is said to *jinejin* both the persons he calls *jinej* and those he calls *feefinej*. I have heard *jinej* used for an older sister on Moen Island in Truk, though I later ascertained that there, too, the term *feefinej* was in common use. The term *jinejisemej* may more properly mean, therefore, "older sister of my father" or "older female relative on my father's side," meanings which correspond more closely with the actual use of the term. It is not to be confused with the descriptive phrase *jinen semej* (my father's mother) which applies to anyone one's father calls *jinej*.

fathers), fellow *jëfëkyr* of one's father's lineage; and (3) *pwiipwi winipwyny* (siblings by spouses), persons who are married to *pwiipwii cëk*. There are no special terms of individual reference for persons in these different categories which are comparable to the other special terms considered so far. Only the collective expressions given above are used.[17] The *pwiipwii cëk* have their relations governed by common lineage membership, common property interests, and the obligations which these imply. The *pwiipwi winisam*, being members of different lineages and not having common property interests except as they are jointly the *jëfëkyr* of the same lineage, have their relationship modified accordingly as well as by the fact that they are considered somewhat remoter kin. The *pwiipwi winipwyny* have a bond based on common membership in a matrilocal extended family (if they are men) or by the fact that their husbands are *pwiipwii cëk* (if they are women).

One general distinction, in addition to that of sex and age, that can be made among persons called *neji* is based upon whether they are members or *jëfëkyr* of one's own lineage. One says *neji jëfëkyr* (my *jëfëkyr* children) in referring to the latter type. A man will speak of *nëwyn feefinej* (my sister's children) to distinguish them from his *neji jëfëkyr*.

NEAR AND REMOTE KIN

No distinctions in terminology are made between near and distant kinsmen. One's relatives, nevertheless, fall into fairly clear-cut groups with respect to distance of relationship. A more distant relative is less intensely subject to the obligations of kinship than is a closer relative, though he is referred to by the same kinship term. It is important to emphasize that closeness of relationship has nothing necessarily to do with the intimacy expressed within the relationship itself. Brothers and sisters are anything but intimate in most aspects of their behavior, yet they consider themselves extremely close kin and observe the taboos and obligations between them most scrupulously. It is the scrupulousness with which a relationship is observed and the seriousness with which a breach of the relationship is viewed which provides the yardstick for the following formulations.

In Trukese thinking closeness of relationship is not simply a function of purely biological considerations. The natives recognize, for example, that biologically a father's brother is as closely related as a mother's brother. Both are of "one flesh" with oneself. But my mother's brother and I belong to the same corporation, to which we must both subordinate our personal interest, while my father's brother and I always belong to different corporations. The interests which my mother's brother and I share jointly as members of the same corporation take precedence over my relations with my father's brother. Measuring closeness of kinship by the scrupulousness with which kinship obligations are observed makes sociological as well as biological factors important as relevant criteria.

There is, therefore, no simple rule by which relative distance of consanguineal rela-

---

[17]One says: *jääm pwiipwii cëk* (we are siblings only), *jäämi pwiipwi winisam* (you are siblings by fathers), or *jiir pwiipwi winipwyny* (they are siblings by spouses).

tionship is determined. Rather, there are several rules which operate simultaneously. These are:[18]

1. Other things being equal, the fewer the intervening genealogical connections, the closer the relative (e.g., brother is closer than mother's sister's son).

2. Beyond primary and secondary relatives, intervening connections are reckoned primarily in terms of the differential solidarity of the several types of matrilineal kin groups and secondarily in terms of genealogical connections (e.g., one's descent line siblings are collectively closer than one's lineage siblings, and one's father's descent line siblings are collectively closer than one's father's lineage siblings, even in cases where members of the descent line are genealogically more remotely related than are other members of the lineage).

3. Other things being equal, relatives in generations closer to one's own are closer than those in generations further removed from one's own (e.g., brother is closer than father). This applies to generations in the Trukese and not in the absolute sense.

4. Other things being equal, relatives connected through females are closer than relatives connected through males (e.g., mother's brother is closer than father's brother).

5. Other things being equal, relatives of the same sex are closer than relatives of the opposite sex (e.g., a man's brother is closer than is his sister); the bond between own siblings of same sex is the strongest in the culture.

In accordance with these five rules, one considers one's primary and secondary relatives to be one's closest. The members of one's own descent line are closer than those of one's father's descent line (rules 2, 3, and 4). A mother's sister's son is closer than a father's sister's son (rules 3 and 4). The *jëfëkyr* of one's father's descent line are in one sense remoter than the *jëfëkyr* of one's own descent line (rules 1, 2, 4) but in another are closer (rule 3). This last example demonstrates that the rules do not all reinforce each other, but one may counteract the effect of another. This raises the problem of weighting the criteria on which the rules are based. Actually, however, the question of weighting is unimportant. The Trukese native does not appraise his relationship with another individual with mathematical precision, and when fairly close relatives are involved he will avoid making a decision in favor of one at the expense of the other if he possibly can.

Among affinal kin, the spouse's consanguineal relatives are equated with the relatives to whom they are married. A mother's sister's husband is thus a closer affinal relative than a father's sister's husband. A brother's wife is closer than a father's brother's son's wife. A man reckons distance among his wife's consanguineal relatives as his wife does, and she does the same in relation to his blood kin. The same rule applies to persons who are married to the consanguineal relatives of one's spouse. Thus a wife's sister's husband is closer than a wife's mother's sister's husband.

By and large, affinal kin are considered less closely related than blood kin. A woman's

[18] It is obvious that no Trukese informant was ever able to make these rules explicit to me. I have derived them by a careful analysis of my field notes and checked them in the only way possible, namely, against my own remembered experiences as one partially acculturated to the Trukese way of life. The systematic collection of data necessary for the formulation of such rules with greater reliability poses a crucial methodological problem.

obligations to her brothers, for example, are considered more important than her obligations to her husband. If her brothers have a dispute with her husband, she is supposed to take their side. Similarly a man's obligations to his siblings take precedence over his obligations to his wife and her siblings.

THE *FUTUK*

Anyone who can be referred to by a kinship term may be called *tefej* (my relative). As noted, however, not all relatives are considered among one's close kin. The group which forms what the Trukese calls his close kin consists of his primary and secondary relatives, the members of his own and his father's lineage, and the *jëfëkyr* of both. The natives call this group a *futuk* (flesh), considering its members to be of "one flesh with oneself." Their use of the concept of "one flesh" is similar to our own concept of consanguinity.

It will be noted that patrilineally as well as matrilineally related persons are included in the *futuk*. As broken down further it consists of:

1. All four grandparents.
2. Both parents.
3. The siblings of both parents (including all members of their respective lineages).
4. Siblings (including all members of one's lineage).
5. The children of all the siblings of both parents (including the *jëfëkyr* of their respective lineages).
6. Children.
7. The children of all siblings (including the *jëfëkyr* of one's lineage).
8. All grandchildren.

It is apparent that the *futuk* represents a modification of the bilateral kindred as defined by Rivers (1926: 16), just as the Trukese kinship system is a modification of an earlier Hawaiian type.[19] The development of matrilineal corporations and of the *jëfëkyr* concept has modified the basis for extending membership in the *futuk* beyond primary and secondary relatives and has unquestionably transferred to the lineage functions which at one time were associated with the earlier kindred.

The *futuk* corresponds to what we mean by the "family," "relatives," or "kin-folk" in the wider sense, as when we speak of family gatherings in connection with such events as Christmas, Thanksgiving, weddings, and funerals. It is the members of the *futuk* who assemble at births, marriages, and deaths on Truk. If there are members of his *futuk* living on other islands, a native can always look to them for food and shelter while away from home. In his own community he can turn to such kinsmen for a meal if there is no food in his own house. Sex relations with persons in one's *futuk* are considered incestuous.

A native may also have active kin relations with persons who are not strictly members of his *futuk*. Such persons are his *määräär*, who may be defined as affinal relatives

19 For the association of the bilateral kindred with the Hawaiian type of kinship system, see Murdock (1948; 1949: 158, 228–31).

and consanguineal relatives who are remoter than those in the *futuk*, but with whom an active relationship is maintained. One's *määräär* may include persons who are not covered by any kinship terms, but who wish to consider themselves related to one another by virtue of some affinal or remote consanguineal tie. The members of one's *futuk* are automatically counted among one's active relatives, but the *määräär* relationship is one which must be activated by mutual consent, though based on the potentialities of a remote kinship connection.[20] As with the *futuk*, one can count on a meal from one's *määräär* when need arises. Visiting at the homes of others within a community tends also to be largely confined to *määräär*. A record of the people who stopped off at one native house on Romonum for visiting and gossiping was kept for a period of several weeks. Virtually everyone who stopped by was at least a *määräär* or ramage mate, if not a closer relative, of one of the adult occupants of the house.

A native may loosely refer to any kinsman by blood or marriage as a *määräär*, provided he is not of the same lineage, and even may use the term collectively to cover all active relatives, including those in the *futuk*. The Trukese regularly refer to a kinsman as a *määräär* when they wish to avoid expressing more precisely the nature of the relationship.[21]

SOME METHODOLOGICAL CONSIDERATIONS

In our discussion of kinship so far, we have presented a set of terms as comprising a "system" and have followed this with other terms which we called "special" in the sense that they did not fit into the system. By what criteria have we decided to treat some terms as belonging and others as not belonging to a terminological system? Little validity can be claimed for the foregoing description without an answer to this question. In order to see its implications more clearly, we can restate it as follows: By what methods can we derive social categories from native terminology; how can the structural relationships of such categories to each other be determined; and what must be the manner of their relationship in order to classify them as members of a system of categories? Our problem starts in linguistics and ends in ethnography with semantics bridging the two, for we start with linguistic forms and, by defining their symbolic

[20] Jejiwe and Söön of Romonum are not considered relatives within the framework of the formal kinship system; neither calls the other *tefej* (my kinsman). Nor do they consider themselves "buddies," which would lead to an artificial sibling relationship. Söön is the older brother of Puruuta, who is married to the own sister of Jejiwe's wife. Jejiwe thus refers to Puruuta as *pwiij*. Puruuta and Söön both live together in adjacent houses in virilocal residence, and this has brought Söön into the relationship between Jejiwe and Puruuta, insofar as it involves doing small mutual favors such as providing food for one another at meal times. For this reason Jejiwe considers Söön to be one of his *määräär*, referring to him as *määrääri* (my *määräär*).

[21] Several men reported dreams in which they had become involved sexually with a taboo female relative. To have used the terms *feefinej, jinej*, or *neji* would perhaps have tipped the listener off to the identity of the person in the dream, and would certainly have made the dream seem more heinous in view of the taboos governing one's relations with persons as referred to by the more specific terms. The woman of such dreams was always, therefore, a *määräär*, vague as to her identity and the nature and distance of her relationship, an anonymous female relative.

values, arrive at the categories of kin which they denote.[22] In the discussion to follow, our methods of analysis in the present instance will be outlined step by step.

In order to isolate the verbal behavior patterns[23] which would be relevant to kinship analysis, it was first ascertained that there is a group of persons any of whom can be referred to as *tefej* (my kinsman). Our genealogical census of Romonum revealed that nearly all people who can be referred to by this term have the common characteristic of being connected genealogically to an ego or to an ego's spouse. It is this fact which led to a definition of *tefej* as meaning "my kinsman." In order to isolate other kinship terms, it was necessary to find verbal behavior patterns which in their role as symbols denote persons who are included among those denoted by *tefej*, but who have more characteristics in common.

Employing the genealogical method, we obtained a series of symbolic behavior patterns which satisfy these criteria, e.g., the terms *jinej, jääj mwään, nëwyn neji* (child of my child), and *sömwomw* (your father). Morphological analysis[24] of these verbal behavior patterns—and there are a great many of them—indicated that whether or not the persons denoted are kinsmen depends on the presence of a limited number of morphemes,[25] some one of which has to be a part of the behavior pattern. These morphemes consist of the following base forms:[26] *sam-, jin-, mwään-, feefin-, mwogej-, nëw-, jëës-,* and *pwyny-*. Some of these have corresponding forms appearing as independent words, uncompounded with other morphemes. They are *mwään, feefin, saam* (sam-), and *jiin* (jin-).[27] The remaining morphemes seem to occur only when compounded with other morphemes or with repetition of their own base form in complex words, e.g., *pwii-j* or *pwii-pwi (pwi-)*.

The independent words *mwään* and *feefin* do not signify kinship at all. The characteristics of persons which they denote are such that they signify "man" and "woman" respectively. Nor do *saam* and *jiin* signify relationship with respect to some ego. The persons which they denote have characteristics in common such that these words signify "father" and "mother" in the sense of "he is a father" and "she is a mother" or "everyone who is a father (or mother)." Thus, they signify social attributes which people may or may not have rather than kinship with respect to a specific ego.

This raises an important distinction that must be made between types of social categories. There are categories to which a person may belong regardless of the category membership of others. For example, an old man is an "old man" regardless of anyone else's age, and he has a social role as such. Similarly a man who has children may have

[22]The term "ethnolinguistics" has recently been adopted in reference to subject matter of this kind (Voegelin and Harris, 1945).

[23]Linton (1945: 45) defines a behavior pattern as "a range of normal responses to a particular situation." Acoustically no two utterances of the same kinship term are ever exactly alike, but all utterances of it which are intelligible fall within a range of normal responses.

[24]For methods of morphological analysis, see Nida (1946).

[25]Bloomfield (1933: 161): "A linguistic form which bears no partial-semantic resemblance to any other form, is a *simple* form or *morpheme*."

[26]For base and stem forms in Trukese, see Dyen (1949: 421).

[27]For the lengthening or doubling of the vowels in monosyllabic words, see Dyen (1949: 422-3).

a role in his community as one who is a father. On the other hand, there are categories to which a person may belong only as they are polar to specified categories of others. In this context, one can be an "older man" only in relation to those who are younger than oneself. A man can be a "father" only in relation to persons who are "children" to him. In deriving the categories into which the members of a society are classified it is necessary to distinguish between these two types. The first may be called *absolute categories* and the second *relative categories*.[28] With this distinction in mind, analysis revealed that there are only two Trukese terms denoting absolute categories of kin: *saam* and *jiin*. Beyond them it is not possible to construct a system of kinship nomenclature based on terms of this semantic type.

We turned our attention, therefore, to the forms denoting relative categories of kin, those categories which exist only with reference to a specified ego or egos. This immediately raised the problem of how such reference is expressed in the Trukese language, and what the possible categories of reference are.

Reference or possession may be expressed for the following categories of persons or egos: first person singular, second person singular, third person singular, first person plural inclusive (we including you), first person plural exclusive (we excluding you), second person plural, and third person plural. Any of the morphemes which may signify kinship can occur compounded with a suffixed form denoting any one of the above categories of ego-reference. There is also a suffix expressing reference or possession for an unspecified category of egos. Any compound with this form must be followed by a specifying word or phrase.[29] All resulting compounds, unless further modified, denote relative categories of kin and may be said to belong to a semantic class of verbal behavior patterns on the basis of this common characteristic.[30]

Having thus derived a series of verbal behavior patterns which regularly denote persons who are genealogically connected with an ego or ego's spouse, our next problem was to define the boundaries of each category of kin. Since relative categories of kin are denoted only by behavior patterns which include referential or possessive forms as one of their components, it was necessary to hold the ego constant; that is we had to ascertain all the persons who can be denoted by each term as given consistently in the first

[28] This distinction is relevant for any comparative or cross-cultural study. In comparing the age-grading systems of different societies, for example, the relative system of categories in one is not comparable with the absolute system of categories in another. For the cross-cultural study of kinship terminology, Murdock (1949: 97–8) points out that terms of address are not necessarily comparable with terms of reference. Even with terms of reference, we cannot compare those denoting absolute categories with those denoting relative categories, for within one culture they may not coincide.

[29] The possibilities can be illustrated with the root *jin-* as follows: *jinej* (my mother), *jinomw* (thy mother), *jinan* (his or her mother), *jinac* (our mother, incl.), *jineem* (our mother, excl.), *jinemi* (your mother, pl.), *jineer* (their mother), *jinen Kinöwus* (mother-of Kinöwus), or the permitted but awkward expression *jinen gaag* (mother-of me). Cf. Dyen (1949: 421).

[30] There are other forms which also belong to this class, e.g., the compounds *semenapej* (my main father), *jinenapej* (my main mother), *jinejisemej* (my father's sister), and *mwääninyki* (my younger sibling of same sex), and also the phrases *jääj mwään* (my older sibling of same sex), *neji mwään* (my adult son), and *neji feefin* (my adult daughter). But such phrases of similar construction as *neji cöön agaag* (my employee) and *semej sömwon* (my chief) do not belong to this semantic class.

person singular or some other referential form. Having derived a set of persons who can be denoted by each kinship term in the first person singular, we proceeded to do the same thing for each term in the second person singular, and so on for all the referential categories. We then compared the set of persons denoted by a term in the first person with sets denoted by it in the other referential categories, and found them all to be congruent. For example, the persons who can be "your father" in relation to "you" have the same characteristics as those who can be "my father" in relation to "me."[31] In our description of the kinship system, therefore, it was necessary to present only the first person singular forms, for the same picture would have obtained had the terms been presented in any other possessive form.

The next step in our analysis was to see how each category of persons denoted by a term is related to the other categories as denoted by the other terms. This involved comparing them with respect to the characteristics by which membership in each category is defined. We shall refer to the characteristics which define what a term denotes as what the term *signifies* or as the *significatum* of the term.[32] Our problem, then, was to derive the significatum of each kinship term and to compare these significata with one another to see how they are related, if, of course, they are related at all beyond the fact that all persons denoted have the common characteristic of being genealogically connected to an ego or ego's spouse.

In order to derive the significatum of a term we compared all the persons who were denoted by it on the occasion of all of its utterances as we had experienced them. The characteristics which these persons had in common, but which they shared with no one who could not be denoted by the term, were considered to be the criteria for membership in the category of persons which they constituted, and hence to comprise the significatum of the kinship term. Thus, for example, the significatum of *semej* (my father) consists of the following characteristics or attributes: (1) kin to ego (as contrasted with non-kin), (2) higher generation than that of ego (as contrasted with same or lower generations), and (3) male (as contrasted with female). According to our data, anyone with this combination of characteristics, and no one else, may be called *semej*.

The method used in comparing significata can be illustrated by analysis of the English words, "go," "went," and "gone." While there is no constant phonemic segment among them, they can all be classed as parts of the same verb because of the fact that when any utterance in which they occur is varied only with respect to tense, the others must be substituted for it. In other words, the differences in their significata are a simple function of a variable of tense. This can be expressed symbolically as follows:

Let A equal the characteristics of motion away from an ego.
Let B equal the variable characteristic of tense with B_1 (present), B_2 (imperfect), and B_3 (perfect).

---

[31]While the congruence thus obtained was to be expected, rigorous analysis does not allow us to assume it as axiomatic. This congruence was established by the process of substitution. It was found that whenever a context in which *semej* (my father) can occur is altered only with respect to the ego referent, then *saman* (his father), *somwomw* (your father), etc., can be substituted.

[32]This usage is taken from Morris (1946: 17).

Thus: "go" has the significatum . . . . AB_1
"went" has the significatum . . . . AB_2
"gone" has the significatum . . . . AB_3

The significata of these words are mutually contrasting and at the same time complement each other with respect to the variable of tense.

For our purposes we must complicate this example further by examining the relation of "come," "came," "come" to "go," "went," "gone."

Let A equal the characteristic of motion.
Let B equal the variable characteristic of direction, with B_1 (towards ego) and B_2 (away from ego).
Let C equal the variable characteristic of tense, with C_1 (present), C_2 (imperfect), and C_3 (perfect).
Thus: "come" has the significatum . . . . AB_1C_1; AB_1C_3
"came" has the significatum. . . . . AB_1C_2
"go" has the significatum . . . . AB_1C_2
"went" has the significatum . . . . AB_2C_2
"gone" has the significatum . . . . AB_2C_3

All of the above forms have the common characteristic of motion in their significata. The differences between their significata are simultaneously functions of two variable characteristics, those of direction in relation to an ego and of tense. Because the differences between the significata of "go," "went," and "gone" in the first paradigm are functions of only one variable, they are forms which belong together in what may be called a *simple semantic system*. Because the differences between the significata of all the forms in the second paradigm are functions or more than one variable, we shall consider them members of what may be called a *complex semantic system*.

We can say that a series of symbolic behavior patterns belong to the same semantic system if (1) their significata include one characteristic in common, (2) the differences between their significata are functions of one (simple system) or more (complex system) variable characteristics, and (3) their significata are mutually contrasting and complement each other.

With this in mind we are now in a position to examine the significata of Trukese kinship terms. Taking them all collectively, their significata involve, in addition to the common characteristic of kinship, characteristics which are expressions of seven different variables. In accordance with the procedure outlined above we may list them as follows:

Let A equal the characteristic of being someone who is *tefej* (my kinsman) to an ego.
Let B equal the variable characteristic of generation in relation to that of ego, with B_1 (higher generation), B_2 (same generation), and B_3 (lower generation), generation here to be taken in the Trukese sense.
Let C equal the variable characteristic of the sex of ego's kinsman, with C_1 (male) and C_2 (female).

Let D equal the variable characteristic of the sex of ego's kinsman in relation to the sex of ego, with D_1 (same sex) and D_2 (opposite sex).

Let E equal the variable characteristic of the age of ego's kinsman in relation to ego's age, with E_1 (older) and E_2 (younger).

Let F equal the variable characteristic of the lineage of the kinsman in relation to ego's lineage, with F_1 (ego's lineage) and F_2 (ego's father's lineage).

Let G equal the variable characteristic of affinal as opposed to consanguineal connection, with G_1 (no affinal connections), G_2 (one affinal connection), and G_3 (two affinal connections).

Let H equal the variable characteristic of lineality versus collaterality, with H_1 (lineal relative) and H_2 (collateral relative).

TABLE 6. SEMANTIC SYSTEMS OF KINSHIP

	Kinship Term	Significatum
System 1	semej	AB_1C_1
	jinej	AB_1C_2
	pwiij	$AB_2D_1G_1$; $AB_2D_1G_3$
	jëësej	$AB_2D_1G_2$
	mwääni; mwogejej	$AB_2D_2G_1C_1$
	feefinej	$AB_2D_2G_1C_2$
	pwynywej	$AB_2D_2G_2$
	neji	AB_3
System 2	jääj mwään	$AF_1D_1E_1$
	mwääninyki	$AF_1D_1E_2$
	jinejisemej	AF_2C_2
System 3	semenapej	$AB_1H_1C_1$
	jinenapej	$AB_1H_1C_2$

Note. There is no term for the complementary possibility of $AB_2D_2G_3$ in System 1, other than the descriptive phrase *pwynywen jëësej.* There are no terms for the remaining complementary possibilities implied by the significata of the three terms in System 2 and the two terms in System 3, both systems being fragmentary.

Comparison of the kinship terms in relation to these characteristics of their significata reveals that they fall into three distinct semantic systems, as illustrated in Table 6.

It will be noted that none of these systems contains terms for all the complementary categories which are made possible by the significata actually represented. In this respect they are all what may be called incomplete semantic systems. The first system is nearly complete with only one unrealized possibility, while the other two are fragmentary.

Each system is composed of kinship terms whose significata meet the requirements of our definition of a semantic system. The first system, for example, consists of terms whose significata have characteristic A common to all of them. The differences between the significata are functions primarily of the variable characteristic of generation (B) and secondarily of other variables which subdivide the major categories of generation into complementary subcategories. All of the significata are mutually contrasting and complement one another with respect to their variable characteristics.

The significata of the kinship terms composing the second and third systems are not mutually contrasting with those of the first system, nor do they complement them, despite the fact that they share the common characteristic A. For example, at least one person denoted by *jinenapej* may also be denoted by *jinej*. People who may be denoted by *jääj mwään* are partially included among those who may be denoted by *semej* and *pwiij*.

This constitutes the method whereby we derived the criteria by which kinsmen are differentiated as presented in our description of the Trukese kinship system. It explains why the kinship system was described with respect to the terms found in the first semantic system given in Table 5, whereas the others were treated as "special" terms which could not be fitted into it. All of the kinship categories denoted by terms belonging to one semantic system are considered as constituting a single system of social categories. It is in this sense that we have used the expression "kinship system."

In the writer's opinion, the method of analysis just presented has important impli-cations for comparative studies of kinship. It reveals what are the primary variables out of which a given kinship system is constructed and what are the secondary variables. Systems can therefore be compared on the basis of the particular variables selected by different societies as the primary ones on which to base differentiation of kin. For ex-ample, the primary variable differentiating the significata of contemporary American kinship terms is that of lineality versus collaterality, with three categories which are expressions of this variable: (1) those who are lineal ancestors or descendants, including siblings; (2) those who are the siblings of lineal ancestors or reciprocally the lineal descendants of siblings; and (3) those who are the lineal descendants of the siblings of lineal ancestors. Within the first two categories we also distinguish by sex and genera-tion of kinsman, but within the third category we make no distinctions at all, referring to everyone as "my cousin" unless the requirements of the situation demand such further description as "second cousin, once removed." This, of course, contrasts markedly with the Trukese system (system 1), where the primary variable is that of generation. Classification of kinship systems for comparative study has so far been based mainly on differences in the way in which relatives in the first ascending or in ego's generation are distinguished.[33] Our method of analysis makes possible the systematic comparison of total kinship systems, taking completely into account the larger range of differ-entiating criteria which were first isolated by Kroeber (1909).[34]

[33] Spier (1925: 69–88), Lowie (1928: 265–6; 1929: 84–6), and Murdock (1949: 223–4).

[34] Kroeber (1909: 78–9) recognized the following criteria for the differentiation of relatives: (1) "The difference between persons of the same and of separate generations," (2) "The difference between lineal and collateral relatives," (3) "Difference of age within one generation," (4) "The sex of the rela-tive," (5) "The sex of the speaker," (6) "The sex of the person through whom relationship exists," (7) "The distinction of blood relatives from connections by marriage," and (8) "The condition of life of the person through whom relationship exists." These considerations are further elaborated by Murdock (1949: 101–6).

In conclusion, we may summarize our procedures for the empirical derivation of the Trukese kinship system as follows:

1. Isolating the symbolic, verbal behavior patterns whose significata included blood or affinal kinship as one of their constituent characteristics.
2. Determining just who could and who could not be denoted by each of these verbal behavior patterns.
3. Deriving the significata of these behavior patterns as defined by the characteristics common to all persons who could be denoted by each of them.
4. Comparing the significata of each of these behavior patterns in order to determine which of them could be included in the same semantic system.

These procedures provide a method for the precise derivation of social categories and systems of social categories. Analysis of the significata of kinship terms in effect establishes the criteria for determining an individual's social category within the framework of a category system. By a social category is meant that aspect of social organization whereby persons are differentiated from each other and classified in accordance with attributes which they may or may not possess.[35] In the present instance the relevant attributes are non-behavioral. There was no need to analyze any interaction patterns between ego and his kinsman in order to derive the Trukese categories of kin. They are quite different, therefore, from what will be referred to as statuses in the next chapter. A status may be defined as a pole of interaction, something which can be isolated only with reference to the combination of behavior patterns which are exclusively and consistently associated with it. In this definition we follow Linton (1936: 113), who defines a status as "simply a collection of rights and duties." We shall define a role, as he does, as "the dynamic aspect of a status." There will be occasion to reexamine this definition of status and role in discussing the implications of our methods for the empirical derivation of status positions in the next chapter.

[35] Since the characteristics comprising the significatum of a kinship term constitute the attributes of the social category which the term denotes, they correspond to what Rouse (1939: 11), in his analysis of material culture, has called "modes," which he defines as culturally patterned attributes of artifacts, i.e., the criteria by which categories of artifacts (types) are defined.

STATUS SYSTEMS AND KINSHIP BEHAVIOR

INTRODUCTION

I T IS not intended here to describe all the aspects of behavior exhibited in interaction between kinsmen. Our discussion of corporations and of the various kin groups has already touched on a number of them. They will be encountered again in connection with marriage and the organization of residential kin groups.[1] The aim here is to discuss the problem of deriving status positions as functions of interaction patterns.

In the last chapter we indicated that analysis of the significata of referential terms provides a means for an empirical derivation of social categories and systems of categories. Statuses, however, must be derived from the roles which are exhibited in social interaction, rather than from the analysis of terminological systems. Our data are sufficient to permit us to outline two status systems. They will be projected against the category systems based on kinship terms, for, as will be seen, it is only with respect to social categories of one sort or another that one can describe the kinds of persons who do or do not occupy a given status.

SETTING ONESELF ABOVE ANOTHER

There are a number of behavior patterns of the Trukese whose occurrence or failure to occur in specific situations is said to be an expression of whether or not a person is "taboo from setting himself above another." *Jii meji pin me wöön* (he is forbidden from above-him) is given as the reason for a number of prescriptions of behavior. The particular behavior patterns or types of behavior patterns which will be analyzed may be summarized as follows:

1. There are persons to whom the verbal behavior pattern *"fääjiro!"* is spoken as a greeting. Such persons are district chiefs or *jitag*.[2] The expression is uttered only if one is "taboo from above" *(pin me wöön)* the chief or *jitag*.

2. There are persons to whom crouching or crawling behavior, known as *jöpwörö*, is exhibited. It is shown only to certain people whom one is "taboo from above." It is not permitted to be physically higher than they are. If such a person is seated, one must crouch or crawl in passing by or in coming into his presence. Persons to whom this behavior must be shown are chiefs and *jitag* by persons of lower rank, brothers by their sisters, and daughters by their fathers.[3]

---

[1] Some aspects of behavior between kinsmen have also been summarized by Murdock and Goodenough (1947).

[2] An *jitag* is a specialist with combined skill in oratory, law, tradition, diplomacy, and military tactics. He stands at the top of the native prestige ladder, (Bollig, 1927:46-60).

[3] The Trukese no longer say *"fääjiro,"* nor do they exhibit crawling behavior today, except possibly toward the few remaining genuine *jitag*, who have the power to inflict illness on anyone who fails to show them the proper behavior. The fact that these prescriptions used to be in force, however, appears still to affect native attitudes toward persons to whom they formerly applied. Informants, for example, stated that a man is "very taboo from above" his daughter, citing the fact that in former times he crawled in her presence. When some Puluwat Islanders visited Romonum, one informant regularly crouched in the presence of their navigator (navigation being a skill on a par with that of the *jitag*) until the latter told him it was not necessary.

3. There are certain people whose presence one tends to avoid when possible, with whom one deals preferably through an intermediary, and toward whom one tends not to initiate behavior. If such a person is visiting in a house other than one's own or that of one's lineage and is observed there, one will normally refrain from entering until he has gone. Not to do so would be considered impertinent. Likewise, if such a person enters a house in which one is visiting, one feels constrained to leave. If such a person approaches with some business, however, one speaks up and withdraws when the matter at hand has been terminated. This pattern can be summarized as an avoidance of direct interaction with another except at the other's pleasure. It is not to be confused with the avoidance of persons who are sexually taboo, though a native may exhibit both types of avoidance in his relations with the same person. One is always "taboo from above" any person whom one avoids in this manner.

4. There are persons whose requests one may not persist in refusing. One may indicate that it would be inconvenient to grant their request, but one may not refuse to comply. One is always "taboo from above" any such person.

5. There are persons to whom one may not speak harshly, whom one may not scold, address with *föös pëcëkkyn* (hard words), or personally take to task for things they have done. To do so would signify a state of anger so extreme as to flout the requirements of normal interaction in the particular relationship. One may or may not be "taboo from above" such persons.

6. There are persons to whom one may not use what the Trukese call *föösun fiwuuw* (fight talk), which involves the use of belligerent or threatening language and certain insulting expressions or gestures. One may or may not be "taboo from above" such persons.

According to informants, all of these prescriptions are connected in some way with being "taboo from above" another. None of them, however, is strictly correlated with any other in regard to the people to whom they apply. They are, nevertheless, associated with each other in a consistent way. For example, anyone to whom one must say *"fääjiro"* is a person to whom one must also crawl, whom one must avoid, whose request one may not refuse, to whom one may not speak harshly, and with whom one may not use fight talk. Similarly, anyone to whom one must crawl is also a person who one avoids, whose request one does not refuse, to whom one does not speak harshly, and with whom one does not use fight talk, but one does not necessarily say *"fääjiro"* to such a person. Thus there is a definite relationship between these behavior prescriptions such that definite statuses are expressed by how many and which of them are applicable in one's relations with others. All of them are associated in such a way that their joint application in any of their combinations is understandable as the function of a single variable. In this case the variable may be expressed as the degree to which a person is or is not "taboo from above" another.

This means that we can construct a scale of these behavior prescriptions.[4] For a set of items to form a scale for a population, their total distribution must be such that both the population and the items can be ranked simultaneously each in a lineal hierarchy on the basis of the distribution. The six prescriptions outlined above constitute just such a set of items. Their distribution and the lineal hierarchies which result are shown in Table 7. If any prescription were such that its distribution in relation to the

[4]The theory and method of "scale analysis" employed here, together with a full bibliography of same, is thoroughly presented by Stouffer *et al.* (1950).

TABLE 7. STATUS SCALE OF "SETTING ONESELF ABOVE ANOTHER"

Status Position	Ego in Relation to Other	Must not Use Fight Talk	Must not Speak Harshly	Must not Refuse Request	Must Avoid	Must Crawl	Must Say Fääjiro
1	Man to semej	No	No	No	No	No	No
	Man to jinej	No	No	No	No	No	No
	Man to feefinej	No	No	No	No	No	No
	Man to Hu of feefinej	No	No	No	No	No	No
	Man to Wi	No	No	No	No	No	No
	Man to Wi's younger pwiij	No	No	No	No	No	No
	Woman to semej	No	No	No	No	No	No
	Woman to jinej	No	No	No	No	No	No
	Woman to own Da	No	No	No	No	No	No
	Woman to Da of pwiij	No	No	No	No	No	No
	Woman to Hu	No	No	No	No	No	No
	Woman to Hu of younger pwiij	No	No	No	No	No	No
	Woman to Hu's feefinej	No	No	No	No	No	No
2	Man to Wi of younger pwiij	Yes	No	No	No	No	No
	Woman to own So	Yes	No	No	No	No	No
	Woman to Hu's younger pwiij	Yes	No	No	No	No	No
3	Man to younger pwiij	Yes	Yes	No	No	No	No
	Man to Wi's older pwiij	Yes	Yes	No	No	No	No
	Woman to younger pwiij	Yes	Yes	No	No	No	No
	Woman to So of pwiij	Yes	Yes	No	No	No	No
	Woman to Hu's older pwiij	Yes	Yes	No	No	No	No
4	Man to male neji	Yes	Yes	Yes	No	No	No
	Man to Wi of older pwiij	Yes	Yes	Yes	No	No	No
	Woman to Da of mwääni	Yes	Yes	Yes	No	No	No
	Woman to Da of Hu's pwiij	Yes	Yes	Yes	No	No	No
	Woman to So of Hu's younger pwiij	Yes	Yes	Yes	No	No	No
	Woman to Da to Hu's feefinej	Yes	Yes	Yes	No	No	No
	Woman to So of Hu's feefinej	Yes	Yes	Yes	No	No	No
	Woman to Hu of older pwiij	Yes	Yes	Yes	No	No	No
	Woman to Da's Hu	Yes	Yes	Yes	No	No	No
	Woman to So's Wi	Yes	Yes	Yes	No	No	No
5	Man to older pwiij	Yes	Yes	Yes	Yes	No	No
	Woman to older pwiij	Yes	Yes	Yes	Yes	No	No
6	Man to female neji	Yes	Yes	Yes	Yes	Yes	No
	Man to Wi's mwääni	Yes	Yes	Yes	Yes	Yes	No
	Woman to So of mwääni	Yes	Yes	Yes	No(?)	Yes	No
	Woman to mwääni	Yes	Yes	Yes	Yes	Yes	No
	Woman to So of Hu's older pwiij	Yes	Yes	Yes	Yes	Yes	No
	Woman to Wi of mwääni	Yes	Yes	Yes	Yes	Yes	No
7	Non-kinsman to district chief	Yes	Yes	Yes	Yes	Yes	Yes
	Non-kinsman to jitag	Yes	Yes	Yes	Yes	Yes	Yes

Note. Abbreviations used are: Da, daughter; Hu, husband; So, son; and Wi, wife. The Trukes-kinship terms are used to cover anyone in the categories they denote.

others did not enable the construction of such hierarchies, it would not belong with the others in the scale. The fact that all of them do form a scale is evidence that they are consistently related as expressions of one underlying variable.

It will be seen from the distribution in Table 7 that the resulting hierarchy of persons consists of seven positions, which are expressions of the different degrees to which people are or are not taboo from setting themselves above others. Position 1, for example, represents the extreme of not being "taboo from above" another, while position 7 represents the opposite extreme of being most heavily "taboo from above" another. A native is not "taboo from above" anyone who, for him, occupies one of the first three positions, though he may respect them, whereas he is "taboo from above" anyone who is in the fourth, fifth, sixth, or seventh position in relation to himself.

There are a number of other behavior patterns which limited information suggests are correlated with these seven positions.[5] Furthermore, additional information on other behavior patterns might well discriminate more positions on the scale of *pin me wöön*.[6] It should be made clear, however, that not all the behavior patterns manifested between any two persons, e.g., a man and his sister, are functions of the positions which they occupy for each other on the continuum of *pin me wöön*. As will be seen, other positions expressing other variable factors in behavior are also relevant to interaction between kinsmen.

Each position derived from analysis of the behavior patterns consistently manifested or not manifested in social interaction constitutes what is herewith called a status. The configuration of prescriptions by which the status is derived constitutes the role for that status.

In deriving social categories from kinship terms, it was possible to start with the assumption that the persons denoted by each term comprise a category as defined by their common characteristics. By comparing the various categories with respect to these characteristics, it was possible to derive a system of categories. Analysis of behavior patterns, however, starts with these patterns as characteristics which may or may not be appropriate to particular status positions and which may or may not be so related that their distribution forms a scale from which status positions may be derived. The fact, however, that status positions are found to be simple functions of a single variable factor, as evidenced by the scalability of the behavior patterns by which they are defined, coupled with the fact that the combinations of behavior patterns which define each status are mutually contrasting and complement one another with respect to the underlying variable, permits speaking of these statuses as comprising a status system in the same way that certain categories of kinsmen can be said to form a system of categories.

It will be recalled that the kinship categories derived earlier are defined by characteristics which have nothing to do with behavior in social interaction. These char-

[5] For example, a father may not enter his daughter's room in the *jimw* because he is "taboo from above" her, whereas a brother may enter his sister's room because he is not "taboo from above" her.

[6] The native expression *pin me wöön* (taboo from above) will herewith be used to designate this scale or status continuum.

acteristics consist of such conditions as generation, sex, lineage membership, and age, the definition of any one of which can be objectively stated in terms of such observable phenomena as time order of birth, physiological sex characteristics, and whether birth was by the same woman as mother or by different women.

It was with such social categories that we described the types of persons who occupy the various status positions on the *pin me wöön* scale in Table 7. By using Trukese kinship categories whenever possible considerable economy was effected. It should be pointed out, however, that the same status positions could have been obtained by using personal names, taking one name as ego and indicating the combinations of behavior patterns which he exhibits to every other individual by name.[7] In short, the behavior patterns form a scale, regardless of how the population is categorized, providing that the categorizations enable us to state accurately who occupies what statuses for any ego.

If personal names alone were used, however, it would be impossible to state the principles which govern the occupancy of statuses. On the other hand, a set of social categories showing a one-to-one correspondence with the occupancy of status positions would provide a means for formulating rules governing the occupancy of statuses precisely and economically. It would be too much, however, to expect a culture to provide a set of category systems which correlate perfectly with all its status systems. The most that can be expected is that the categories based on linguistic terminology provide a means for a relatively economical description of status occupancy. In view of these considerations, it is pertinent to see to what extent the status system based on distinctions of *pin me wöön* is actually correlated with the various kinship categories. The degree of correlation is shown in Chart 1.

Chart 1 shows the relationship between occupancy of *pin me wöön* statuses and the categories of consanguineal relatives of a male and of a female ego. The numbers in the chart represent the status positions of each relative for ego as given in the *pin me wöön* scale (Table 7). Under each number is given the kinship term by which ego refers to his kinsman. Below this is the native word which a person uses when talking about any behavior oriented towards a kinsman.

In speaking of kin-oriented behavior, a man is said to *samasam* (behave as child to father) anyone whom he calls *semej*. He is said to *jinejin* (behave as child to mother) anyone whom he calls *jinej* or *feefinej*, there being no separate term for behaving as a brother to a sister. A man is said to *pwiipwi* anyone whom he calls *pwiij*, to *newynew* anyone whom he calls *neji*, to *pwyppwyny* anyone whom he calls *pwynywej*, and to *jëkkëës* anyone whom he calls *jëësej*.

Comparison indicates that consanguineal kinsmen who occupy status position 1 for a male ego may be called *semej*, *jinej*, or *feefinej*. Thus the kinship terminology makes distinctions which are not related to distinctions in the status positions which kinsmen occupy for ego. The kinship terms correlate better, however, with the status positions ego occupies for them, ego being in status 4 to *semej*, in status 2, 3, or 6 to *jinej*, and in status 6 to *feefinej*. The fact that he occupies any one of three statuses for persons he

---

[7] Personal names are, of course, merely a method for signifying social categories of one member each.

may call *jinej* accounts for the special term *jinejisemej,* which refers to those *jinej* for whom a man occupies status 6.

It is now becoming apparent how social categories serve as descriptive devices for indicating who occupies what status positions in relation to whom. A Trukese father can instruct his child by saying that he must exhibit certain behavior patterns to his *jinej, semej,* and *feefinej,* that his *semej* must in turn behave in certain ways to him, his *feefinej* certain other ways, and his *jinej* in still others, among whom his *jinejisemej* must behave like his *feefinej.* The terms denoting social categories are such that they have a ready applicability to a number of status systems at once, rather than correlating exactly with the occupancy of statuses in any one status system. This will become clearer when the kinship terms are projected against the status system derived by scaling behavior prescriptions which are functions of the variable of sexual distance.

The usefulness of the special term *jääj mwään* for an older sibling of same sex is made apparent by the fact that persons who are called *pwiij* may be in status 5 or 3 for an ego depending on whether they are older or younger. The term *neji* is correlated with the fact that a male ego occupies position 1 for any of his *neji,* but fails to correlate with the positions which his male and female *neji* occupy for him. These distinctions are readily made by the descriptive phrases *neji mwään* and *neji feefin* (my adult son and my adult daughter, respectively).

It will be noted that the lack of difference in the behavior directed by a man toward the persons he calls *jinej* and *feefinej* is reflected in the behavioral terminology, a man being said to *jinejin* persons in both of these categories. In other respects, however, the behavioral terms do not correlate exactly with the positions which persons occupy on the scale of *pin me wöön.* A man will *nëwynëw* both a son and a daughter, though he behaves to a son (status 4) in a different manner from the way he behaves to a daughter (status 6). This is even more apparent in the case of persons who call each other *jëësej.* A sister's husband is in status 1 for a male ego, while a wife's brother is in status 6, yet each is said to *jëkkëës* the other. Behavioral terms, then, are not correlated with the different positions people occupy in any one status system, but refer to a complex of statuses which two people may occupy in their interactions with one another regardless of the time and place of these interactions. They can be expected to reflect to some degree the distinctions made in any status system, just as do the categories of kin designated by the kinship terms; but rather than referring to the behaviors appropriate to any one status on any one continuum of statuses, they tend to summarize the behaviors exhibited to persons of a certain social category. These persons, on the other hand, simultaneously occupy a number of status positions on a number of different continua, no one of which is necessarily correlated with their social category.

SEXUAL DISTANCE

Behavior patterns which express degrees of sexual distance and availability are susceptible of the same kind of analysis. Our data permit us to establish four types of behavior prescriptions reflecting sexual distance.

1. There are certain persons of opposite sex who are forbidden to be seen alone in one another's company or to interact socially outside the home. This applies only to persons who are *mwääni* and *feefinej* to one another. If they belong to the same lineage, they may have direct dealings with each other only when they have specific business to transact and are at their lineage house. Correlated with this is the prohibition against such persons sleeping in the same house together, when they are both past puberty. This prohibition is relaxed when a man is ill. It is then appropriate for him to be cared for by his *feefinej* in her house. This type of avoidance may be called "sexual avoidance" to distinguish it from the type of avoidance behavior discussed in connection with *pin me wöön*.

2. It is forbidden or highly disapproved for a man to see the breasts of certain women, or for a woman to let certain men see her breasts. When such a man approaches, a woman who is exposed must turn her back or cover her breasts in some way.[8]

3. There is a class of behavior patterns which involves sexual joking and horseplay. Included in it are attempts by a man to peer underneath a woman's skirt without her knowledge, and speaking to a woman in public in a suggestive or openly provocative manner (provided no

TABLE 8. STATUS SCALE OF SEXUAL DISTANCE

Status Position	Ego in Relation to Other	Joke Sexually in Public	Have Inter-course	See Breasts Exposed	Be Seen in Company	Sleep in Same House
1	Man with pwynywej (other than Wi)	A	A	A	A	A
2	Man with Wi	D	A	A	A	A
3	Man with affinal jinej	D	D	A	A	A
4	Man with consanguineal jinej	F	F	A	A	A
5	Man with Da of Wi's mwääni	F	F	D	A	A
6	Man with female neji (except 5)	F	F	F	A	A
7	Man with feefinej	F	F	F	F	F

Note. Abbreviations used are: A, approved; D, disapproved; F, forbidden; Da, Daughter; Wi, wife.

one whom she calls *mwääni* is present). Such behavior is approved only between persons who call each other *pwynywej* (my spouse) but who are not married to one another, and is actually directed mainly towards one's wife's more attractive sisters, whether they are married or not.

4. There are persons with whom sexual intercourse is forbidden as incestuous, and there are others with whom intercourse, while not strictly forbidden, is strongly disapproved.

The distribution of these prescriptions for a male ego is such that they form a scale. This is shown in Table 8, from which it is possible to derive six different status positions on the continuum of sexual availability, from most available (position 1) to least available (position 7). These positions are strictly reciprocal in any relationship. That is, if a woman occupies position 3 for a man, he occupies position 3 for her. In this respect the statuses of sexual availability differ from those of *pin me wöön*, wherein persons may interact in terms of any two positions on the scale.

[8] Such persons are not allowed to see each other's genitalia, either. Since this prohibition has a wider application, the boundaries of which were not determined in the field, it has not been possible to include it in the scale of sexual distance, where it would unquestionably fit, were our data complete.

As in the case of *pin me wöön*, additional information might yield more positions on the scale of sexual availability, and should enable us to include non-kinsmen as well as kinsmen in the population for which these behaviors form a scale.

Chart 2 compares these status positions with the distinctions made in the kinship and behavioral terminologies by a male ego. The status positions correlate most closely with the kinship terms which a man uses for his female relatives, and less well with the behavioral terms (cf. mothers and sisters). This correlation is especially high if we treat as one those status positions which are differentiated only as to whether a behavior pattern is disapproved or forbidden, which would, for example, equate positions 1 with 2 and 3, 2 with 4. This illustrates that while social categories may be correlated with status positions on a scale of behavior, the correlation may be with several adjacent positions taken together rather than with each one separately.

CONCLUSION

In this chapter status positions have been derived in relation to two variables, that of *pin me wöön* and that of sexual distance. Unquestionably there are a number of other variables or continua in terms of which other status positions could be derived by the scaling of behavior-patterns. A full analysis of the behavior exhibited between kinsmen would require exhausting all of these variables. Once this was accomplished, one could note just what status positions any two individuals simultaneously occupy in their dealings with one another. The sum of the status positions which a person simultaneously occupies for an ego in their interaction would determine the total range of behavior patterns which ego would exhibit toward him. The sum of the status positions thus occupied by a person in an interaction situation would constitute what we may call the *composite status* of that person in that interaction. The sum of the configurations of behavior patterns, which when directed toward that person define his composite status, may be called the *composite role* of ego toward him.

It should be pointed out that what is here called a role differs in one important respect from what Linton (1936: 114) calls a role. He defines a role as the behaviors which emanate from a person occupying a status. To us a role consists of the behaviors which are directed towards a person occupying a status. This by no means denies that a status has a dynamic aspect to which Linton gave the name "role." It merely recognizes that a status can be empirically derived only from the behaviors which are directed toward its occupant. It is ego's role in reacting to another which defines the status of the latter with respect to him, while the other's role toward ego defines the status of ego in the relationship. If in Linton's words a status is simply a collection of rights and privileges, these can be manifested in behavior only as others respect these rights and privileges in their dealings with the person who occupies the status. If they fail to do so, they indicate that for them the person toward whom they are directing their behavior does not occupy the status which he thinks he does. The things which a chief can and cannot do in his dealings with his subjects do not define the status of the chief, but define the composite status which his subjects occupy for him as chief, while the things the subjects can and cannot do in their dealings with him define the composite status which the chief occupies. This is demonstrated in connection with the status positions on the *pin me wöön* continuum. The behavior of an ego toward someone in position 1 is in no way an indication of ego's status with respect to that person. If the person in position 1 is a *semej*, ego is in position 4, but if the person in position 1 is a *pwynywej*, ego is in position 1. The behavior of ego toward *semej* and *pwynywej*, insofar as it is a function of *pin me wöön*, is identical, though ego's status with respect to the two relatives is markedly different. Ego's role, therefore, does not define his status.

The *pin me wöön* scale revealed that persons who are not kinsmen can be assigned positions on it as well as those who are. The interaction between any two individuals, whether they are kinsmen or not, is in part a function of the status positions they occupy relative to one another on the *pin me wöön* continuum. That we have been unable to present the two status systems as they relate to all possible categories of persons is due to the fact that attention during the course of the field work was largely concentrated upon kinsmen alone.[9]

[9] Were I to do the field work over again, I should try to collect the behavior prescriptions which an informant must observe to everyone in the community, regardless of what social categories they occupy. Unfortunately the field work was done without a full appreciation of where the analysis of the materials collected would ultimately lead.

RESIDENTIAL KIN GROUPS[1]

MARRIAGE[2]

IT HAS already been indicated that while marriage with a sib mate is disapproved, marriage with a subsib mate is forbidden. It is equally forbidden with a member of one's ramage, lineage, and descent line. Marriage prohibitions are likewise extended bilaterally. It is forbidden to marry anyone in one's *futuk*, in fact to marry anyone who is recognized as a consanguineal relative. It will be noted that this prohibition includes the members of one's father's lineage among the taboo relatives, a fact which makes it impossible for two lineages to intermarry regularly generation after generation and excludes cross-cousin marriage as a possibility.[3] On the other hand, there are no prohibitions against marriage with affinal relatives, even in the case of plural marriages. The prohibition against marriage into one's father's lineage does not extend to members of his ramage, subsib, or sib. In fact, if his lineage is divided into two well defined descent lines, each with its own separate house, marriage into a descent line other than the father's may occur. Any violation of these marriage prohibitions is considered incest. In aboriginal times a person guilty of having sexual relations with a member of his own or his father's lineage was killed by his relatives.

There are no apparent rules of preference governing first marriages. As just indicated, the extension of incest taboos bars any kind of marriage with first cousins and with at least half of one's second cousins as well.[4] Analysis of the genealogies reveals no consistent preference for marriages based on particular sib or lineage affiliations, though in any one generation a majority of the members of a given lineage will frequently be married into one lineage or ramage. Again, however, there are no consistent patterns, and the apparent tendency for lineage siblings to marry into the same lineage or ramage may well be a function of such factors as the chance distribution of available spouses at a given time or the fewer obstacles afforded a man conducting a love affair with the sister of his brother's wife.

Courtship starts when boys are about seventeen or eighteen years old and when girls pass puberty (at fourteen or fifteen years of age). Sexual freedom is allowed adolescents of both sexes until marriage. Sexual intercourse, therefore, is a normal part of courtship activities. It is supposed to be conducted in secret, but if it becomes known

[1] The term "residential kin group" is used in this report as defined by Murdock (1949: 41–2).

[2] Much of the information presented here on marriage is based on the notes of T. F. Gladwin. We shall here but summarize his data.

[3] Cross-cousin marriage, i.e., marriage with a father's sister's child or a mother's brother's child, while forbidden on Truk is reported by Tolerton (personal communication) as the preferred marriage in the Mortlock Islands. Bollig (1927: 79) appears to be in error when he states that marriages occur between uncle and niece and between cousins, if they belong to different sibs.

[4] Marriage with the following groups of second cousins is permitted: the children or grandchildren of one's father's father's brother, father's father's sister, mother's father's brother, and mother's father's sister. Marriage with the last, however, is likely to be considered bad, depending on the degree to which the connection is remembered and recognized.

that an unmarried couple is sleeping together there is no objection on the part of the community, though the youth may be teased by his fellows. Courting, therefore, involves trysts in the bush and secret visits at night to the house in which the girl lives.

The age of marriage is between 17 and 20 for girls and between 19 and 25 for boys. It varies somewhat depending on the sex ratio in a given community at a given time. Men feel that they should marry women who are somewhat younger than themselves. They say that women, who sit around the house while doing much of their work, age faster, while men, who are more active, remain vigorous longer.

The early stages of any marriage are looked on as an experiment. If it doesn't work out, there is little hesitancy in getting a divorce. Young people, even though married, engage in numerous extra-marital affairs, so that in a sense coutship activities continue even after marriage.[5] Even when a husband and wife feel themselves well matched, it is assumed that if they must be separated for a while they will satisfy their sexual urges with other partners until they can be reunited. Husbands are jealous of their wives in this connection, however, and a wife may be compelled to live with her husband's mother while he is away. This is especially likely if gossip gets started about her.

There are four ways of entering into a marriage. The most usual and socially most approved is where the young people themselves initiate the match. After courtship and the couple's decision to marry, the boy informs his parents and the *mwääniici* of his lineage of his intentions. If there are no objections from them, he requests the permission of the girl's parents, who also refer him to the members of her lineage. The *mwääniici* of the girl's lineage, her oldest brother, her mother, and her father have individually the power to veto the match. It is usual to get the consent of all the adult members of both lineages, whereupon the couple starts living together. The groom normally moves into the household in which the bride has been living. At present, a young man also gets the consent of the district chief and the local native policeman. Marriages are now recorded by the district secretary as well, and either an administrative chief or a Catholic priest may conduct a brief ceremony. It was customary in former times to ratify the marriage with an exchange of food between the two sets of parents involved, and to have a small feast attended by the district chief and by the *futuk* of the bridge and groom.

The second way of arranging a marriage is for the match to be instituted by the parents of the couple. This is the only type of marriage which is normally preceded by a definite betrothal *(kköföt)*. In betrothal it is customary for the girl to live with the boy's parents and for the boy to live with the girl's. This exchange of residence continues theoretically until marriage, but may last for shorter periods. Infant betrothal also occurs. The usual reason is because the parents desire the match for political or property considerations. Such marriages are frequently incompatible and are likely to result in divorce, a fact which the natives recognize. For this reason, they consider this type of marriage less desirable than the first. The relative ease with which a divorce may be obtained, on the other hand, does not make such marriages overly burdensome. Arranged marriages sometimes included brother-sister exchange, the parents arranging that both a son and a daughter will marry the daughter and son of another couple.

---

[5]For a fuller discussion of the problems involved in courtship and extra-marital relations, see Goodenough (1949).

Elopement is rare, but may occur. Its purpose is to force parental approval of a match, or to abduct another man's wife and thus force a divorce. Elopement cannot result in marriage in the former case unless the parents ultimately give their consent. Its purpose is to force the issue by indicating that if the couple are further frustrated in their desire to marry they may be driven to suicide. In the case of wife stealing, the brothers of the woman go in pursuit of the eloping couple in order to restore their sister to her husband. The man's brothers also join the pursuit in order to prevent the woman's brothers from taking her back. This frequently led to a fight in former times. Nowadays the couple is jailed for adultery on such occasions, and it seems that the injured husband usually gives up his claim.

The final method of marriage is by surreptitious purchase. The would-be husband secretly gives the father of the girl lavish gifts. By this he makes the father feel obligated to him so that it is difficult for him to refuse his consent.[6] The daughter is then forced or tricked into the marriage. The payment is for the father's consent and help in the matter and is not considered a bride-price. The girl may, and usually does, divorce such a husband at the first available excuse, in which case the husband does not get his property back. In aboriginal times such a purchase was often made for a girl under puberty, though the marriage was not consummated until after she had reached puberty. Old men used it as a technique for getting young brides. Informants reported that this type of marriage has always been in disfavor.

While both men and women look for compatible sex partners in marriage, they look even more for good workers. A person incapable of work is not likely to get married. Physical beauty in one's spouse, while desirable, is subordinate to industry and skill. There are, however, no formal marriage tests. A native already knows the character and abilities of the members of his community. In view of the premarital freedom in sexual matters, virginity is expected of neither the bride nor the groom.

It should be emphasized that while divorce is frequent among young couples, once children come on the scene it is taken much less lightly. Relatives bring pressure to bear to keep the marriage intact because of the children. It should also be noted that the reshuffling of spouses during the experimental period tends to bring together in marriage those couples capable of making the best adjustment.

SECONDARY MARRIAGES

Both the sororate and levirate were practiced in former times. The usage is said by informants to be less strongly adhered to today. The sororate required that when a man's wife died, he must remarry if possible a woman of his deceased wife's lineage, e.g., a sister or sister's daughter of his wife. In order to marry someone else, the wife's lineage had to release him. This was regularly done, of course, if his former wife's lineage could not supply him with a new wife or if the only woman available was unwilling. The betrothal of a girl was broken in case she was needed for a marriage to her dead sister's husband.

[6] Gifts designed to coerce a favor from another are called *jefisifis* (clinchers). See above in connection with the discussion of *niffag*.

Similarly a widowed woman was supposed to remarry some man of her deceased husband's lineage, normally a brother or a sister's son of the husband. Such levirate remarriages sometimes resulted in a man's having two wives. In one case a woman passed successively to two brothers and then to a sister's son of her deceased first husband.

It should be noted that while the levirate not infrequently resulted in polygyny, the sororate did not result in polyandry. No woman was required to take an extra husband to satisfy the demands of the sororate. If her first husband was in disfavor with her brothers, however, she might divorce him in order to remarry her dead sister's widowed husband.

Not all instances where the sororate or levirate could operate actually resulted in the appropriate remarriages. With the consent of their own lineage mates, widowers and widows sometimes went their own way without obtaining a release from their former spouse's lineage. Also, a lineage with a woman to supply for the sororate might let her marry someone else. In this event, the injured widower might claim back any property he had given to his wife and her lineage during their marriage, and such action usually resulted in a nasty quarrel. However, the Trukese say that people usually did not bother with the property angles in such cases in order to avoid unpleasant consequences.

In aboriginal times polygyny was permitted. A man might legally be married to two sisters or two unrelated women. Rarely did a person have more than two wives at one time, though cases have occurred. If the wives were unrelated they continued to live each in her own lineage house, the husband alternating his residence between them. The natives consider marriages to sisters undesirable on the grounds that they will quarrel because they live together in the same house. They consider marriage to two unrelated women equally undesirable because the husband is likely to experience frequent difficulties with one or the other of his two sets of brothers-in-law. Actually most polygynous marriages result from the customary remarriage of a widow to a member of her former husband's lineage. Only six of the 397 marriages recorded in the Romonum genealogies were polygynous and only one was polyandrous.[7] There may have been other polygynous marriages which escaped record in the genealogies, but if so they were few.

The first wife of a polygynous union outranks the second wife. The problem resulting for the husband is put by one informant as follows: "The first wife is angered if the husband divides his favors evenly. But the second wife gets angry if he doesn't. The brothers of the two wives also make it difficult for the husband if he shows favoritism to either set of brothers-in-law."

Polygyny is still practiced to a slight degree on Truk. The genealogies record that at the present time a Polle man is married to two women, one the daughter of the other

---

[7] Polyandry, like polygyny, is not considered illegal, but is not practiced. The one case of polyandry resulted when a man made payment of goods to another to secure permission to share his wife with him. Any marriage is legal where the relevant persons have consented to it, even though the community may consider it odd.

by a former marriage. The present district chief of Neeman in Fëëwyp on Tol Island is said to have two wives and to be negotiating for a third.[8]

THE NUCLEAR FAMILY

The nuclear family on Truk consists of a woman, her children, and whoever is her husband at the time. Many of the activities and responsibilities which we associate with the nuclear family in America are associated on Truk with the lineage or the extended family household.

The most important function of the nuclear family is the socialization of the children. Corporal punishment may be inflicted only by the father, mother, mother's brother, and grandparents. Scolding, too, is confined to these relatives of the child, unless others are specifically authorized by the parents to take a hand. It is the actual parents who are primarily responsible for a child's conduct. Although a child acquires special knowledge, as he grows older, from the most skilled of his senior lineage mates, even in these matters his parents are mainly responsible for his education.

It is one's actual parents (or their surrogates, should they be dead) who play the most important role in marriage negotiations. The position of the father in this regard is particularly important. It is true that consent to a marriage must also be obtained from the lineage, but the father may, if he feels strongly in favor of the match, persuade the more reluctant members of his wife's lineage to accept it. In marriage and the education and care of children, then, the nuclear family appears as a distinct and important social unit.

THE EXTENDED FAMILY

The group of people who lived in a lineage house of aboriginal times must not be confused with the lineage itself. A lineage house was occupied by the women of the lineage, their husbands, and the boys of the lineage who were below puberty. This group, differing from the lineage in its male members, constituted the core of the extended family, which ideally was based on uxorilocal residence.[9]

Extended families frequently had other members as well, such as a former husband of a deceased lineage woman who wished to continue to reside with his children and look after their economic interests. Moreover, one or two women from other islands or from nearly extinct lineages might live in virilocal residence with women of their

---

[8] The people of Romonum were under the impression that polygyny had been outlawed by the United States Administration. This impression was apparently the result of a campaign on Udot Island, conducted by a Spanish Catholic priest, who passed himself off as a spokesman for the government to get the native chiefs to enact decrees favorable to the Catholic precepts. He even sought to require that existing polygynous marriages be broken up, only the first wife being allowed to remain with the husband. The natives told a couple of lurid stories of refusal to comply, attempted suicide, and subsequent sentencing to jail when the man who was then administrative chief of Udot tried to enforce what he mistakenly believed to be required by the United States Government. The Naval Administration subsequently cleared up the misunderstanding.

[9] A native refers to the members of his extended family as *cöön imwej* (the people of my house) to distinguish them from *cöön ääj faameni* (the people of my lineage). For the terms uxorilocal and virilocal, see Adam (1947).

husband's lineage. The daughters of these women might continue to reside with their father's lineage after marriage. Thus an extended family might contain the women of two distinct lineages, the members of one being the *jëfëkyr* of the other,[10] as we have seen in connection with lineage clients. Frequently an extended family includes dependent relatives of its nuclear lineage or of one of the husbands. It is customary, for example, for an old person or other dependent to be cared for by a "father" (if the real father is dead, some member of the father's lineage). In fact, the rule that care of dependents is the responsibility of the nearest "father" explains the rule that in case of divorce, the children reside with their father, not with their mother, unless they are infants. This arrangement continues until puberty, or even until marriage, when the children become functioning members of their own lineage. The inclusion of dependents, women in virilocal residence, and other client members of the lineage in an extended family sometimes creates a situation in which the women of a lineage are outnumbered by the men and women from outside their lineage who reside with them. This does not alter the fact that the organization of the household is typically that of a matrilocal extended family.

As previously noted, an important descent line within a lineage may have a separate house of its own. An extended family, therefore, may be based on a descent line of high lineage potential rather than on an entire lineage, the husbands in one household working as a group apart form the husbands in the other on most occasions.

The internal organization of an extended family is derived from that of the lineage whose women form its nucleus. Husbands are organized into generations, each with its age-graded hierarchy. They derive their postions in the age hierarchy of husbands from the positions their wives occupy in the age hierarchy of women in the lineage. The senior husband, therefore, is the man who is married to the *finniici*, the senior woman. Thus a younger man who is married to a senior woman has seniority over an older man who is married to a junior woman. The husbands of a generation of "sisters" constitute a generation of husbands. The women of the Jacaw 2 lineage on Romonum and their husbands are given in rank order in Table 9. In this extended family Nikommy is the senior husband and Jakawo the junior one. Nikommy may ask any of the other husbands to help him in work connected with the extended family, but not to do work relating to his own lineage's interests. Japen is the senior husband of the second generation. If he should divorce Naapi, her new husband would become the senior husband even if Japen should remarry the as yet unmarried Tarajimen and thus remain a member of the extended family. Japen would then rank next to the bottom as indicated by Tarajimen's position.[11]

[10] Usually when the *jëfëkyr* women became sufficiently numerous to organize as a separate extended family, they went to live in a house of their own, built on land owned by one of their husbands or belonging to a member of their own newly established lineage.

[11] Unfortunately I failed to inquire as to the ranking of a man whose wife died but who remarried a younger woman in accordance with the sororate. I do not know whether he acquires the rank of his new wife or retains that of his deceased wife. I have not listed Setin (Pwëën) in Table 9 because his wife is dead. His wife belonged to the first generation of Jacaw 2 women. Setin is still senior husband over Japen, Jejiwe, and Symijer in their household, where he continues to reside, not having remarried.

Not only is the age grading of husbands important in the organization of activities which they undertake as a group; it is also important in etiquette. For example, it is always the senior husband present who opens the packages of mashed breadfruit at meal times and who starts the eating.

As a group, the husbands are subordinate to the men of their wives' lineage. If Jakiwo, for example, who is a brother of the women of the second generation in the Jacaw 2 lineage, is present for a meal in the home of his sisters, it is he who opens the food packages and starts the eating, and who becomes head of the house over all the husbands present. He may call on them to help him in any task of importance to his lineage. In aboriginal times, he would expect them to support him in a feud between his lineage and another, provided they were not themselves members of the enemy lineage. In

TABLE 9. RANK IN THE EXTENDED FAMILY OF JACAW 2 WOMEN

Generation	Rank Order	Jacaw 2 Woman	Husband	Husband's Lineage
First	1	Jijoopa	Nikommy	Wuwäänyw 3
	2	Cajïppwe	Taan	Wuwäänyw 3
Second	1	Naapi	Japen	Söör 2
	2	Nesäw	Jejiwe	Wuwäänyw 1
	3	Kasija	Pwuna	Pwukos
	4	Sitaje	Puruuta	Pwukos
	5	Fyciko	Siro	Pwereka 1
	6	Namako	Symijer	Jacaw 1*
	7	Tarajimen	—	—
	8	Jaruko	Jakawo	Wiitëë 1

* This is the case of sib endogamy which caused such a stir on Romonum, see above p. 83.

the latter event he could terminate the marriage. Jakiwo can also appropriate the personal belongings of his sisters' husbands, who must make a *kiis* of them to him.

Now that the extended family is broken up into smaller households there appears to be less cooperation between the husbands than there was in former times. The husbands of the two or three women in a house continue to cooperate, however, frequently fishing together and jointly providing the food for their wives and children. For example, Japen, Jejiwe, and Symijer live in one house with their wives. They work together one day to prepare food in quantity, which their wives distribute to the women of the entire lineage. The next day Nikommy, Jakawo, and Siro (living in an adjacent house) do the same thing. Pwuna and Puruuta have separate arrangements and do not participate to the same degree in this exchange.

Although the house belongs to the lineage or descent line of their wives, the husbands have the immediate responsibility for its maintenance and for building a new one, if necessary. Ultimately this is the responsibility of the men of the lineage rather than of the husbands of its women. The latter, however, are charged with the actual job as a *kiis* which they render their wives' brothers.[12]

[12]The description of the extended family given here is contradictory to that given by Hall (Hall and Pelzer, 1946: 18-19). By failing to recognize the lineage organization, Hall tried to show that men

RULES OF RESIDENCE

The discussion of the lineage and extended family implied that there are definite customs which regulate the choice of residence on the part of a newly married couple. It has been apparent that the preferred arrangement is for the husband to live with his wife in her lineage house. It has been noted, however, that under certain circumstances alternative arrangements can be made whereby a man may bring his wife to live in a small house adjacent to the lineage house of his sisters. We have also seen that, in addition to the women of the lineage, a lineage house may contain women who are its *jëfëkyr*, even after their marriage. These considerations raise the problem of determining when it is the rule on Truk for residence to be uxorilocal and when virilocal.

As already noted, the organization of the lineage as a tight cooperative group is strengthened by its being localized in a particular place in a house occupied by its women, who operate as a cooperative team. For such a team to be effective, there have to be enough women to satisfy certain minimum working requirements. Fishing, for example, is an important feminine activity. The techniques involved require a minimum of about four women in order to get a reasonable catch. For an extended family to function adequately, therefore, there must be enough young women to do the necessary work and at least one woman of sufficient age and experience to direct it intelligently. There have to be men in the form of husbands or brothers to prepare those foods (such as breadfruit) which it is a male responsibility to provide. If there are no men in a lineage, its women are dependent on their husbands, whose primary responsibilities are with their own lineage. If the men of a lineage are few, their share of responsibility toward their lineage sisters is proportionally greater. All these factors are of importance in determining whether or not the women of a lineage will be organized in a single household and whether or not the men of a lineage can afford to live in uxorilocal residence when responsibilities to their sisters are heavy.

To achieve its localization, a lineage also has to have land. That is, some member of it has to have at least a provisional title to the soil of some plot which is suitable for building a lineage house. Otherwise, the lineage cannot establish a house except on land provided by the husband of one of its women. In this event, the husband customarily makes a *niffag* of the land and house to his children, thus giving their lineage a suitable house site.

There are other considerations as well. If a man marries a woman on another island, he may live there in uxorilocal residence. On the other hand, he may become head of his own lineage; or he may be one of only a few men in his lineage; or he may control a sizable amount of land on his home island while his wife's lineage has little land for him to work. Any one of these considerations favors his taking his wife to his own

---

have the dominant position in their wives' homes, where they are actually subordinate to their wives' brothers. The latter, while avoiding their sisters in public, come frequently to their sisters' home, and in fact keep their important personal possessions there in order to prevent their wives from appropriating them and giving them to their brothers.

island. There he can look after his lineage's interests or provide his wife and children with more land than they can command at home.

The necessary conditions for uxorilocal residence, therefore, can be summarized as follows: (1) there must be sufficient women to form the nucleus of an adequately functioning extended family; (2) there has to be at least one woman of sufficient experience to be head of a household; (3) there must be lineage land on which to build the house; (4) the husbands must not be too urgently needed with their own lineage sisters; (5) the husbands must not come from lineages located too far away.

If the first of these requirements cannot be satisfied, the few surviving women of the lineage go in virilocal residence to become a part of the extended families based on their husbands' lineages. If the second requirement cannot be satisfied, the first in all probability cannot be satisfied either. This requirement is evident when two descent lines establish separate houses. If the women of one are all young, but there are two older women in the other, then one of the latter will join the household of the younger women, each house now having a senior woman of experience. Thus lineages do not always divide strictly along genealogical lines. If the third requirement cannot be satisfied, a husband may provide the necessary land, but if no husband is willing to accommodate an entire lineage, then its women are forced individually to join the extended families of the respective lineages of their husbands. A husband who is pressingly needed with his own lineage, or who has married too far away, may also take his wife in virilocal residence.

The history of lineages on Romonum demonstrates that these considerations not infrequently arise, and that they often provide the initial situation giving rise to the fission of old lineages or to the establishment of new ones and the introduction of new sibs. A recent illustration of the working of these considerations was provided when the United States administration required that, whenever possible, houses be built along the shore so that their occupants might have ready access to outhouses located over the water. On Romonum it turned out that some lineages had no members with provisonal title to land along the shore. In order to comply with this requirement, the women of these lineages are now living in virilocal residence or are living together on land controlled by one of their husbands.

In summary, then, uxorilocal residence is preferred but can be realized only when certain conditions are satisfied. Virilocal residence is the standard alternative. While we may, therefore, characterize the Trukese as typically uxorilocal, we must remember that the need for membership in a functioning extended family is more important than strict adherence to one type of rule. In fact, so thoroughly accepted is virilocal residence as the standard alternative that when questioned about residence, many informants said that there is no fixed rule.

[13]From the standpoint of field method, it should be pointed out that Trukese residence patterns were isolated only after tracing the history of each lineage as far back as informants could remember. It was this which revealed the conditions under which virilocal residence regularly occurs.

TERRITORIAL AND POLITICAL ORGANIZATION

THE DISTRICT

SIZE AND COMPOSITION

ALTHOUGH districts[1] on Truk are concrete political and territorial units, they are not necessarily communities. A community has been defined as "the maximal group of persons who normally reside together in face-to-face association."[2] Such a group on Truk may be composed of the people of a single district or of several adjacent districts. For example, the island of Romonum is at present divided into two independent political districts, but the entire island is a single community. The part of Tol called Fëëwyp is similarly a single community, but divided into two districts. On Uman the adjacent districts of Neesaraw, Söönnuuk, Nuukan, and Mwööcun appear to form a single community of people living in daily personal contact. On Pata, on the other hand, each district is also a separate community.

Prior to 1900, each district was politically independent of all others. The district chiefship was the highest political office. In both territory and population, however, the Trukese districts are very small. Their average area and population on each island are given in Table 10. In aboriginal times there were probably a few more districts than those listed on the table. Some of them were very small and intimately associated with a neighboring district to form a community. Within the past 50 years, some of these tiny districts have been merged with the larger ones with which they formed communities. Apparently the present district of Penija on Udot, for example, was formerly two independent districts: Penija and Nykynyfëw. These two districts formed a single community, regularly intermarrying. After the establishment of the German Administration of Truk, they were merged, and the chief of Penija was given jurisdiction over both.

The old district of Nykynyfëw is said to have been composed of several lineages, all of the Pwereka sib. No other sibs were represented, and all the lineages were organized as a ramage and shared a single meeting house. They regularly obtained their spouses from neighboring Penija, where three other sibs were represented. Nykynyfëw is the only case reported where a district was composed entirely of persons belonging to the same sib.

Prior to about 1890 the present districts of Söönnuuk and Nuukan on Uman Island were organized as a single district called Söönnuuk. The composition of this district as of that time is given in Table 11. The Fesinim lineage was divided into two descent lines each with its own house but sharing the same meeting house and *fanag*. The elder of the two *mwääniici* was the district chief. Rowoow, in turn, had a complete establishment

[1] The term "district" is used instead of "village" because of the connotations which the latter word has as referring to a definite cluster of dwellings whose inhabitants comprise a single community. The word "district" also more closely represents the meaning of its Trukese name, *sööpwun fëny*, "section of the land."

[2] Murdock *et al.* (1945: 29).

with a house, meeting house, and *fanag* of its own. Wiitëë had at one time maintained a meeting house, but had given it up. Its men attended the meeting house and *fanag* of Fesinim or Rowoow, according to whether they considered themselves the *jëfëkyr*

TABLE 10. AVERAGE DISTRICT AREAS AND POPULATIONS FOR TRUK'S VOLCANIC ISLANDS

Island	Number of Districts	Average District Area	Average District Population
Dublon	18	0.188 sq. mi.	64 persons
Eot	1	0.187	90
Eiol	0	0.000	0
Eten	1	0.219	?
Falabeguets	2	0.303	90
Falo	1	0.128	127
Fefan	11	0.464	94
Moen	14	0.520	127
Param	3	0.192	94
Pata	5	0.260	94
Polle	5	0.700	94
Romonum (Ulalu)	2	0.144	115
Tarik	0	0.000	?
Tol (less Pata and Polle)	18	0.467	94
Tsis	1	0.235	94
Udot	6	0.317	90
Uman	10	0.182	92

Note. Dr. Karl Pelzer, who mapped the districts of Truk for the first time, has kindly allowed me to use his maps in calculating the areas given in this table. I have followed his maps entirely, except in the case of Eot, for which he gives three districts. This does not agree with my information and seems highly unlikely in view of Eot's size. No accurate data are available on the one inhabited reef island of Pis. The table gives the picture roughly as of 1947.

TABLE 11. COMPOSITION OF SÖÖNNUUK DISTRICT, UMAN, CA. 1890

Sib and Lineage	Number of Houses	Number of Meeting Houses	Number of Fanag
Fesinim	2	1	1
Rowoow (Rogowu)	1	1	1
Wiitëë	1	0	0
Wiisuusuu	0	0	0
Söör	0	0	0
Cëëcija	0	0	0
Neewow	0	0	0
Totals	4	2	2

of one or the other. The Wiisuusu, Söör, Cëëcija, and Neewow sibs were all too sparsely represented to maintain separate households. Their women lived in virilocal residence with their husbands or continued to reside after marriage in the lineage houses of their fathers. Their men, in turn, "followed their fathers" in determining which meeting

TABLE 12. COMPOSITION OF THE DISTRICTS ON PATA

District	Sib and Lineage	Number of Houses	Number of Meeting Houses	Number of Fanag
Söpwötä	Maasanë 1	1	1	1
	Maasanë 2	1	0	1
	Sowuwefeg	1	0	1
	Jimwö	1	0	1
	Fesinim	1	0	1
	Wiitëë	1	0	1
	Totals	6	1	6
Nuukaf	Wiitëë	1	1	1
	Maasanë	1	0	1
	Pwereka	1	0	1
	Wuun	1	0	1
	Jacaw	1	0	1
	Totals	5	1	5
Jepin	Jacaw 1	1	1	1
	Jacaw 2	1	1	1
	Mwööc	1	0	0
	Wiitëë	1	0	0
	Maasanë	1	0	0
	Söpwunupi	1	0	0
	Totals	6	2	2
Pwowukocow	Söpwunupi	2	1	2
	Jacaw 1	1	0	0
	Jacaw 2	1	0	0
	Maasanë	1	0	0
	Wuwäänyw	1	0	0
	Totals	6	1	2
Jetijamar	Söpwunupi	1	1	1
	Pwereka	1	0	1
	Wiitëë	1	0	1
	Mwööc	1	0	1
	Nuukan	1	0	1
	Wuwäänyw	1	0	1
	Totals	6	1	6

house or *fanag* they attended. Thus there were eight lineages and four extended families.[3]

[3] It is possible that the sibs without houses of their own should be treated as client members of the other lineages rather than as independent lineages in their own right.

The part of Tol known as Fëëwyp is organized into two districts, though together they form a single community. The district of Neeman has about 80 people representing three sibs: Fesinim (Pesinim), Söpwunupi, and Sowuwefeg (Cëwykkyk). The district of Söpwuwu has about 165 people in the following sibs: Jacaw (two lineages united in a ramage), Söör, Niippwe (Tiniik), Jipeges.

The composition of the five districts on Pata is given in Table 12. In each case where a lineage was without a meeting house or *fanag*, its men "followed their fathers" as in

TABLE 13. COMPOSITION OF ROMONUM, CA. 1900

Sib and Lineage	Number of Houses	Number of Meeting Houses
Jacaw 1	1	1
Jacaw 2 and 3	2	1
Jeffeg	1	1
Pwereka 1	1	2
Pwereka 2	2	1
Pwereka 3	2	2
Pwëën	1	1
Söör 1	1	1
Söör 2	3	1
Wiitëë 1	2	2
Wiitëë 2	3	1
Wuwäänyw 1	2	1
Wuwäänyw 2	1	1
Wuwäänyw 3	1	1
Wuwäänyw 4	1	2
Totals	24	18

Note. Pwereka 1, Wuwäänyw 4, and Wiitëë 1 each had a meeting house for meetings and another for the storage of canoes. Pwereka 3 was temporarily split into two pseudo-lineages each with its own house and meeting house. I am sure that not all of the lineages had their own meeting houses at this time. This reconstruction is based mainly on one informant's memory of conditions as of the time when he reached puberty. Kubary (Kubary and Krause, 1889: 60) reported only the Pwereka, Jacaw, Wiitëë, and Pwëën sibs on Romonum in 1887, and estimated the population at 200.

Söönnuuk on Uman. It will be noted that in some districts only the chief's lineage maintained a meeting house, which was attended by all the men of the district. Lineage meetings were confined to the *fanag* or some other convenient place. In all of these districts the lineage house has given way to a cluster of smaller houses, except in Jepin, where one old lineage house is still in use by one of the Jacaw lineages.

In aboriginal times the houses were usually located well back from the shore, up on the mountain slopes, as a defense against a surprise night attack from the sea. Today, the dwellings have all been moved down to the sandy coastal strips, except on Fëëwyp. The new arrangement, with the increased number of houses confined to a narrow coastal area, has created a situation in which the various lineages are bunched closer together, making for a more compact "village" in some cases.

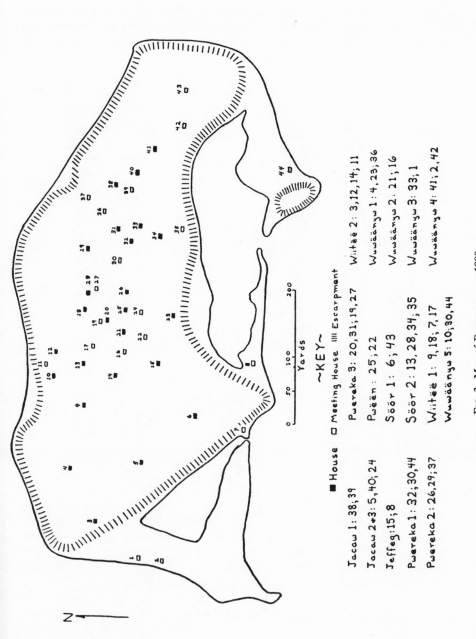

~KEY~

■ House   □ Meeting House   ⅢⅢ Escarpment

Jacaw 1: 38;39
Jacaw 2+3: 5,40;24
Jeffeg:15;8
Pwereka1: 32;30,44
Pwereka 2: 26,29;37

Pwereka 3: 20,31,19,27
Pwëën: 25;22
Söör 1: 6;43
Söör 2: 13,28,34,35
Wiitëë 1: 9,18;7,17
Wuwäänyu 5: 10,30,44

Wiitëë 2: 3,12,14;11
Wuwäänyu 1: 4,23,36
Wuwäänyu 2: 21;16
Wuwäänyu 3: 33;1
Wuwäänyu 4: 41;2,42

Yards
0   50   100   200

Fig. 3. Map of Romonum, *ca.* 1900.

134

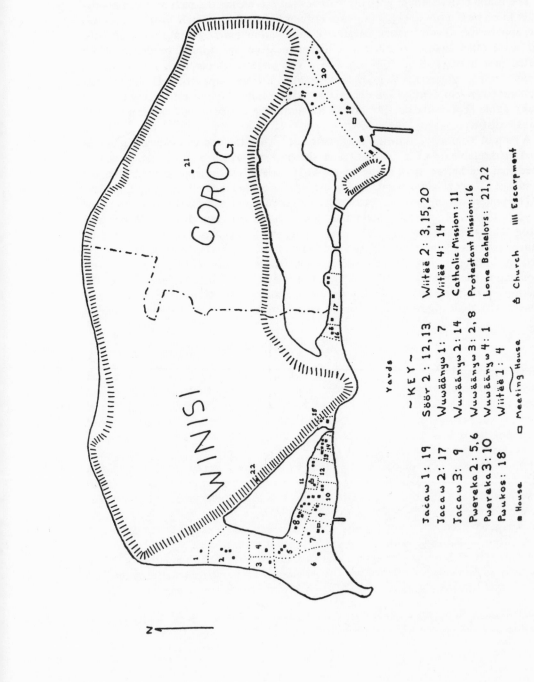

~ K E Y ~

Jacaw 1: 19	Sȫr 2: 12,13	Wiitȫ 2: 3,15,20
Jacaw 2: 17	Wuwáányw 1: 7	Wiitȫ 4: 14
Jacaw 3: 9	Wuwáányw 2: 14	Catholic Mission: 11
Pwereka 2: 5,6	Wuwáányw 3: 2,8	Protestant Mission: 16
Pwereka 3: 10	Wuwáányw 4: 1	Lone Bachelors: 21,22
Puukos: 18	Wiitȫ 1: 4	

■ House   □ Meeting House   ⓑ Church   ⅢⅢ Escarpment

FIG. 4. Map of Romonum, 1948.

The island of Romonum presents a somewhat more complex picture. Even aboriginally there were more lineages than are ordinarily found in a single district. This was due, apparently, to two factors. Because of its isolation, marriages into other districts, and hence other islands, resulted in a higher incidence of virilocal residences which started new lineages. Since the island is a flat plateau, rather than steeply mountainous, and is equipped with good taro swamps, it could support a relatively greater population (present density: 798 persons per square mile, the greatest for any island in Truk). Table 13 gives the composition of Romonum as of about 1900, when it was still a single district.

A map of Romonum, showing the location of each of the houses and meeting houses listed in the table (see Fig. 3), illustrates the physical layout of a district. It will be noted that the houses were scattered about the island on the high ground after the manner of a loose neighborhood, each house with its extended family forming a hamlet.[4]

The present arrangement of houses on Romonum contrasts markedly with that of 50 years ago. Moreover, Romonum is now divided into two districts: Winisi and Corog. The present location of dwellings along the low coastal strips is dictated by sanitary policies of the United States Administration. However, the houses are clustered by lineage or descent line,[5] as is indicated in Figure 4, and stand on land belonging to some member of the lineage or to one of the husbands of its women. The requirement that houses be built by the shore has led to a situation in which some lineages with their houses in one district are politically a part of the other district.

THEORY OF DISTRICT CHIEFSHIP

The organization of the several lineages of a district into a sociopolitical unit depends, in part, on property relationships. The boundaries of a district enclose a piece of real property apart from the plots of soil and trees held under the various types of tenure by the several lineages which belong to the district. When discussing divided ownership, we indicated that there is a form of property which we called territory. Territory refers to the district insofar as it is a piece of property.

Full title to territory is initially established by staking a claim to hitherto unclaimed and virgin land. This is done by setting up small piles of stones as base markers (paas) between which run the boundaries (jijään). Such a claim constitutes a söpwun fëny (literally: "section of land'), which is the name used for a district. Since before this the land was unclaimed, the claimant and full title holder has absolute sovereignty over the territory he has created for himself. He holds it from no one.

As his natural heirs, the claimant's children inherit full title to the territory, which they hold as their corporate property. The matrilineal corporation which they found is said to have started the land in the district which results. As administrator of his

[4]Informants did not confirm Kubary's observation (Kubary and Krause, 1889:60) that the natives of Romonum lived along the sandy coastline.

[5]In both Figures 3 and 4, when more than one house or cluster of houses is given for a lineage, it means that the lineage is divided into more than one descent line, each with its own house and extended family.

corporation's property, the *mwääniici* of this founding lineage is the *sömwonun fëny* (chief of the land), which is the title held by the district chief.

Fundamentally, then, the territory consists of virgin land which has been claimed as property. The title holder of this territory has the right to clear it and make it productive. In doing so he establishes title to soil on those plots which he has cleared and title to any other improvements he proceeds to make on it.

With considerable land to clear, the men of the founding lineage can provide for their children handsomely by bringing their wives into virilocal residence in the new district. They clear the as yet uncleared portions of the territory and plant breadfruit and other food-producing trees on them. Their children duly inherit full title to these plots of soil and trees and found new lineages affiliated with other sibs. While the new lineages have full title to plots of soil which they acquire in this way in the territory, they hold only provisional title to the territory from the founding lineage. In other words, by creating property in the form of soil and trees for their children, the men of the founding lineage make them a *niffag* of certain portions of the territory. Residual title to the territory is held by the original lineage. In this way the various lineages in a district owe the founding lineage the permanent obligations of a provisional title holder to a residual titler holder. The new lineages are also directly or indirectly started as the *jëfëkyr* of the founding lineage.

It is this situation, at least in theory, to which the natives always refer when talking about the history of a district. The chief of Winisi district on Romonum always spoke of his sib, Pwereka, as having started the land on Romonum (formerly a single district) and as having sired *(nëwynëw)* all the other sibs there, which, he said, hold their lands from Pwereka. The people of Jepin district on Pata speak of the Jacaw sib in the same way. Jacaw began Jepin and sired the other sibs there. Jacaw, therefore, furnishes the chief of Jepin.

All previous writers on Truk note that the sibs are ranked. Ranking is primarily local to a district and is based on the principle of seniority as determined by the time of a sib's establishment as a lineage in the district. Certain sibs may have the reputation of having been the first on an entire island, and are hence ranked higher than any other on the island (e.g., the Jacaw sib on Pata), though it may have established title to only one part of the island as its territory and district. The ranking of sibs has no particular function other than to express the order of their immigration into a district, the sib first there being that of its chief.

Older lineages are, of course, likely to hold full or residual title to larger portions of soil in a territory than are younger lineages, the latter being established when there was less uncleared land remaining in the territory. Any lineages founded after the last land had been cleared would be without any soil to which they could hold full or residual title. They would hold only provisional title to soil, though in time they might acquire full title when the lineage holding residual title became extinct. The tenure situation on Romonum clearly reflects this. Full or residual title to soil on the various plots is held entirely by the older lineages, younger lineages holding only provisional title. Of those holding full or residual title to soil, the older lineages have many such plots, which are largely contiguous, while the younger ones have only a few, which are scattered.[6]

In summary, then, a district consists of a piece of real property, a territory, in whose confines there are usually several lineages. The oldest lineage holds residual title to the entire territory, while the newer lineages hold various portions of it under provisional title and consider themselves to have been sired directly by the oldest lineage or by one of the other lineages, which was in its turn sired by the oldest.

The District as a Kin Group

As the above discussion implies, district membership for the individual Trukese is based entirely on his lineage membership. Unless his lineage is a part of a given district, he is not considered a member. There are thus political reasons, in addition to the economic ones discussed earlier, which require anyone moving to a new district to join a local lineage as a client member or to activate his membership in a local lineage with which he has subsib ties. Otherwise he remains a stranger without a place in the district's social structure.

A lineage's district membership, as we have seen, is based in part on its organization as a corporation with property rights in the district's territory. Normally, it can acquire these rights only through a patrilineal inheritance from a father who is already a member of a lineage in the district or through a *niffag* from his lineage. Kinship ties of the *jëfëkyr* sort, therefore, are ordinarily prerequisite to the establishment of property rights in a district. Property rights, however, cannot be considered the determinant of a lineage's district membership, because lineages frequently have such rights in more than one district, though having political membership in only one.

More closely associated with political affiliation is the place in which a lineage is localized as an extended family. But a shift of localization from one district to another does not automatically result in a corresponding shift of political affiliation. The Pwereka 2 and Jacaw 3 lineages of Romonum are presently localized in the district of Winisi, but are still classed as members of the Corog district and remain under the jurisdiction of its chief. This situation appears to be rare, having arisen in the present instance in response to the government's requirement that houses be located near the shore, and it should be noted that in moving to the neighboring district these lineages have not left their larger community. It demonstrates, none-the-less, that localization is not *per se* a necessary criterion of district membership.

Normally, both the possession of property rights and the consequent ability to localize in a district depends on a prior *jëfëkyr* connection with either the chiefly lineage or some other lineage already affiliated with it politically. The importance of such ties as determinants of district membership is clearly revealed by the events connected with the division of Romonum—which until about 1900 had been one district—into its

[6] It should be pointed out that the newer lineages are at no disadvantage with the older ones in terms of the number of plots to which they hold provisional title. The *niffag* of land from father to son and from corporations to their *jëfëkyr*, serves to keep the actual use of land under constant redistribution in accordance with the changing sizes of the various lineages.

present districts of Winisi and Corog. On this occasion, the territory of Romonum was divided between the Pwereka 1 and Pwereka 3 lineages, which thereby acquired the chiefship of Corog and Winisi respectively. Pwereka 2 joined Corog on the basis of its ramage connections with Pwereka 1 and its history of hostility to Pwereka 3. The rest of Romonum's lineages affiliated according as their nearest or most important *jëfëkyr* connections with the chiefly lineages and their satellites indicated, even though they were localized in the territory of the opposite district and had the bulk of their *sööpw* lands there. What happened in each case and why will be discussed in detail in the next chapter. On Uman, the present districts of Söönnuuk and Nuukan were formerly united under a lineage of the Fesinim sib as a single district. Around 1890 the present division was made under political pressure from the great *jitag* Genimun, who had united all of northern Uman under his leadership in war against Fefan Island. The chiefship of each district was taken by a descent line of the Fesinim lineage. The other lineages affiliated in accordance with their *jëfëkyr* connections with the Fesinim descent lines. These examples, together with the Trukese habit of regarding the chiefly lineage as having "sired" the others in its district, make it clear that kinship is the basic criterion of district membership.

We have already seen how the Trukese lineage functions sociologically as an individual in connection with ownership (where it can be a party to a transaction), in connection with inheritance (where it has its "natural" heirs), and in connection with kinship (where it has its "children," its *jëfëkyr*). If we extend this consideration to district affiliation, viewing lineages as in a "father-child" relationship, as is the case when one is the *jëfëkyr* of another, then the social composition of a district is revealed as a group of lineages which are in theory, at least, the patrilineal descendants of the chiefly lineage, which is in the position of founding "father." The lineages sired by it and ranking next to it in time order of their establishment are its "children," who in their turn may have sired new lineages as their "children." As titular father of his district, a chief is regularly referred to in the possessive as *semej sömwoon* (my-father chief). He is considered responsible for the welfare of his district in a way analogous to a father's responsibility for the welfare of his dependent children. A Trukese district is structured, therefore, as a consanguineal kin group, composed of patrilineally related matrilineal lineages. We are presented with the interesting phenomenon of a society whose individuals are organized into matrilineal lineages, which groups are in their turn further affiliated matrilineally into ramages and subsibs and patrilineally into districts.[7] It is the patrilineal tie, coupled with territorial localization and cemented

---

[7]The linking of kin groups into larger social units by applying to them the same unilinear considerations applied to individuals has been noted in other societies, such as the Kazak (Hudson, 1938: 17-23) and the Nuer (Evans-Pritchard, 1940: 193-4), group kinship among the latter being called *buth*. In these cases, however, as well as in the more conventional cases of phratry organization, and also as with the Trukese ramages and subsibs, the rule of descent affiliating individuals into groups and groups into larger groups is the same throughout. Truk presents the only instance known to the writer wherein one rule of descent is used to affiliate individuals while the opposite rule of descent is used to affiliate the resulting kin groups into a larger kin group. This situation differs from the usual ones involving double descent (Murdock, 1940) in that in the latter both patrilineal and matrilineal descent apply only to individual affiliations.

with the obligations of divided ownership, which makes a district a social as well as a territorial unit.

The position of the Pwukos lineage on Romonum today presents an interesting test case for the view of district social structure outlined above. This lineage was founded when a Chinese trader named Siko settled in what is now Corog district. Instead of marrying a Romonum woman, he brought with him two wives from Moen Island. Because of his peculiar economic position and his identification by the natives with the German administration he never operated as a client member of any local lineage, ordinarily a necessity for an immigrant native. Through debts to his store he gradually acquired a number of land holdings. By each of his two wives he had several children who now constitute the Pwukos lineage and who inherited from Siko the lands he had accumulated. This lineage is localized in the present district of Corog and has property interests in its territory, but has not been sired by any established lineage on Romonum, nor has it acquired its property through inheritance or *niffag* from a native father. It is, therefore, without a patrilineal tie which would integrate it into Corog's social structure. In line with our analysis, the Pwukos lineage does not give allegiance to Corog's present chief and in other respects seems to occupy an anomalous position. Although there are conflicting claims, for example, as to whether or not this lineage has full title to the soil of its holdings, the residual title of Pwereka 1 to the territory involved does not appear to be questioned. But Pwukos does not, apparently, give Corog's chief the food gifts to which he is presumably entitled. Informants would sometimes refer to Pwukos as a part of Corog district and would sometimes refer to it as a separate district unto itself. When, moreover, Catholicism was introduced to Romonum, the rest of Corog remained Protestant, but Pwukos, as if to accentuate its independence, joined the Catholic congregation of Winisi. The peculiar position that this lineage occupies has undoubtedly been enhanced by the fact that a Marshallese son of Siko occupied a high administrative chiefship under the Japanese and American regimes. Nevertheless, the fact that Pwukos is not considered a full-fledged member of Corog district tends to corroborate our conclusion that the patrilineal tie is a critical criterion by means of which the district membership of a lineage is determined.[8]

From the point of view of the individual native, one might say that a Trukese district forms what Murdock (1949: 62–4) has called a "deme," a local group whose members are consanguineally related through both male and female (bilateral) connections and have a feeling of kinship thereby. It is also true that with each generation the arrangement of *jëfëkyr* connections between lineages in a district is modified, due to the taboo against a woman's marrying a member of her father's lineage. A lineage which is in a child relationship to another today may be in the opposite relationship to it in a generation's time. The fact remains that the Trukese themselves think of a district as a group of matrilineal lineages which, as units of descent, are patrilineally derived

---

[8]Needless to say, the Pwukos lineage represents an exceptional case made possible only by Siko's position as a foreign trader. Otherwise a new lineage on Romonum could have started only through a patrilineal tie with one of the lineages already present.

from the founding lineage of the chief. In these terms, the structure of the Trukese district is clearly that of a non-exogamous patrilineal kin group.

SUCCESSION TO CHIEFSHIP

A district chief is *mwääniici* of the lineage holding residual title to the district's territory. Chiefship is exercised, therefore, by the oldest man of the founding lineage, just as the *mwääniici* of any lineage is its oldest male member. Only a man may be chief. If the founding lineage should find itself without any adult men, the situation is considered to be the same as when a lineage becomes extinct.

It will be recalled from the discussion of divided ownership that when a lineage holding residual title to soil becomes extinct, the provisional title holders acquire full title to their portions. In accordance with this rule we would expect that if the chiefly lineage died out, the other lineages would each get full title to those portions of the territory to which they had been holding provisional title. This would result in a set of smaller districts, each consisting of an aggregate of plots which were not necessarily contiguous. For this reason such a course would be undesirable. There are other factors which make it impossible.

As already noted, it frequently happens that one lineage may hold provisional title to the soil and trees on a plot of land, while two other lineages respectively hold residual title to its soil and trees. All three lineages, however, are simultaneously holding provisional title to the same piece of territory as represented by this plot, for only as holders of provisional title to territory do any of them have any rights there. If the chiefly lineage dies out, therefore, all three of them are presumably in a position to get full title to the same piece of territory. Each of these three lineages is similarly involved with other lineages on other plots of land. This means that it is impossible to apply to territory the rule that on the death of the residual title holder the provisional title holder gets full title.

It will be recalled that when a lineage holding full title to soil or trees becomes extinct, the title is inherited by its *jëfëkyr*, the children of its men. It is this rule which is followed when the chiefly lineage becomes extinct. Since its *jëfëkyr* may be distributed over several lineages, residual title to the entire territory is inherited by the children of the last man who held the chiefship before the chiefly lineage became extinct. Residual title to the territory now becomes the corporate property of his children, and is administered by the *mwääniici* among them. When a chief's lineage has no adult men, the same thing happens. The *jëfëkyr* of the former chief take over the chiefship which continues to be held by their lineage, even though the surviving women of the older lineage bear sons who eventually grow to maturity.

In one respect, then, the rights of the younger lineages to territory resemble those of a provisional title holder, while in another respect they are like those of a borrower. The chiefly lineage is not free to take back the use of territory from the other lineages without cause, namely their defaulting in the obligations which they owe the chief. In this respect the relations between the chiefly lineage and the others correspond exactly to those between the parties to divided ownership.[9] On the other hand, the fact that the other lineages do not acquire full title to portions of the territory on the extinction of the chiefly lineage puts them in a position comparable to having only the loan of territory. In short, in relation to the other lineages of a district the chiefly lineage has the rights of a residual title holder to territory, but has the rights of a full title holder when the question of inheritance by its *jëfëkyr* arises.

Once the residual title to territory has passed from one lineage to another, the latter also acquires the right to have said of it that it began the land and sired all the other lineages in the district. It is now considered the oldest lineage in the district and ranks in the number one position.

The same thing occurs when a lineage defeats the chiefly lineage in war and drives it out of the district. The victorious lineage wins the chiefship, the residual title to the territory, and the right to have said of it that it began the land. In cases where outsiders conquer another district and drive out its entire population, the vacated district is apparently regarded in the same light as a newly staked claim to virgin land.

The lists of chiefs obtained for the five districts of Pata, for a district on Uman, and for Romonum, all go back only a short way to the first chiefs of those lineages, which are now said to have begun the land. While the present distribution of property holdings on Romonum is very complex, if one carries the history of the various plots back to about the time of the first Pwereka chief there (approximately 150 years), one finds that nearly all the lands to whose soil lineages now hold residual title were then held by them under full title, the soil not having been given away to children of their men in *niffag*. There are enough exceptions to this, however, to indicate an older stratum of holdings that were perhaps as complex in their distribution as they are today. It is remembered on Romonum that the chiefship was once held there by the Jimwö sib, which was defeated in war and driven off the island by the Pwereka sib, whose then one lineage acquired the chiefship by this conquest. The other lineages on Romonum are said to have supported Pwereka in this undertaking. It would appear that this conquest led to the redistribution of many holdings and their consolidation into sizable blocks of contiguous plots at that time. The processes of transfer by *niffag* and inheritance have gradually scrambled holdings again. While the lists of chiefs are short, districts must be presumed to have much longer histories. Otherwise it would appear that the opening up of Truk by immigration from other islands took place only within the past few hundred years.

Whether or not the theory of chiefship results from a pioneering tradition surviving from the time of the original settlement of Truk, it is now impossible to say. It is equally possible that the gradual development of the tenure system led to a set of relationships which were subsequently extended by analogy to the political organization as well, older political forms being modified to conform to the property system as successive wars and conquests recreated pioneering situations.[10]

[9] Cf. what was called "the eminent domain of the district chief" in Murdock and Goodenough (1947: 337).

[10] There is a tradition, for example, that the population of Uman Island was almost entirely exterminated in a war with Fefan. The survivors gained allies on another island and recaptured Uman, which is said to have been resettled by the other island which befriended the survivors. Many of the present sibs there claim to have come from the other island in connection with this event.

CHIEFS AND SUBJECTS

As noted above, the relations between a chief and the people of his district are patterned largely after the relations between the parties in divided ownership. As provisional title holders to territory, the various lineages owe the chief periodic gifts of produce from the land. These gifts are rendered at stated times in connection with feasts given in the chief's honor. He fixes the time for these feasts in accordance with a seasonal calendar: two feasts during the breadfruit season, and two more during the turmeric season.[11] The men of the various lineages prepare breadfruit in giant wooden bowls while the women fish. Other types of food are also collected. On the day of the feast each lineage brings its food in a procession, the men carrying the giant bowls on frames and chanting as they walk. The food is carried into the meeting house of the chief's lineage. The chief then selects the largest bowl for himself and his lineage mates and redistributes the rest of the food to the assembled population. The distribution is made according to lineage and is roughly proportional to the size of each lineage. The contributions which each lineage makes are also proportional to the size of its membership and the amount of productive land which it controls. If a lineage fails in this obligation, the chief has the right to confiscate its holdings. Should he indicate dissatisfaction with the contribution of a particular lineage, its members will hasten to prepare additional food and other gifts to mollify him.

It is the chief's privilege to call out his entire district on large fish drives. To him always go the first fish obtained on such drives. Today, the chief decides whether his district will hold a feast in connection with some event such as Christmas, and how the feast will be conducted and prepared.

Aside from his prerogative as administrator of the residual title to the territory which his lineage holds, a chief has relatively little jurisdiction over the members of his district, except as their titular father. In aboriginal times, for example, he had no legal right to interfere in quarrels and feuds among his subjects. He had no judicial powers. He could exert his influence against troublesome individuals or lineages by throwing his own lineage onto one side or another of a feud. To do this, however, without the support of the majority of the lineages in the district was risky, for a chief who threw his weight around too much would find the rest of the district taking sides against him in open feud. He would be killed, and his lineage would be exterminated or driven out of the district. In event of a serious violation of the mores, however, a chief could interfere with impunity, since he would have the support of the rest of the district against the offender.

In this connection, if a man contemplated trying to steal another man's wife to marry her, he would secretly bring his chief a bowl of mashed breadfruit at night as a gift and ask his permission to marry the woman. If the chief was sympathetic he would agree to keep his hands off the affair, and if it came to a feud to support the wife-stealer. If the chief anticipated serious trouble from the proposal, he would refuse his per-

[11] The Trukese divide the year into two main seasons, each of approximately six months' duration: *rääs*, the breadfruit season, lasting roughly from July to December, and *jefen*, the turmeric season, lasting from January to June.

mission. This meant that the would-be wife-stealer could go ahead with his plans only at his own risk, and that in the event of a feud he would find the chief's lineage arrayed against him.

Similarly, if the action of one lineage was such as to cause another to seek vengeance, the *mwääniici* of the latter would take a present to the chief at night and invite the chief and his lineage to join him in going after the person he sought to kill. If the chief refused, those seeking revenge would have to proceed with caution.

A good chief was expected to use his position in this way to try to keep peace in his district and see that no injustices were done by one lineage to another. At assemblies in his meeting house, he would preach to the people against theft, murder, and adultery, the three acts mostly likely to lead to a serious breach of the peace. When disputes arose, he would try to act as mediator and bring quarreling lineages to a peaceful solution of their problem.

It was expected of a good chief that he would be *mösönösön* (a person of humility) in his dealings with others and not display *namanam tekija* (arrogant behavior). For example, it was bad form for a chief personally to express his displeasure with people, to scold them publicly, or personally to order them to prepare for one of the regular feasts which were his due. When dealing authoritatively with his people, he was expected to do so indirectly. It was his *mwääniinyk* (younger brothers) and children who came to the people and told them that their behavior was not meeting with the chief's approval, or who let it be known that a feast would be held in the chief's honor on a certain day.[12] A chief who orders people around directly is likely to be unpopular.[13]

As potential heirs to the chiefship, the children of a chief were accorded special privileges in aboriginal times. They, the *jëfëkyren sömwoon* (*jëfëkyr* of the chief), were not classed with the rest of the people, *jaramas*. Together with the next younger brother of the chief, they occupied seats of honor in the meeting house and were privileged to harangue the people. A chief's death, followed by his younger brother's assumption of office, did not terminate the privileges enjoyed by the children of the former chief. They continued to exercise them until their death, for they were still among the potential heirs to the chiefship. These privileges were held only by a chief's own children. They could not in turn be passed to their children or lineage mates.

No regular religious duties were attached to the chief's office. They were performed, instead, by various specialists. A chief was concerned, however, that the proper spe-

[12]In this respect, the younger brothers and sons of the chief filled the role fo the so-called "talking chiefs" of many Polynesian people, without having their position as such so highly formalized. This role now tends to be exercised by the local policeman and secretary.

[13]It is interesting to contrast the behavior of the man who held the office of councilman on Romonum Island, a new administrative post, with that of the man who had held the administrative chiefship over Udot and Romunum. The former was throwing his weight around, publicly scolding people, threatening them to get them to work on the paths, which work is now required once a week under the United States administration. The people were constantly grumbling about him. The other chief, however, never acted directly in any matter which would be distasteful. He had his policeman and secretary do his dirty work for him. The man who had been his policeman and later his assistant chief was, therefore, unpopular, but I never heard a bad word said against himself.

cialists engage in their respective activities at appropriate times, at least when the welfare of the entire district was involved. He also used to set the times for dances, which were a popular form of entertainment before the missionaries banned them.

As administrator of the title to the territory and as father of the district as a kin group, a chief has a definite say as to the kind of reception strangers are to receive. A visitor must make sure that he is welcome to the district and to be fed and housed there during his visit. Assurance of this is given by the chief. In the old days he signified it by inviting visitors to lodge the mast and sails of their canoe in his meeting house.

A chief represents his district in inter-district relations and in aboriginal times led the people of his district in war. He organized the military campaign, ascertained that all necessary preparations were made, had diviners determine auspicious days for attack, and saw to it that the available magical specialists employed all the magic they knew in order to inflict sickness upon the enemy and render all counter-magic harmless. If his district was getting the worst of it, the chief made proper representation to the victors for ending the war and making peace. A decision to go to war, however, did not rest entirely with the chief. His wish for war could be vetoed by the adult men of his district, who assembled in his meeting house to discuss the matter. A chief, in turn, could veto a desire for war expressed by his people, the approval of both being required. When war was decided on, a chief assembled the adult men to determine appropriate plans of action. The man with most prestige as a strategist and tactician was the one whose words carried the most weight, regardless of whether or not he was a chief, while the man most skilled as a fighter led the military expedition. The chief acted as manager and coordinator. He had no legal right to compel any person in his district to go to war. If someone refused to take part, the chief would be angry but could not force him. He would assign such a person the job of staying home as a guard for the women and children.

Because of his role in war and his position as mediator in intra-district disputes, it was desirable that a chief have had training in the lore of *jitag*. An *jitag*, it will be recalled, is a sort of combined lawyer, general, diplomat, and orator. His knowledge includes the history of the district and its land tenure, the special language and magic of diplomacy, strategy and tactics in war with its related magic, and rhetoric. A chief could handle the affairs of his district much more adroitly if he commanded such knowledge. By no means all district chiefs were *jitag*. Frequently, however, a chiefly lineage would be in possession of the lore of one of the several *jitag* schools. In this event, though the chief himself might not be skilled as an *jitag*, some member of his lineage would be. If there was no *jitag* in his own lineage, but there was one in another lineage in the district, a chief would call upon him to apply his knowledge on behalf of the district. In times of war, a district without an *jitag* might hire the services of one from another, friendly district.

In former times an important item in a chief's equipment was the conch-shell trumpet (*sewi*). It could be blown only by the chief, himself, and was not used except to summon his people to an important meeting on an emergency matter. Nowadays the conch is used to call the people to routine meetings, to community work, and to Protestant church services. The prohibition against unauthorized persons blowing it has been relaxed.

Certain trees and plants (breadfruit, coconut, and the dryland, elephant-ear taro) growing near a chief's residence were formerly reserved exclusively for his use, no matter who actually owned them. This also applied to certain fragrant flowers and herbs used in making a chief's leis.

Everyone who was not a consanguineal or affinal relative of the chief was heavily "taboo from setting himself above" him.[14] This involved saying *"fääjiro"* as an expression of respect on meeting a chief. It further required that one crouch or crawl in the chief's presence if he was seated, for it was forbidden to have one's head on a higher plane than his. One avoided initiating social interaction with a chief, unless the need was urgent, in which case one made him a gift and then waited the chief's pleasure. One could not persist in refusing a chief's request without being guilty of *namanam tekija* (arrogant behavior), nor could one address him harshly or belligerently. For persons other than his relatives, a chief occupied the most heavily taboo status with respect to behavior of this kind.[15] His consanguineal and affinal kinsmen, however, behaved toward him in accordance with the status positions which he occupied as their kinsman, at least as far as their being "taboo from above" him was concerned. Other formalities were also accorded a chief. When he walked along a path with a party of people, he went first, unless the path was difficult. In the latter event someone went ahead to clear the way. While crawling behavior and the expression *"fääjiro"* are no longer exhibited, a chief still walks first today and the people still feel themselves to be "taboo from above" him.

THE COMMUNITY

Since a community of people living in daily face-to-face contact with one another may consist of the members of more than one district, it is necessary to look beyond the political structure for those features of organization which hold the community together as a social unit.

It is the community within which most marriages take place. People are not restricted to their district for their spouses, but do tend to restrict themselves to their community.[16] Regardless of district membership, therefore, the members of a community are linked together by the bonds of consanguineal and affinal kinship. While no one individual counts all the members of his community as kinsmen, each person's *futuk* and *määräär* overlap with the next person's so that the entire population of a community is included in a set of closely interlocking kin relationships.

The *niffag* of property from fathers to their children also creates a network of

[14] See above in the discussion of behavior between kinsmen and the derivation of statuses on the *pin me wöön* scale.

[15] The other categories of persons who shared this status with the chief were *jitag* and *pwëny* (navigators).

[16] Since matrilocal residence takes the men away from their home lineages, most of them marry women whose lineage houses are within a few minutes' walk of their own (cf. Murdock, 1949: 213–14).

146

interlocking parties in divided ownership, not only within the district, but in the community as well, property holdings frequently cutting across district lines as a result of inter-district marriages. The result is that one individual may owe payments to two different district chiefs, and the several district chiefs in a community may all owe payments to each other for those plots which each holds in the others' districts.

Another set of relationships helping to unite the members of a community in a social group is based on age groupings, which are particularly important among the men.[17] Such groupings are continuations of boyhood play-groups. All of the men with whom one regularly played as a youth are in one's age group. The members of an age group start courting at the same time, start learning fighting skills at the same time, get married at about the same time, and engage in post-marital affairs with one another's wives. It is in the age group that friendships are likely to crystallize into artificial sibling relationships.

While a native is not "taboo from above" unrelated persons in age groups senior to his own, he is supposed to show them respect, his respect increasing in proportion to the distance between their respective groups. If a gang of men are working together, the members of the younger age groups start the work out of respect for the older men. The older age groups expect the men in the youngest group present to run errands and, if they are away from home, to do the cooking and other necessary chores. Thus the position of the younger men is in some respects like that of the *setipwitur* (youngest sibling) in the lineage and household organization.

Between members of the same age group no holds are barred in conversation. They are free to tease and joke with one another (except when the obligations of kinship require modifications of such behavior). It is largely with members of his own age group[18] that the Trukese man establishes intimate relationships of an equalitarian sort with other men.

The fact of daily association and residential proximity puts the members of a community in a position where they are most likely to call upon one another rather than strangers for assistance in the many little tasks that come up where an extra hand or two may be needed, as, for example, in launching a canoe. The members of a community tend, therefore, to be more or less obligated (*kinissow*) to one another in informal matters as well as in more formal property relationships. Similarly, recreational activites frequently involve the entire community membership. Dancing appears to have been

[17] The word *tetten* (rank, line, file), used for a generation in a lineage, is also used to refer to such age groupings.

[18] Age groupings of this kind should not be confused with the system of absolute categories classifying the population on the basis of age and sex, e.g., *mënukön* (infant), *semiriit* (small child), *jäät* and *neggin* (boy and girl), *jënywën* and *fëëpwyn* (young man and young woman), *mwään* and *feefin* (middle aged man and middle aged woman), and *cinnap* (oldster). Among those men on Romonum who were all classed as *jënywën*, an informant distinguished between five different age groups of "contemporaries," one above his own and three below it in seniority. There were fourteen men whom he included in his own age group, some of them three or even four years older than he and others a year or two younger. Absolute age is less relevant to membership in such a group than are the rate at which one matured and the persons with whom one played and fought as a youth.

the most important activity of this kind in aboriginal times, but under the influence of missionaries it has come to be considered sinful and no longer serves this purpose. Its place has been taken by baseball, a sport introduced by the Japanese. When services are over, every Sunday on Romonum is devoted to baseball in which the entire population participates as players or spectators. Many communities are now split into Catholic and Protestant congregations, but the indications are that in former times participation in religious ceremonies was largely a community affair.

The frequency of interaction between members of the same community is, of course, higher than between members of different communities. An important consequence is that each community tends to have minor peculiarities of dialect and culture which provide for its members a means for greater mutual understanding and consequent trust than can obtain between comparative strangers. The writer was struck with the fact that on Moen Island, for example, each community had a few definite linguistic features of its own, mainly in vocabulary. The Trukese are fully conscious of them and use them to identify an individual's community affiliation.

In summary, a Trukese community is composed of a group of people who live in fairly close proximity. Though they may have no over-all political unity, they have common interests in that they depend on one another for minor assistance in the daily routine of living, marry largely among themselves, and jointly participate in a local system of interlocking kin relationships, a local network of mutual property obligations, a single hierarchy of age groups, and local recreational and ceremonial activities.[19] Their sense of unity as a group is enhanced by their sharing in local peculiarities of language and culture.

[19] In the Mortlock Islands, Tolerton and Rauch (1950) find that lineages of the same sib within a community are organized as a ramage, of which the head of the senior lineage is chief. At the same time, the community consists of several small districts, each with its chief, as in Truk. It is possible that what we have called ramages are not confined to districts, but are similarly of community scope in some parts of Truk.

As in the case of *pin me wöön*, additional information might yield more positions on the scale of sexual availability, and should enable us to include non-kinsmen as well as kinsmen in the population for which these behaviors form a scale.

Chart 2 compares these status positions with the distinctions made in the kinship and behavioral terminologies by a male ego. The status positions correlate most closely with the kinship terms which a man uses for his female relatives, and less well with the behavioral terms (cf. mothers and sisters). This correlation is especially high if we treat as one those status positions which are differentiated only as to whether a behavior pattern is disapproved or forbidden, which would, for example, equate positions 1 with 2 and 3, 2 with 4. This illustrates that while social categories may be correlated with status positions on a scale of behavior, the correlation may be with several adjacent positions taken together rather than with each one separately.

CONCLUSION

In this chapter status positions have been derived in relation to two variables, that of *pin me wöön* and that of sexual distance. Unquestionably there are a number of other variables or continua in terms of which other status positions could be derived by the scaling of behavior-patterns. A full analysis of the behavior exhibited between kinsmen would require exhausting all of these variables. Once this was accomplished, one could note just what status positions any two individuals simultaneously occupy in their dealings with one another. The sum of the status positions which a person simultaneously occupies for an ego in their interaction would determine the total range of behavior patterns which ego would exhibit toward him. The sum of the status positions thus occupied by a person in an interaction situation would constitute what we may call the *composite status* of that person in that interaction. The sum of the configurations of behavior patterns, which when directed toward that person define his composite status, may be called the *composite role* of ego toward him.

It should be pointed out that what is here called a role differs in one important respect from what Linton (1936: 114) calls a role. He defines a role as the behaviors which emanate from a person occupying a status. To us a role consists of the behaviors which are directed towards a person occupying a status. This by no means denies that a status has a dynamic aspect to which Linton gave the name "role." It merely recognizes that a status can be empirically derived only from the behaviors which are directed toward its occupant. It is ego's role in reacting to another which defines the status of the latter with respect to him, while the other's role toward ego defines the status of ego in the relationship. If in Linton's words a status is simply a collection of rights and privileges, these can be manifested in behavior only as others respect these rights and privileges in their dealings with the person who occupies the status. If they fail to do so, they indicate that for them the person toward whom they are directing their behavior does not occupy the status which he thinks he does. The things which a chief can and cannot do in his dealings with his subjects do not define the status of the chief, but define the composite status which his subjects occupy for him as chief, while the things the subjects can and cannot do in their dealings with him define the composite status active leadership. This was exercised by the eldest of his sisters' sons, named Jöku. To insure success against Jimwö, the Pwereka people appealed for aid to subsib mates in Nykynyfëw district on Udot, who sent over a contingent of reinforcements under the leadership of Wowunuppwyn (P1). As subsib mates they enjoyed automatic membership in the Pwereka lineage of Romonum for as long as they remained there. This served, apparently, to complicate relations within the Pwereka group because Wowunuppwyn and his *mwääninyk*, Nusumwacej (P1), were both senior in age to Jöku. After the defeat of Jimwö, Wowunuppwyn returned to take over the chiefship of Nykynyfëw, leaving Nusumwacej on Romonum. The latter's sisters also came over from Udot to establish a distinct descent line in the Pwereka lineage with a household at Mwej (680–400), alongside the older one at Neewuukec. The members of the present-day lineage of Pwereka 1 are descended from this group.

As victors over Jimwö, Pwereka presumably had a claim to the chiefship and to the lands which Jimwö had formerly held under full title. Normally, the chiefship would have gone to Jöku, but as his senior, Nusumwacej now had a prior claim. Nor did Pwereka's victory stand uncontested, for the *jëfëkyr* of Jimwö had a legal right to inherit the lands to which their fathers' lineage had held full title, and the children of the last Jimwö chief were heirs to the chiefship. Moreover, Jimwö's *jëfëkyr* were duty bound to avenge the death of their fathers, if at all possible, vengeance being a duty of one's "sons," "brothers," and "fathers." It is for these reasons, apparently, that we find a descent line of the Wiitëë lineage feuding against Pwereka. The members of this group were probably the children of the former Jimwö chief, for among their land plots is reckoned Fääkomon (530–430), which is said to have been the site of Jimwö's lineage house or *wuut*. As will be seen, they succeeded in taking over at least some of the Jimwö lands which were theirs by right of inheritance. It was this, apparently, which led to their establishment as a separate lineage, Wiitëë 3, with their house at Fäänifac (580–440) and *wuut* at Fääkomon (530–430). They are said to have been fairly strong in numbers and are remembered as formidable fighters and skilled sorcerers, capable of presenting strong opposition to Pwereka. One of their *jëfëkyr* in turn, however, was the aforementioned Jöku, the displaced Pwereka *mwääniici*. Since he was their "son," they were "taboo from above" him[5] and could neither persist in refusing his requests nor agress against him. Jöku was thus immune from their vengeance and at the same time in a position to use them to advance his own ends. He is said to have entered into a conspiracy with his "fathers" of Wiitëë 3. They were to kill Nusumwacej, the present Pwereka head. This would satisfy the demands of vengeance, Jöku would take over the chiefship without personally being guilty of fratricide, and the land claims of Wiitëë 3 would be recognized, at least in part, by Jöku as Pwereka's *mwääniici*. Success would depend on Jöku's ability to control the Pwereka lineage, but with the backing of his powerful Wiitëë "fathers" and the neutrality of the Pwereka group native to Romonum, he should have the immigrants from Nykynyfëw in too weak a position to fight back, as well as at a moral disadvantage in the face of his now manifest seniority. Everything went according to plan: Nusumwacej was cut down by the men of Wiitëë

[5] See above, p. 113.

3 when he was out alone gathering breadfruit, Jöku became chief of Romonum, and Wiitëë 3 was confirmed as heir to a good portion of the Jimwö lands.

There remained, however, the problem of keeping the other Pwereka men from seeking reprisals against Wiitëë 3. It appears that the death of Nusumwacej left the Mwej branch of Pwereka without responsible adult males. This strengthened Jöku's hand, except for the fact that there remained two adolescents, Nitej and Jätäna (P1), who had a reputation as hot-heads, and who were strongly backed in everything by their father, Jitimä (U5). Whether or not it was a part of the original plan, Jöku found it necessary to persuade his Wiitëë 3 "fathers" to give them some plots of land as a *kiis* in compensation for the killing.[6] He could justify his role as arbitrator on the grounds that, as *mwääniici*, he could not countenance an attempt by his "younger brothers" to kill his "fathers," though recognizing that the former had a right to compensation. This represents the only instance known to informants where a form of wergild was used to settle a feud. They stated emphatically that it was without precedent, was tried this once and never again. As will be seen, its success was temporary only, but it testifies to the genius of Jöku nonetheless. It also reveals the kind of situation which can lead to establishment of a recognized wergild system in a unilinear society.[7]

Jöku's assumption of Romonum's chiefship, with the backing of Wiitëë 3, settled Pwereka's claim to it. Jöku is now spoken of as Romonum's first chief and founder of the land, although older informants are aware that this is true in a figurative sense only. Although Jöku's manipulations stabilized affairs for some time, the lack of precedent for wergild meant that his Pwereka "brothers" continued to have a legal basis for seeking vengeance from Wiitëë 3, if circumstances should become sufficiently altered to make such action feasible and profitable. And circumstances did so change.

Since the death of Nusumwacej had apparently left the Mwej branch of Pwereka without responsible adult males, its affairs were delegated to one of the older men of the Neewuukec branch as guardian. This would explain the fact that Meejiwen (P1 or P2), born a member of the Pwereka line native to Romonum, succeeded Nusumwacej as *mwääniici* of the immigrant Pwereka line from Nykynyfëw. This group, it appears, was subsequently joined by Jecag (P1) and his brother, Mwënefëw (P1), from Nykynyfëw. Thus, in a few years' time, the Mwej group acquired considerable manpower, with the now maturer Nitej and Jätäna scheming for vengeance against Wiitëë 3.

The Neewuukec branch of Pwereka also increased in numbers to the point where it was necessary to build another house. This was erected at Neemwon (650–450), not far from the old house at Neewuukec, where Jöku's two sisters and their four daughters (P3) continued to reside. The remaining women of Neewuukec moved into the new house where they formed the nucleus of a new descent line (as distinct from Jöku's). It came under the leadership of Jaamew (P2), who was next in line to Jöku as lineage head, and also counted Meejiwen, guardian-leader of the Mwej group, as a member.

[6] This transaction involved the plot of Neefëw (390–500) and parts of Penijenyk (400–550).

[7] For analogous considerations leading to a modification of vendetta justice in a bilateral society, see the excellent account of the Kalingas by Barton (1949).

The Pwereka lineage was thus divided into three discrete and powerful descent lines, each with its own house: that at Neewuukec under Jöku (P3), that at Neemwon under Jaamew (P2), and that at Mwej under Meejiwen (P1), with the latter two closely linked through Meejiwen's joint membership. Both Jöku's and Meejiwen's descent lines held full title to a number of land plots independently from the over-all Pwereka lineage, whose lands were exploited largely by Jaamew's descent line. How these independent properties were acquired is no longer remembered, but it is difficult to account for them, particularly in the case of the immigrant Mwej group, except as spoils taken from the defeated Jimwö lineage. The major share of such spoils would have fallen to Jöku, as *mwääniici* of the Pwereka line native to Romonum, and to Nusumwacej, as *mwääniici* of the immigrant line, whose needs would have been most pressing.[8] In any case, the lineage potentials of both the Neewuukec and Mwej groups were now strong not only in personnel but also in property.

As its strength increased, the Mwej group became more openly hostile to Jöku because of the Nusumwacej incident, but cooperated closely with Jaamew. As his leadership of the Pwereka lineage became less secure, Jöku was forced increasingly to rely for support on his "fathers" of Wiitëë 3 and his sons in the Jeffeg lineage in order to maintain unchallenged his position as Romonum's chief. He continued, of course, to command the active support of the Neewuukec group, particularly from the children of a sister's daughter who had married Jösoomä of Wiitëë 3. Like himself, they were *jëfëkyr* of the enemies of the Mwej group.

The growing cleavage in the Pwereka lineage led finally to a plot by the people of Neemwon and Mwej to assassinate Jöku. It was carried out by Jaamew in the Pwereka *wuut* at Neepiiköw. The writer heard the story of this event on several occasions, and each time its narrator stressed what for the Trukese was its really tragic aspect: its effect on old Misyk (P2), who was still alive and who was mother's brother to both Jaamew and Jöku. So old that he could not walk, totally blind, he was present in the *wuut* when Jöku was killed. The stunned silence which followed was broken only by Misyk, who, crawling on hands and knees and weeping from his sightless eyes, was groping for Jöku's body. He had lived to see his lineage defeat Jimwö, acquire Romonum's chiefship, grow strong in numbers and capable leadership, and then tear itself apart with fratricide.[9] The story was never told without presenting this tableau as its climax.

[8] Lands to which full title was held by Mwej: Corog (850–150), Fääjiccyk (850–320), Fäätuutu (850–230), Janapa (810–240), Neejin Pënë (620–400), Neejöör (600–420), Neminaany (770–160), Söpwunifëw (710–150), Sowujëëwyr (710–120), Wuunög (710–200), and part of Nëëry (820–170). Lands to which full title was held by Jöku's descent line: Fääkanaw (550–520), Fäänikep (500–560), Mäjefëw (880–240), Neefanag (780–200), Neejöör (540–470), Neekus (570–400), Neenyk (470–500), Pwynypeges (560–400).

[9] As the reader can well infer, fratricide is, next to incest, about the most serious crime which a Trukese can commit. Since it involves only lineage mates, no vengeance is possible except by the victim's sons and fathers, if he has any, for vengeance within the lineage would require further fratricide. A popular story on Truk today, told the writer on a number of occasions, is the well known European folktale of "Big Claus and Little Claus" (Korusunap and Korusukis). Its popularity rests on the fact

As next in line to Jöku, Jaamew succeeded to Romonum's chiefship. Jöku's assassination, however, had serious consequences. Both his "fathers" of Witëë 3 and his sons in the Jeffeg lineage had the duty of vengeance against Jaamew. This pitted them in feud against the Neemwon group. At the same time, the Mwej group had an old score to settle and had been privy to the plot against Jöku, so that its feud with Wiitëë 3 was reopened. The latter's old claim to Romonum's chiefship remained as additional cause for quarrel. A further complication arose from the fact that the Neewuukec group could no longer operate within the same lineage with the people of Neemwon and Mwej. It duly declared its independence under the leadership of Sijajer, Jöku's sister's son, to form the Pwereka 3 lineage. This put Sijajer in a position to claim Romonum's chiefship for himself as *mwääniici* of the lineage which in a retroactive sense had supplied the last chief. One branch of Pwereka 3 had further potential differences with Neemwon and Mwej, for as the sons of Jösoomä (W3) its members were bound to aid their Wiitëë "fathers" in the growing feud. Having outgrown the house at Neewuukec, this branch of Pwereka 3 built a new house at Fääkanaw (550–520), somewhat removed from the other Pwereka houses and nearer to that of Wiitëë 3 at Fäänifac (580–440).[10] To protect its occupants, they surrounded the house with a stone wall, whose brush-covered ruins still stand, the only entrance being a small hole through which it was necessary to crawl. The date of this move may be estimated at about the year 1850. The other branch of Pwereka 3 remained at Neewuukec under the leadership of Tuumwaw (P3b), who was also a sister's son of Jöku. Thus from its inception, the Pwereka 3 lineage had two distinct descent lines, each with its own house, the one at Fääkanaw (P3a) and the other at Neewuukec (P3b). Both branches shared a new *wuut* which they erected at Neenyk (470–500).

The Pwereka 2 lineage (the Neemwon and Mwei groups) concentrated on disposing of Wiitëë 3 as the most formidable among its opponents. Finding themselves in a not too favorable position, its members again sought help from their subsib mates in Nykynyfëw.[11] Wowunuppwyn returned to Romonum, where his wife was a member of

that, as told on Truk, Little Claus manages to bring about the death of Big Claus, who was guilty of unbrotherly behavior, without ever once departing from the strict requirements of respect and obedience to his older brother or ever once lifting his hand against him. Not only was Jaamew's act a "shocker" because Jöku was his brother; it was particularly shocking because Jöku was his older brother and *mwääniici*.

[10]There is a possibility that this move had already been made before Jöku's death. Informants' memory for the timing of events was often hazy. At one time they indicated that the move was made by Jöku, at another time by Sijajer.

[11]Very little of the time during which two lineages are feuding involves open acts of violence. Most of the time is spent in waiting for an opportunity in which damage can be inflicted with a minimum of risk. Meantime, of course, tension in the community mounts. There are secret midnight conferences with possible allies. People are careful not to go out alone. Each side practices sorcery against the other and takes countermeasures against the other's sorcery. At the same time, the daily round of domestic and economic activities goes on. Persons who are parties to the feud jointly take part in the community's life, acting as though on the best of terms, but overdoing it. Gossip, of course, mounts with the increase in tension, as the community feels that something must happen soon. Finally, the break comes. There is a violent emotional outburst, somebody is killed or badly hurt. The resulting shock concludes the vio-

the Wiitëë 1 lineage, and drew up a plan of action for the complete extermination of Wiitëë 3. The opportunity to strike presented itself one day when the men of Wiitëë 3 were out fishing. The Pwereka forces surrounded their enemy's house at Fäänifac and in a surprise attack slaughtered all its occupants. Proceeding thence to the Wiitee 3 landing place at Söpwutiw (090–450) on the west end of the island, they ambushed the fishing party as it was bringing its canoes in over the reef and annihilated it.

The Fääkanaw branch of Pwereka 3 was now brought openly into the feud to avenge the death of its Wiitëë 3 father, Jösoomä. Leagued with their *jëfëkyr* in Jeffeg, the members of this group continued hostilities with Pwereka 2. In the subsequent jockeying for advantage, however, the Neewuukec branch of Pwereka 3 appears to have refused to take an active part.[12] As their position became increasingly insecure, and tension mounted, the members of the Fääkanaw group and the Jeffeg lineage fled, taking refuge with kinsmen on other islands. The scattered *jëfëkyr* of Wiitëë 3 in other lineages were either too weak to do anything or had other kinship ties with Pwereka 2 which rendered them neutral.[13] At any rate, no one felt in a position to challenge Jaamew further, so that he and the Pwereka 2 lineage gained a decisive victory with the flight of their opponents.

DISPOSITION OF WIITËË 3 LANDS

The annihilation of Wiitëë 3 led to an extensive reshuffling of land holdings. Jaamew and his lineage mates, for example, are said to have acquired full title to the soil of a number of plots at this time, plots which appear to have been held by Wiitëë 3.[14] The *jëfëkyr* of Wiitëë 3 also acquired full title to plots which their fathers had held or which had already been given them in *niffag*. The resulting division of property was as follows:

1. To Pwereka 3a as children of Jösoomä (W3): Fääkomon (530-430), Fäänimëryp (550-460), Neemwar (500–420), Söpwutiw (090-450), Winifëw (800-380), Woccofëw (330-580), and parts of Fäänifac (580-440) and Penijenyk (400-550). Söpwutiw and Winifëw were later seized by Jaamew after the flight of Pwereka 3a from Romonum.

---

lence, the community settles back, and as it recovers from the trauma starts wondering what the next move will be, and the cycle of mounting tension starts all over again. Thus two lineages may be at feud for many years without either directly attacking the other.

[12] My notes show considerable disagreement as to just what happened in this case. One account has both branches of Pwereka 3 actively involved, while a subsequent account, which seems more reliable, suggests that only the Fääkanaw branch prosecuted the feud.

[13] Different accounts, sometimes by the same informant, give conflicting pictures of the line-up of other lineages in connection with this feud. One problem is that some lineages unquestionably shifted their support from one side to the other as the death of older members brought new *jëfëkyr* and affinal connections into prominence. It appears, however, that at least passive support was given to Pwereka 3a and Jeffeg by Jacaw 1, Pwereka 3b, Söör 2, Wuwäänyw 2, and Wiitëë 1; while Pwereka 2 had the support of Jacaw 2, Söör 1, Wuwäänyw 1, Wuwäänyw 3, Wuwäänyw 4, and Wuwäänyw 5.

[14] This is suggested by the location of these plots in relation to the holdings of Wiitëë 1 and other known Wiitëë holdings as well as by the coincidence that their unexplained acquisition by Pwereka occurs precisely at the time of the extermination of Wiitëë 3.

2. To Pwëën as children of Wupweewyn (W3): Neejäsep (820-470), Nëëwuwë (360-520), and part of Neepwyg (500-410).

3. To Söör 2c as children of Nykynap (W3): Neeceece (540-380), Neejör (550-400), Neepwinijepwin (180-270), and part of Fäänifac (580-440). Since Nykynap was without daughters, these properties were inherited on the death of his sons by their children in Pwereka 2b.

4. To Wuwäänyw 2 as children of Nippwör (W3): Jenigemaram (760-400) and parts of Fäänifac (580-440), Neepwyg (500-410), and Penijenyk (400-550).

5. Seized by Jaamew and the Neemwon branch of Pwereka 2: Faajë (not on map), Fään Acapar (140-390), Kyny (not on map), Neemaji (090-350), Neesöpworeg (130-370), Söpwötä (130-430), all of which Jaamew gave to his children in Wuwäänyw 3; Jepinifëny (100-250), the western half of Mwyyn (150-220), Sömööry (not on map), Winifatafat (100-170), and Wocamwoc (050-250, 090-280), all of which became the corporate property of the children of one of Jaamew's sisters, who became thereby the Pwereka 2b descent line (see below).

6. Seized by Jecag and the Mwej branch of Pwereka 2: Fään Öför (180-450), Mesejijag (160-440), Neetëttën (180-390), Tunnuköc (310-520), and Winipwëët (330-550).

The subsequent disposal of the seizures by Jaamew and Jecag reveal that they were prompted not so much by the enhancement of economic power at the expense of others as by a desire to fill genuine needs. For example, Jaamew gave half of what he took to his children in Wuwäänyw 3, a new and landless lineage, which was now well provided for without Pwereka 2 losing any of its former holdings. Pwereka 2 was itself expanding in numbers with increasing pressure on its holdings. Jecag, in turn, was an immigrant from Nykynyfëw without land on Romonum. He had married a woman of Wiitëë 2, which was another new, immigrant, and landless lineage. By his seizures he was able to provide for his otherwise landless children.

THE RISE OF PWEREKA 1

While Jaamew was chief of Romonum, the Neemwon branch of Pwereka 2 outgrew its house, whose inhabitants included Jaamew's aging mother, Nesär, who was *finniici* of the lineage; her two married daughters, Jinesan and Jinefä; her deceased sister's young, newly-married daughters, Toowuc, Tipiis, and Nesecip; Jinesan's married daughter, Jinäämën; and the latter's four young daughters. Jinaamën's husband, Kokkan (S2c), built a house for her at Neejör (550–400), land which he had inherited from the extinct Wiitëë 3 and which his children would inherit from him since he was without a sister.[15] The widowed father of Toowuc, Tipiis, and Nesecip built them a house at Fäännäjaas (600–460), land which they held under provisional title from their own lineage. Since they were still young, Nesär had her daughter Jinefä move in with them as *finniici* of their household. With her other daughter, Jinesan, Nesär continued to reside in the old house at Neemwon, which was abandoned on their death.

[15] It is possible that this move was made because Kokkan, as a son of Nykynap (W3), was put in a somewhat awkward relationship with his wife's lineage, which was responsible for the extermination of his father's lineage. The fact that he was married into Pwereka 2, however, made it impossible for him to avenge Wiitëë 3 without destroying his marriage and losing his children.

The separation into two houses at Neejör and Fäännäjaas divided the Neemwon branch of Pwereka 2 into two distinct descent lines, Pwereka 2b and Pwereka 2a respectively. This division was accentuated by the fact that Jaamew turned over to Pwereka 2b half of the lands he had seized from Wiitëë 3, giving the other half to his own children as noted above. As a minor corporation, therefore, Pwereka 2b came to have full title to a significant number of land plots, enough to give it economic independence from Pwereka 2a. These two descent lines have never severed their ties, however, maintaining their over-all corporate organization down to the present time as one lineage (P2), though the Mwej group has since split off to form the Pwereka 1 lineage. Jaamew and the brothers of Jinaamën looked after the interests of Pwereka 2b, while Mwaatejinyk and Jögömataw, sons of Jinefä, looked after the interests of Pwereka 2a, of which descent line they are now considered members.

When Jaamew died, the oldest surviving member of Pwereka 2 was Meejiwen (P1), *mwääniici* of the Mwej branch, who duly succeeded to the chiefship. It was at about this time, apparently, that relations with Pwereka 3 were sufficiently patched up so that the exiles in Pwereka 3a (the Fääkanaw group) were permitted to return to Romonum. They established a house at Näämärew (500–450), which they held under provisional title from Wiitëë 1, and attended the *wuut* which the Pwereka 3b descent line at Neewuukec had built in their absence at Fäänimëryp (550–460).

When Meejiwen died, the oldest surviving man in Pwereka 2 appears to have been Jecag (P1), an earlier immigrant from Nykynyfëw, who now became *mwääniici* of the Mwej group. He was passed over for Romonum's chiefship, however, the office being filled by Mwaatejinyk, *mwääniici* of Pwereka 2a. Either because of this or in consequence of the later assassination of Mwaatejinyk, the Mwej branch became formally established as an independent lineage, Pwereka 1. The reasons are not clear, but relations between Pwereka 1 and Pwereka 2 became increasingly strained.

One evening, Mwaatejinyk was eating with his lineage mates and his *jëfëkyr* (the men of Söör 2a) in the Pwereka 2 *wuut* at Neepiiköw. Wunnunö of Pwereka 1 and his wife's brother, Paasegeni (A1), sneaked up on them, each armed with a rifle. They intended to kill Mwaatejinyk. Wunnunö carefully pushed his rifle through the loose thatch wall of the *wuut*, drew a bead on Mwaatejinyk, and pulled the trigger. His gun missed fire. Still, no one in the *wuut* noticed anything. While Wunnunö stood fumbling with his rifle, Paasegeni pulled him out of the way, took aim with his own rifle and struck Mwaatejinyk in the chest, killing him instantly. All of the occupants of the *wuut* fled in panic except for Wenejög (S2a), Mwaatejinyk's grandson. He picked up his grandfather's body and carried it out of the *wuut* to prevent its falling into the assassin's hands. Carrying it down to the north shore of the island, he proceeded west along the rocks on the shore and then climbed back up to Neeceemej (420–460), where Mwaatejinyk had lived in the house he had built there for his wife and children (the Söör 2a descent line). Here Wenejög buried his grandfather in an upright position, leaving his head above ground and facing in the direction of the Pwereka 1 house at Mwej. He then propped Mwaatejinyk's mouth open with a stick so that his ghost would go and "devour" the Mwej people in revenge.[16] This deed earned for Wenejög a great reputation for bravery.

Mwaatejinyk's ghost does not appear to have penetrated the counter-magical defenses of Pwereka 1, at least immediately, though our informant insisted that it was the reason why the latter group has since died out except for one old man. In any case, there was no further attempt at retaliation. Jögömataw, the new *mwääniici* of Pwereka 2, refused to continue the quarrel. Wunnunö and Paasegeni were considered the most formidable men on Romonum at the time and were backed by considerable manpower, both locally by the Pwereka 1 and Jacaw 1 lineages and potentially by the Pwereka kinsmen in Nykynyfëw on Udot. The children of Mwaatejinyk in Söör 2a were unable to seek vengeance on their own and had to let the *soojëny* sorcery by Wenejög suffice.

Jecag was now installed as chief by Wunnunö, the chiefship thus passing to Pwereka 1. A new *wutten sömwon* (chief's *wuut*) was built at Neejöör (600–420) by the men of Pwereka 1, who erected another *wuut* for canoes at Söpwunifëw (710–150).[17] At about this time, the women abandoned the house at Mwej for a new one at Neejin Pënë (620–400), next to the new *wuut*. Jecag lived only a short time after becoming chief, and was succeeded by Wunnunö.

WUNNUNÖ'S CHIEFTAINCY

During Wunnunö's term of office Romonum engaged in two native wars with people of other islands, one against the district of Mwäänitiw on Udot and the other on Tol. Romonum had been involved in a war against the Wonej district of Tol while Jöku was chief. This war had been continued by Jaamew and concluded by him— informants did not indicate with what results.

The men of Mwäänitiw are said to have come frequently to sleep with Romonum's women. The Söör 1 lineage had originally come from Mwäänitiw, where it maintained close subsib ties, and this may have provided entree for Mwäänitiw's people into the Romonum community. When these amorous expeditions got out of hand, Wunnunö went to Kuumar, the chief of Mwäänitiw, and said that they would have to stop. Kuumar's reply was unsatisfactory, so Wunnunö declared war. All the districts on Udot but one joined with Kuumar as his allies. These were Fönömö, Jëët (an ad-

[16] This type of sorcery, called *soojëny*, is a standard one in warfare. A corpse of either one's own or the enemy's slain will do. Its "devouring" ghost brings pestilence on anyone toward whom it is directed (the "bite" of a ghost is a standard cause of sickness). It was important for Wenejög to keep Mwaatejinyk's body from falling into the hands of the Pwereka 1 people lest they do the same thing with it, directing the ghost towards Pwereka 2 or Söör 2a. Once it has served its purpose, a *soojëny* is quickly destroyed, for as long as it stands it remains a potent source of harm to anyone who gets in its way.

[17] The *wuut* at Neepiiköw had been the *wutten sömwon* from Jöku's chiefship through that of Mwaatejinyk. It continued as the lineage meeting house of Pwereka 2 until abandoned after a mysterious and deep hole developed in the ground at its "exact center." This was diagnosed as caused by an evil sea-spirit, the *cënykken* Nykynaajo (sharp-water of Nykynaajo), bent on bringing harm to Pwereka 2. To escape this spirit, the members of Pwereka 2 destroyed the *wuut*, but the declining numbers and fortunes of their lineage since then are attributed to its malevolence.

jacent island), Mwonowe, Nykynyfëw (Pwereka 1's old ally), Penija, and Wöönipw. Tuunnuuk district, which already had a quarrel with Fönömö, sided with Romonum. For about two months both sides made preparations. A Japanese trader named Jijemeseta (Yamashita) and two American (?) traders, Piicë and Janisin (Peter and Hanson or Allison ?), were located on Romonum at the time, Jijemeseta having married into the Wiitëë 2 lineage. From them rifles were purchased in return for copra. During this preparation period, hostilities were kept down to small raids by individuals. From one of these raids the body of an Udot man was brought to Romonum where it was set up as a *soojëny* against Mwäänitiw. When all weapons were readied, and divination by the *jitag* Kiijenë (P2a) indicated the moment was auspicious, Romonum sent a fleet of canoes under Kiijenë's command against Mwäänitiw. The attackers landed successfully at dawn, were met on the beach by the defenders, and fought along the shore for the entire day, during which Mwäänitiw is said to have lost seven men while Romonum lost none. When the fighting was resumed on the following day, Mwäänitiw lost two more men. The survivors fled up the mountain where the women and children had already been removed for safety, and Kuumar sued for peace, signifying that he had lost the war. Romonum's fighters returned home, and the poeple of Udot got together canoes, large wooden bowls, and other valuable *pisek* to give to Wunnunö as a "peace price." They then prepared a large feast which they brought to Romonum together with the goods they had assembled. With this feast and the presentation of goods peace was formally declared. Wunnunö divided the booty among Romonum's lineages, giving a share to his allies from Tuunnuuk, according to the number of fighting men which each group had supplied.[18] This venture considerably enhanced Wunnunö's prestige.

Wunnunö did not fare so well in the war on Tol, in which he became embroiled through an alliance with Meejinis, then chief of Fëëwyp district on Tol. When Meejinis became involved in a war with some neighboring districts, Wunnunö took a contingent from Romonum to help him. Since the Jacaw lineages on Romonum had strong subsib ties with lineages on Fëëwyp, this action was doubly appropriate. While no men from Romonum are reported to have been killed, Meejinis suffered severe enough losses to force him to sue for peace. In order to extricate himself, Wunnunö also had to pay a "peace price." This was the last native war in which Romonum participated, occurring around the year 1900.

Wunnunö terminated the amicable relations which had obtained between his lineage and its Pwereka subsib mates in Nykynyfëw on Udot. This may have resulted from Nykynyfëw's alliance with Mwäänitiw in Romonum's war with the latter, or may have occurred earlier. Informants gave no reasons for Wunnunö's actions.[19] In any case, some Pwereka men from Nykynyfëw came to visit Wunnunö, their kinsman, on a

[18] While this ended Romonum's part in the war, the quarrel between Tuunnuuk and Fönömö was continued, until the chief of the latter called a halt and peace was concluded with an exchange of gifts from both sides.

[19] The story was told as an illustration of what is meant by *raaw*, which we may translate roughly as "diplomacy combined with treachery."

mission concerning their relations with him as chief of Romonum. Wunnunö received them in his *wuut*, where he entertained them in a friendly and courteous fashion. He apologized for the fact that his men were not present, saying that they were preparing food. In reality, he had told his men to assemble armed and ready to exterminate the visitors. Gradually his men began drifting into the *wuut*, unobtrusively sitting in strategic spots that would prevent their visitors' escape. The latter, sensing a mounting tension, intercepted a sly exchange of glances between Wunnunö and his men. They, too, exchanged glances and made a sudden break from the *wuut*, racing to the shore and their canoes in an effort to escape. Some were killed in the meeting house. Wunnunö and his men pursued the others to the water's edge and shot down all but one with rifle fire as they tried to get their canoes over the reef. Badly wounded, the one escapee managed to swim to a coral head about a half mile off of Nykynyfëw, whence his cries led to his ultimate rescue. Relations between Pwereka 1 and Nykynfëw remained hostile until a few years before the recent World War, when Taapen (P1), the present chief of Corog, reestablished subsib ties.

THE PARTITION OF ROMONUM

Wunnunö died at about the time when the Germans pacified Truk in 1903. His younger brother, Sëwynyk (P1), followed him as chief for a brief period and was succeeded by his sister's son Ceejejög (P1). By this time Pwereka 1 was considerably weakened in numbers, facing extinction in another generation's time. Pwereka 3, meanwhile, had grown to substantial size and reasserted its claim to Romonum's chiefship. The litigation which followed, apparently under German supervision, ended with the division of Romonum into its present districts of Winisi and Corog, with Nijap (P3a) becoming chief of the former and Ceejejög (P1) remaining chief of the latter. Nijap built Winisi's *wutten sömwon* (chief's *wuut*) at Näämärew, where the Pwereka 3a house was located, and the old wuut at Fäänimëryp was abandoned. The new building was named Winisi, which means "transformed" or "changed over," in commemoration of the rebirth of Pwereka 3's fortunes. It was from this that the new district took its name.[20]

In accordance with their kinship ties with the two chiefly lineages, the rest of Romonum's lineages affiliated with the two new districts. When asked what the basis for affiliation was, informants regularly replied that the *jëfëkyr* of the chiefly lineages followed their fathers respectively, and that their *jëfëkyr* in turn followed them. The facts of the situation can be summarized as follows:

To COROG:

1. Jacaw 1. This lineage included the children of Wunnunö among its members and had all of its *sööpw* lands within Corog territory.

[20] Corog took its name from the section of lagoon (850–150). The districts are also referred to as Söpwuwu (Outer District) for Winisi, and Söpwönög (Inner District) for Corog. Commemorative naming is apparently fairly common. For example, the people of Jiräs district on Moen were displaced during the war to Tuunnuuk district. When the writer left Truk, an order had just been given permitting them to return to their own territory. To commemorate the event, they said they were planning to rename their district Gasanö (Sigh of Relief).

2. Jacaw 2. Its three main descent lines were descended from Nusumwacej, Meejiwen, and Sëwynyk, all of Pwereka 1, although at least half of its *sööpw* lands were in Winisi territory. Both of this lineage's houses were located in Corog.

3. Pwereka 2. Although it had quarreled with Pwereka 1, its differences with Pwereka 3 were of longer standing. It had established ramage relations with Pwereka 1 after the latter's separation as a lineage and its oldest *sööpw* lands were in Corog territory. Its affinal connections were largely with Jacaw 1, Jacaw 2, and Wuwäänyw 4 at the time, and all of these became Corog lineages.

4. Söör 2. Its members were *jëfëkyr* equally of Pwereka 2 and Pwereka 3. Söör 2a and 2c also had strong *jëfëkyr* ties with Jacaw 2. These, plus the fact that its *sööpw* lands were in Corog territory, apparently tipped the scale. Two of its houses were located in Winisi and one in Corog. This lineage now is located entirely in Winisi territory and is considered a part of Winisi, having shifted its affiliation in the past 30 years.

5. Wuwäänyw 4. Its members were *jëfëkyr* of Jacaw 2 and married into Pwereka 2. Its *sööpw* lands were located mainly in Corog and so was its lineage house.

6. Wuwäänyw 5. Its members were closely identified with Pwereka 1, in which they operated largely as client members.

To WINISI:

1. Jeffeg. Its members were *jëfëkyr* of Pwereka 3, and its house and *sööpw* lands were in Winisi territory.

2. Söör 1. Its members were *jëfëkyr* of Jeffeg, and its house was in Winisi territory. Today its two survivors are clients of Pwereka 2 and classed as members of Corog.

3. Pwëën. Its members had *jëfëkyr* ties with the old Wiitëë 3 lineage and with Wiitëë 1. It was on bad terms with both Pwereka 1 and Pwereka 2, which had seized some of its lands. Its house was located in Corog territory.

4. Wuwaanyw 1. Its *mwääniici*, Jesooriik, was an *jëfëkyr* of Pwereka 3, though the rest of its personnel was equally connected with Winisi and Corog by *jëfëkyr* ties. Both its houses were located in Winisi territory.

5. Wuwäänyw 2. Its members were *jëfëkyr* of Jeffeg, and before that of Wiitëë 3, which had been identified with Pwereka 3. Its house was located in Winisi territory.

6. Wuwäänyw 3. Its main *jëfëkyr* connections at the time were with Wiitëë 2, Söör 1, and Söör 2b (the Söör 2 descent line which was sired by Pwereka 3), hence predominantly with Winisi, though the bulk of its lands were held from Pwereka 2, by an older *jëfëkyr* connection. These lands were located in Winisi territory while its house was located in Corog.

7. Wiitëë 1. Its members were equally the *jëfëkyr* of Jacaw 2 and Pwereka 1 on the one hand and of Pwereka 3 on the other. The latter, however, were the children of Nijap, chief of Winisi, and hence heirs to Winisi's chiefship. This lineage had both its *sööpw* lands and house in Winisi territory.

8. Wiitëë 2. This scattered lineage has two main descent lines today, one the *jëfëkyr* of Pwereka 1 and the other including the children of Terejaas (P3), who succeeded Nijap as chief of Winisi. Because of the latter, the lineage is now classed as belonging to Winisi. Its earlier affiliations were with Corog, though its houses were all in Winisi at the time when Romonum was divided. It may at first have been classed with Corog.

Nijap was already an old man when he became chief of Winisi. He died at about the time when the Japanese took over the administration of Truk in 1914. His grandnephew, Terejaas (P3a), succeeded him as chief, though technically Cënyn (P3a) was next in line. Romonum had been placed under the jurisdiction of an area or "flag" chief by the German and, subsequently, the Japanese administrations. This office was created for administrative purposes, having no native counterpart, and was filled at the time by a district chief on Udot. To what extent he may have been instrumental in elevating Terejaas instead of Cënyn is not clear.

Terejaas and Ceejejög are remembered for their extremely cordial relations. It became customary for the two districts to engage in competitive feasting, first one giving a feast for the other and then turn about. Popular memory has it that the two chiefs discussed everything between themselves and always took action jointly, appearing as of one mind, so that the island's affairs were handled as though its districts were reunited under one chief.

PWEREKA TODAY

After Ceejög died, which was shortly before the war, his successor should have been Taapen (P1). But Taan (U3), a Winisi man living uxorilocally in Corog, was appointed chief in his stead by the Japanese. Pwereka 1, whose membership now included but one woman, moved its house site to Nëëry (820-170), where the sole surviving woman of Wuwäänyw 5 also moved by virtue of her client membership in Pwereka 1. Taapen built a small *wuut* at Nëëry as well, replacing the older chief's *wuut* at Neejöör. During the war, the last woman of Pwereka 1 died, the house at Nëëry was abandoned, and the land was sold to the Pwukos lineage. The sole survivor of Pwereka 1 today is Taapen, who became chief of Corog when Taan resigned in his favor at the end of the war. Pwereka 1 also includes several client members: the Protestant preacher and his family, two immigrants from Uman who have a remote kinship connection with Taapen, the members of Wuwäänyw 5, and a young man, Rooke, of Pwereka 3a, who has been adopted by Taapen as a son. What will happen to the chiefship when Taapen dies is in doubt. After the war, Winisi's present chief, Cyyw (P3a), attempted to consolidate the island into one district under his jurisdiction, an attempt which failed to meet the approval of the administrative chief of Udot, who held that Taapen's claim was, if anything, better than Cyyw's. Informants suggested three possibilities: that the client member Jerinis (U5) will succeed; that Rooke (P3a) will take over as adopted *jëfëkyr;* or that Söön, *mwääniici* of the Pwukos lineage and Romonum's storekeeper, will be appointed as chief.[21]

Winisi's chief, Terejaas, also died shortly before or during the war. There were two candidates from different descent lines within Pwereka 3a to succeed him, Mwäär and Cyyw, men of about the same age. Cyyw's descent line had died out except for two other men, but Mwäär's was numerous and thriving. Although Mwäär is considered *mwääniici* of Pwereka 3 today, because almost its entire population comes

---

[21]The last possibility was based on the fact that Söön's half brother, Ayster Irons, had been administrative chief of Udot, and was currently assistant atoll chief, with all of Fääjicuk (the western half of Truk) under his administrative jurisdiction. There has been considerable reorganization of the entire administrative system since 1948, the system of chiefs being officially abandoned in favor of elected magistrates.

from his descent line, it was Cyyw whom the administrative chief of Udot named as Terejaas' successor, and who is Winisi's chief today. When the writer was on Truk, Cyyw also held the administrative post of councilman, representing all of Romonum to the administrative chief of Udot, who controlled the Pwukos lineage, of which his half-brother was *mwääniici*. After the war a new *wuut* was erected, therefore, at Neminaany (770-160), on Pwukos land, to be the island's meeting house, where in his capacity as councilman Cyyw presided as *de facto* island chief.

During the war, the Japanese took over all the upland parts of Romonum for military installations. Pwereka 3a had, therefore, to give up its house at Näämärew and is now located in a cluster of houses on Mwäär's land at Mwyyn (190–220, eastern half). The old Pwereka 3b descent line died out during the war except for one young woman and a little girl. Its house at Neewuukec was abandoned, the surviving woman and her husband now living with Raany (W2), an *jëfëkyr* of her lineage.

The Pwereka 2 lineage is now considerably reduced in numbers. Around 1937 the Pwereka 2b descent line moved its house from Neejör to its present location at Jepinifëny (100–250). The adult women of Pwereka 2a were shortly thereafter reduced to one, who abandoned the house at Fäännäjaas and with her daughters joined her lineage mates at Jepinifëny. The daughters, now married, occupy a hamlet with their mother's brother and his wife at nearby Neemasan (120–300). There are no indications that Pwereka 2 can expect to regain the chieftainship, either of Romonum as a whole or of Corog district, to which it still belongs though located physically in Winisi. When the writer left the field, indeed, it appeared that in a few years—barring administrative changes from outside—the history of Romonum's chiefship would come full circle, with the two districts reunited under the Pwereka 3 lineage. With the approaching extinction of both Pwereka 1 and Pwereka 2, the descendants of Jöku have finally prevailed, as it were, over those of his rivals, Nusumwacej and Jaamew.

APPENDIX A: COMPLEX INSTANCES OF LAND TENURE

ILLUSTRATIONS of most aspects of the Trukese property system as well as of the complex situations which can develop on particular plots of land are provided by an analysis of the *jejif* of Neettimaras (230–240) and the combined *jejif* of Fäässic (320–220) and Mekyr (340–220).

Several generations ago, full title to the soil of Neettimaras (Fig. 5) was held by the Wiitëë 1 lineage. Within Wiitëë 1 provisional title was held by Wotyr. With the consent of his lineage, he made a *niffag* of the entire holding to his children in Söör 2c, a son, Määsijan, and a daughter, Notup, who formed a minor corporation within their lineage. As such they held provisional title to the soil, while Wiitëë 1 held residual title. Notup's children, a daughter, Neejipwi, and a son, Mwëcygeni, automatically became members of the minor corporation holding provisional title. The plot had actually been allotted to Määsijan, but since it needed planting it was subsequently allotted to Neejipwi, whose husband put it in breadfruit trees. Neejipwi's son, Wyseg, automatically a member of the corporation holding provisional title to the soil, was allotted the plot in his turn, getting provisional title to the soil and full title to the trees which his father had planted. Residual title to the soil, of course, remained with Wiitëë 1. Wyseg was the last surviving member of his minor corporation. With the permission of Wiitëë 1 he could have passed the land on to his daughter in Wuwäänyw 3, or on his death and the extinction of the line holding provisional title, full title to the soil would have reverted to Wiitëë 1. Not wishing to do the former, and in order to forestall the latter, Wyseg brought in his younger lineage mate, Woto (S2c), on the holding with him. This, in effect, made it the corporate property of the entire Söör 2c descent line, for Woto was Wyseg's successor as its *mwääniici*, and its remaining members were either Woto's own siblings or their offspring. Woto planted trees on a part of the holding. His daughter, Rufiina (P3a), inherited them and received the soil on which they stood (Section II on Fig. 5) as a *niffag*. The remainder of Neettimaras (Sections I and III) were taken over by Jatoonif, who succeeded Woto as *mwääniici* of Söör 2c. He assigned a small part of it (Section III) to Jemeter, the only living child of his sisters, where her father was allowed to plant trees for her. The situation at the present time is as follows.

Section I. Provisional title to the soil is held by Söör 2c, residual title by Wiitëë 1. Provisional title was allotted to Jatoonif within Söör 2c. He planted and holds full title to 35 coconut, 1 pandanus, and 20 banana trees. The Catholic church and mission house (6) are maintained by Peeta, Jatoonif's younger brother.

Section II. Provisional title to the soil is held by Rufiina (P3a) and her siblings, residual title by Wiitëë 1. Provisional title was allotted to Rufiina. She and her siblings as a corporation hold full title to 16 coconut and 8 breadfruit trees which they inherited from their father, Woto, who planted them. She has planted 27 banana trees, which she holds under full title. Five houses (1–5) owned by Rufiina and other members of her lineage, who live there, were built with Rufiina's permission.

Section III. Provisional title to soil held by Söör 2c, residual title by Wiitëë 1. Provisional title allotted to Jemeter. She holds provisional title to two breadfruit, one coconut, and one pandanus tree, planted by her father, Mwäär (P3a), who holds residual title to them. With Jemeter's permission, Mwäär maintains a taro patch for their common household.

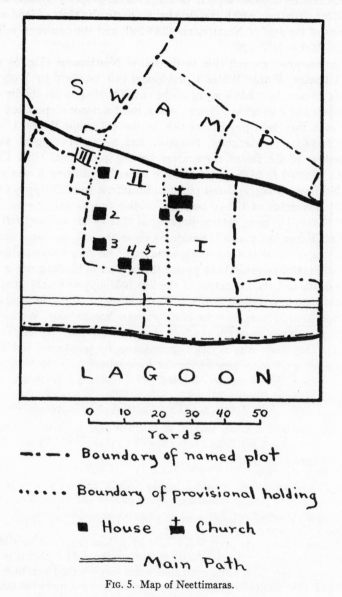

Fig. 5. Map of Neettimaras.

Full title to the soil of the adjacent plots of Fäässic and Mëkyr (Fig. 6) was formerly held by Wiitëë 1. This lineage allotted the rights of provisional title to four of its male members: Niffyg (Sections V and VI), Koomi (Section III), and the brothers Kaamët (Section IV) and Gininö (Section II). Niffyg obtained permission to give part of his share (Section VI) to his children in the Pwereka 1 lineage, the rest of his share (Section V) being reallocated to his sister's daughter's son, Pwöönyn, who received permission to give it to his children in the Söör 2 lineage. Koomi did not alienate his share, which was reallotted to his sister's son, Cemenijor, who gave it to his daughters in the Pwereka

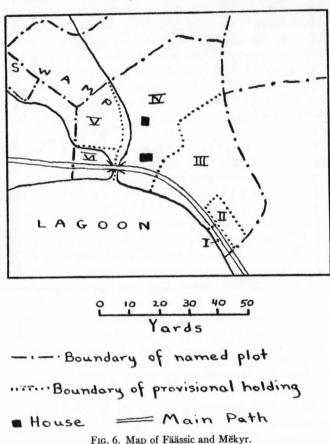

O   10   20   30   40   50

Yards

—·—·Boundary of named plot

·····Boundary of provisional holding

■ House   ══ Main Path

FIG. 6. Map of Fäässic and Mëkyr.

3 lineage. Kaamët and Gininö likewise gave their shares to their children, all of whom were members of Pwereka 3. There is no one in Wiitëë 1 today exercising provisional title to any of the soil of these plots, though the lineage still has full title to a short strip of soil (Section I) between the coastal path and the sea. All the present provisional title holders owe the *mwääniici* of Wiitëë 1 gifts of food. Since the original set of *niffag* alienating the soil, one of the recipients has passed on his holding to his children in the Wiitëë 2 lineage. Through guardianship and loan other individuals have gained rights to soil and/or trees. The present situation is as follows:

Section I. Full title to the soil is held by Wiitëë 1. Pwinipwinin (S2a) has planted two young coconut trees, which he holds under full title, by permission of Wiitëë 1, his father's lineage. He holds the soil on a loan basis.

Section II. Provisional title to the soil is held by the children of Gininö. Their *mwääniici* is Mwäär (P3a), who holds the provisional title himself, not having alloted it. There are four coconut trees planted by Gininö. Full title to them is held by his children, Mwäär having the provisional title allotment.

Section III. Provisional title to the soil is held by the children of Ceminijor and their matri-lineal descendents. Their *finniici* is Jijoona (P3a). They also hold full or provisional title to twenty coconut, fourteen breadfruit, and one orange tree. The provisional title allottment of both trees and soil is held among them by Jijoona jointly with her daughter, Nejisi. Nejisi's husband, Riiken (W2), has recently planted six young coconut trees and eighteen banana trees, to which he holds full title, but he has no rights in the soil except as his wife's husband. The banana trees are for immediate use, while the coconut trees will be given to or inherited by his and Nejisi's children.

Section IV. Provisional title is held by the children in Wiitëë 2 of Terejaas (P3a), who gave them the holding he had received in turn from his father, Kaamët (W1). Manas, the oldest son of Terejaas, is still a boy. Guardian and executor, and therefore co-holder, of the property is Siipen (W2), who is *mwääniici* of the larger descent line to which he and Manas both belong. Provisional title to the soil is now considered the property of this larger descent line by virtue of Siipen's guardianship. This group also holds full or provisional title to 23 coconut, 28 bread-fruit, 1 orange, and 1 mango tree. Provisional title to these and to the soil is allotted jointly to Siipen and Manas. Siipen has full title to 39 banana trees which he planted himself. He has also given his father, Wyres (S2b), permission to keep taro at the swamp edge. While Wyres has full title to the taro he has only the loan of the soil. Siipen has given permission to one of his wife's brothers, Jejipu (U3), to grow a lime tree. Jejipu has, like Wyres, full title to this tree but only the loan of the soil, in which he has no other rights. Houses belonging to Siipen's and Manas' descent line have also been built on the holding. Before giving the soil to his chil-dren, Terejaas permitted his lineage mate, Cyyw (P3a), to plant six ivory-nut palms. Cyyw has full title to these trees but no further rights to soil.

Section V. Provisional title to the soil is held by the children of Pwöönyn (W1), of whom Pwinipwinin (S2a) is *mwääniici*. Their holding consists solely of swamp and is not used at present. Since it remains unallocated, the provisional title is said to belong to Pwinipwinin.

Section VI. Provisional title to the soil is held by the children of Niffyg (W1), of whom the sole survivor is Taapen (P1). Taapen has no trees or crops here, but has permitted his wife's brother, Jaatoonif (S2c), to plant fourteen coconut and six banana trees. Whether he has made a *niffag* of the soil to Jaatoonif as well, with the permission of Wiitëë 1, is not clear from the record.

The complexity of interests that can develop on a plot of land is clearly revealed by these examples. They demonstrate the tendency for holdings to become divided and subdivided through successive *niffag*. They also reveal why anyone trying to purchase full title to a sizable plot of land and trees is confronted with so many interested parties to be paid off, as indicated by Murdock and Goodenough (1947: 339).

APPENDIX B: DISTRIBUTION OF LAND HOLDINGS ON ROMONUM

AN IMPORTANT feature of the Trukese property system is its tendency to keep provisional title holdings in soil and trees fairly equitably distributed through time. The writer encountered no instance of a lineage or extended family hard-pressed for lack of access to food, except where war had temporarily dislocated the local economy, or where an immigrant had been unable to assimilate himself into his new community. There are times, to be sure, when a growing lineage has more members than it can conveniently provide for, but *niffag* from fathers and inheritances make up the deficiencies in a generation's time. As one lineage grows, another declines in numbers, and as the latter gives away more and more of its surplus holdings the former is enabled to add to its own. While old lineages on Romonum which are now numerically small may have extensive residual title holdings, there is no tendency for a few lineages to acquire a corner on land resources. The number of provisional holdings, which are the important ones for purposes of economic exploitation, enjoyed by the membership of a lineage tends to vary directly with the size of its population. While successive *niffag*, therefore, may complicate the land tenure picture, they serve to keep the distribution of land equitable. This can hold, of course, only with a stable population such as Truk's. No tenure system can remain equitable under conditions of sharp population increase.

Tables 14 and 15 have been drawn up to give a rough picture of the present distribution of land on Romonum. Table 14 gives in alphabetical order the name of each *jejif* (named plot), its coordinates on Figure 7, the lineage or descent line holding full or residual title to the soil (or lagoon),[1] and the lineages or descent lines to which belong the present holders of full or provisional title to soil and/or trees. Table 15 shows the present population of each lineage and the total number of plots in which the members of each lineage hold full or provisional title to soil and/or trees, these being the titles which are economically important. To obtain precise data on the square yardage and number and type of trees in each provisional holding on Romonum proved a task of such magnitude that it was abandoned after surveying only a fraction of Romonum's *jejif*. But the simple number of provisional title holdings on every *jejif* was obtained, though unquestionably subject to underestimation through the boredom and oversights of informants. Even on the basis of these crude data, Table 15 shows a high correlation between size of lineage and extent of its members' provisional holdings.

---

[1] Where such title is held by an individual or small minor corporation, his lineage or important descent line alone is listed.

TABLE 14. THE NAMED PLOTS ON ROMONUM AND LINEAGE MEMBERSHIP OF THEIR OWNERS

Name and Map Coordinates	Full or Residual Title Holders	Full or Provisional Title Holders
Cëësinifë (130–500)	U3 fr P1 fr E	U3, W2
Corog (850–150)	P1	U5, W2
Faajë (reef, not on map)	U3 fr P2b fr W3?	U3
Fääggypë (540–200)	A3	A2
Fääjiccyk (850–320)	U3 fr P1	U3
Fääjinömw (500–290)	W1	A2, P1, U3, U5
Fääkanaw (550–520)	P3	P3, U3
Fääkomon (530–430)	P3a fr W3	P3a, S2a, W2
Fään Acapar (140–390)	P2b	U3
Fään Cuuk (880–400)	A3	A3, U3
Fääneecë (400–470)	W1	P1, P2a, W2
Fääneejö (810–400)	A1	P2a
Fääneettow (600–300)	A3	A3
Fäänifac (730–440)	A1	A1
Fäänifac (580–440)	? fr W3	A2, A3, P1
Fäänikep (500–560; 500–590)	P3a	P3a, W2
Fäänimëryp (550–460)	P3a fr W3	U3
Fäänimwacag (200–320)	W1	U3, W1
Fäänimwön (820–350)	W1	A1
Fäänippan (690–500)	P2	A2, P2b, U3
Fäännäjaas (600–460)	P2	A2, A3, U4
Fään Öför (180–450)	P1 fr W3?	W2
Fääsöton (750–300)	U4	A1, A3
Fäätuutu (850–230)	P1	A1, A2, U3, W4
Fäässic (320–220, land)	W1	P3a, S2, W2
Fäässic (250–160, lagoon)	W1	W1
Fenessic (island not on map)	S2a fr W1 fr P3a fr A2	S2a
Fënykytiw (630–310)	S2	S2c
Fënywejipap (700–080)	U4	U4
Fëwysep (680–310)	S2	U3
Fëwywepeep (700–420)	A1	A1, W1
Janapa (810–240)	P1	A1, A3, U3
Jenigemaram (760–400)	U2 fr W3	U2
Jepinifäässic (280–250)	P1 fr E	A1
Jepinifëny (100–250)	P2b fr W3?	A1, A3, P2b, U3
Jijään (800–050)	P1	P1, U5, W2
Jinipw (750–360)	U4	P2a, P3a, U4
Kyny (island, not on map)	P2b fr W3?	U3
Mäjefëw (880–240)	P3b	P3b
Mesejijag (160–440)	P1 fr W3?	W1
Mesekajinömw (650–180)	U4	A3
Mëkyr (340–220)	W1	P3a, W2
Mwej (680–400)	P1	A1, A2, P1, U5
Mwönon (150–340)	U4	U1, U4
Mwyyn (190–220, eastern half)	W1	P3a, U3, W2
Mwyyn (150–220, western half)	P2b fr W3?	U1
Näämärew or Winisi (500–450)	P3a fr W1?	P3a

TABLE 14. THE NAMED PLOTS ON ROMONUM AND LINEAGE MEMBERSHIP OF THEIR OWNERS
(CONTINUED)

Name and Map Coordinates	Full or Residual Title Holders	Full or Provisional Title Holder
Neeceece (540–380)	P2b fr S2c fr W3	P2b
Neeceemej (420–460)	S2a? fr P2a	S2a, P3a
Neefanag (780–200)	P3a	Pu, S2a, W1
Neefäne (630–460)	P2	A3
Neefäreen (870–190)	P1	Pu, W2
Neefëw (390–500)	P1 fr W3	U5, W2
Neefëwyfëw (400–230)	? fr E	U3
Neefëwynap (350–490)	P2a	S2a
Neeggë (250–480)	A2	P2b, P3a, U1
Neejagery (450–440)	W1	A2, U5, W1
Neejä (300–500)	W1	A3, P2a, P3a
Neejäsep (820–470)	A3 fr P2a fr Pw fr W3	A3
Neejimwafë (350–350)	? fr E	P2b, S2a, W2
Neejimwetä (680–440)	P2	A1, A2
Neejimwetä (390–450)	P2a	W2
Neejimwetiw (720–350)	A3 fr U4	A3, S2b
Neejimwowu (500–470)	U4	W1
Neejimwonö (550–370)	A2	A2, P2b
Neejin Acaw (550–320)	A2	S2c
Neejin Acaw (320–450)	W1	A2
Neejin Pënë (620–400)	P1	P1
Neejö (790–410)	A1	A1
Neejöör (600–420)	P1	A2, Mission
Neejöör (540–470)	P3a	S2b
Neejöpwös (430–220)	A2 fr E	A2
Neejör (550–400)	P2b fr S2 fr W3	A3, P2b
Neekkar (800–280)	P2b	A2, P2b, S2b
Neekköötiw (470–280)	A2 fr E	A2
Neekuc (360–440)	W1	A2, P2a, U1
Neekus (570–400)	P3a	Pu
Neemasan (120–300)	U4	P2a, W2, W1
Neemaji (090–350)	P2b fr W3?	U3
Neemään (380–310)	P3a fr W1 fr E	P3a
Neemäsä (750–440)	A3	A3, P2b
Neemes (430–340)	? fr E	P3a, W2
Neemwar (500–420)	P3a fr W3	W1
Neemwar (550–280)	W1	U5
Neemwëc (720–470)	P2	P3b, S2a
Neemwon (650–450)	P2	P2a, U3
Neemwöco (660–410)	P3	A1, P3a, W1
Neeniga (420–240)	? fr E	S2a, W1, W2
Neenisäpiwu (420–530)	P2	U1, W2
Neenyk (470–500)	P3a	S2a
Neepëëk (510–380)	A2	(See Neepiru below)
Neepiiköw (680–570)	P2	A2, A3, U3
Neepiitä (580–470)	S2	S2b

TABLE 14. THE NAMED PLOTS ON ROMONUM AND LINEAGE MEMBERSHIP OF THEIR OWNERS
(CONTINUED)

Name and Map Coordinates	Full or Residual Title Holders	Full or Provisional Title Holders
Neepijenap (750–180)	Pu fr P2	Pu
Neepiru (500–360)	A2	A2, P3a, U5, W1
Neeppiijenefen (270–240)	U2? fr E	S2, U2
Neepwinijepwin (180–270)	P2b fr S2 fr W3?	S2b, U1, U3, W2
Neepwöötög (540–340)	A2	U1
Neepwör (940–370)	A3 fr P2	A2, A3, Pu, S2b, U3
Neepwörö (460–200)	? fr E	Pu, Mission
Neepwyg (500–410)	? fr W3	P1, U3
Neeram (460–490)	S2a fr P2a fr ?	S2a
Neeröötiw (900–320)	A2	S2c
Neeripwyyg (520–350)	A2	A2
Neerup (450–300)	Pu? fr P3a fr W1 fr E	Pu
Neesöpworeg (130–370)	P2b fr W3?	U3
Neetёttёn (180–390)	P1 fr W3?	U1, U3
Neetin (800–320)	A3 fr U4	A1, U3, W2
Neettifёw (440–520)	A1 fr P2a	A1, P3a, S2c, U1, U3
Neettijööc (860–340)	W1	W1
Neettimaras (230–240)	W1	P3a, S2c
Neettow (620–350)	S2	A2, P3a, U3
Neetupw (580–350)	S2	P3b, S2b, U3, W2, P2a
Neewa (750–320)	U4	A1, P2b
Neewerejijaw (830–260)	P1	W2
Neewёwyyn (750–480)	A2	A1, S2a
Neewoonö (640–380)	U3 fr P2b	A2, U3, W1, W2
Neewootä (380–200)	P1 fr E	P1
Neewoow (680–360)	P1	A1, A2, P1, S2b
Neeworoor (700–400)	A1	A1
Neewyr (460–370)	A2	Pu, Pw, S2b, W2
Neewuunö (450–250)	A2 fr E	A2
Neewuukec (630–430)	P3	A1, S2a, P3b, U3, W1
Negenimwär (300–460)	W1	P3a
Neminaany (770–160)	Pu? fr P1	Pu
Nёёmёgy (570–190)	S2	P2a, U3
Nёёry (820–170, western half)	A2	Pu
Nёёry (820–170, eastern half)	Pu? fr P1	Pu
Nёёwuwё (360–520)	Pw fr W3	P3a, S2b, W2
Nёwynareg (250–360)	A2	P2b, W1
Nёwynёёmaw (400–290)	P1 fr E	U4
Nёwyyfё (510–200)	S2	P1, Pu
Nömwuccu (430–200, land)	A2 fr E	A2, P3a
Nömwuccu (500–150, lagoon)	A1 fr P1 fr Pw fr E	A1
Nuuken Fёny (480–400)	U2 fr E	P2b, S2c
Nykiiso (800–420, land)	P2	A1, U3, W1
Nykiiso (820–450, lagoon)	P2	P2b
Nykiisöton (200–530, land)	A2	A2, P2b, P3a
Nykiisöton (200–550, lagoon)	A2	A2

TABLE 14. THE NAMED PLOTS ON ROMONUM AND LINEAGE MEMBERSHIP OF THEIR OWNERS
(CONTINUED)

Name and Map Coordinates	Full or Residual Title Holders	Full or Provisional Title Holders
Nykynaajo (750–500)	P2	A2, P2a, U1
Nykynyfanag (670–480)	P2	A2
Nykynyför (400–500)	U5	U5
Penijenyk (400–550, 400–570)	P1, P3a, U2 all fr W3	P1, P3a, S2a, U2, U5, W1, W2
Penipat (600–190)	S2	A2
Piijessic (200–510)	A2	U1
Pisiinaakkic (720–210)	P2	U3
Pissitijon (not on map)	W1	A2
Pwööjeew (320–320)	P1 fr E	A1
Pwynypeges (560–400)	P3b	U3
Säärec (170–480)	? fr E	P3a, U1, U3
Sömööry (reef, not on map)	P2b fr W3?	P2b
Söpwonotow (620–550, land)	P2	A1, S2a, U1, U3
Söpwonotow (620–570, lagoon)	P2	P2
Söpwötä (130–430)	P2b fr W3?	W1
Söpwunifëw (710–150)	Pu? fr P1	Pu
Söpwunuwar (270–210)	W1	A2
Söpwutiw (090–450)	P2b fr P3a fr W3?	U3
Sowujëëwyr (710–120)	Pu? fr P1	Pu
Tunnuköc (310–520)	P1 fr W3?	Pw, U2
Wäänap (660–440)	P2	P3a, U1
Wäännap (260–520)	A2	A2, W2
Wiicuk (850–370)	A3	A3, U3
Wiinen (360–470)	W1	A2, P1, W2
Wiiseejinyk (410–420)	U5	S2c, W2
Wiisefään (850–280)	P2	A1, A3, P2, U4
Wiiton (720–390)	A3 fr U4	A1, A3, P2b, U3
Winifatafat (100–170)	P2b fr W3?	U1
Winifej Römönum (670–150)	U4	Pu, U1, U4
Winifëw (800–380)	P2 fr P3 fr W3?	P2a
Winifëw (200–490)	U1	U1
Winijä (700–330)	U4	U1
Winijaas (250–450)	A2	A2, P3a, Pu
Winimejë (370–270)	A2 fr E	P3a
Winimwër (600–500)	P2	U3
Winipiru (800–360)	U4	A1, W2
Winipisin (320–270)	S1 fr E	A1, S1
Winipisipis (460–220)	A2 fr E	A2
Winipwëët (330–550)	P1 fr W3?	S2a
Winipwëw (300–420)	A2	P1, P2b
Winipwökur (200–450)	A2	W2
Winisi (same as Näämärew above)		
Wocamwoc (090–280, land)	P2b fr W3?	A2, W2
Wocamwoc (050–250, lagoon)	P2b fr W3?	U1
Wocäänej (050–140)	S1 fr E	S1
Woccofëw (330–570, 330–590)	P3a fr W3?	A2
Woconuuk (same as Nykynaajo)		

TABLE 14. THE NAMED PLOTS ON ROMONUM AND AND LINEAGE MEMBERSHIP OF THEIR OWNERS
(CONCLUDED)

Name and Map Coordinates	Full or Residual Title Holders	Full or Provisional Title Holders
Wonejaas (reef, not on map)	A2	W2
Wonosop (270–300)	? fr E	S2a
Wönaggat (350–410)	A2	W2
Wynynaw (620–140)	U4	U4
Wukupw (410–390)	U2 fr E	P3a, P2b, U2, W4
Wunuupw (360–390)	U5	U3, U5, W2
Wunuupwan (400–180)	? fr E	W2
Wuraany (island, not on map)	Several parties have recently planted on this hitherto unused and unowned island	
Wuroroor (500–320)	U1	Pu
Wuroroor (220–410)	A2	Pu
Wuunög (710–200)	P1	S2c

TABLE 15. SIZE OF LINEAGE BY NUMBER OF PLOTS IN WHICH ITS MEMBERS HOLD FULL OR PROVISIONAL
TITLE TO SOIL OR TREES

Lineage	Number of Members	Number of Plots
Söör 1*	2	2
Pwëën*	3	2
Wuwäänyw 5	4	12
Jacaw 3	5	21
Pwereka 1	6	12
Wuwäänyw 1	8	15
Wuwäänyw 4	9	7
Pwereka 2	9	28
Wiitëë 1	10	18
Wuwäänyw 2 and Wiitëë 4	15	5
Pwukos	17	16
Jacaw 1	20	27
Jacaw 2	20	35
Söör 2	25	32
Wuwäänyw 3	25	38
Pwereka 3	32	31
Wiitëë 2	34	29

* Clients of other lineages.

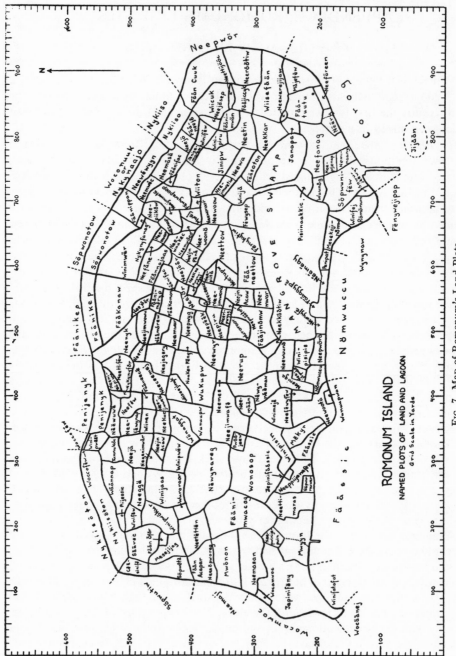

FIG. 7. Map of Romonum's Land Plots.

ROMONUM ISLAND

NAMED PLOTS OF LAND AND LAGOON

Grid Scale in Yards

APPENDIX C: ROMONUM'S LINEAGES[1]

THE JACAW LINEAGES

AT PRESENT there are three lineages of the Jacaw sib (A1, A2, and A3). Jacaw 2 and 3 cooperate closely as a ramage, whereas Jacaw 1 functions more independently. Until recently the first two were united as one lineage (A2), with which Jacaw 1 had earlier been linked in a ramage.

It is not clear when the Jacaw sib was first established on Romonum. According to their own traditions, the Jacaw people came to Truk from an island called Kacaw (equated with Kusaie). Migrating to Truk as a result of wars, they settled in the western part of the atoll on Tol. One of their early settlements was in Fëëwyp district, whence they established themselves in Wonej and Pata. Both Jacaw 1 and 2 on Romonum were founded by women who came from Jepin (a district of Pata) in virilocal marriages. What groups they married into is no longer remembered, though an informant on Jepin thought it was the Söör 2 lineage in the case of Jacaw 2's ancestress. The distribution of residual title holdings in soil on Romonum is quite compatible with this hypothesis. Jacaw 2 was apparently the first of the two lineages established, another immigrant woman founding Jacaw 1 somewhat later. Since both lineages had the same subsib ties with Pata, they cooperated closely as a ramage, sharing one meeting house, though independent with respect to their corporate holdings. This was the picture when the Pwereka people succeeded in wresting Romonum's chieftaincy from the Jimwö lineage. At that time, or shortly thereafter, Jacaw 1 had its lineage house at Fëwywepeep (700–420), while that of Jacaw 2 was at Nëwynareg (250–360). Their joint *wuut* was on land belonging to the latter lineage at Neepëëk (510–380). Ramage chief was Cööpwa (A2), who was succeeded in this office by Gynyn (A1), Wusööpw (A3), Jakkinö (A2),and Nëwyta (A3). Following the latter's chieftaincy the ramage organization was terminated. It was at this time that the feud between Pwereka 1 and Pwereka 2 was under way, leading to the assassination of Mwaatejinyk (P2). Paasegeni, *mwääniici* of Jacaw 1, was the actual killer and supported his brother-in-law Wunnunö (P1). The men of Jacaw 2, on the other hand, had married into Pwereka 2 which they tended to support. The dissolution of the ramage was formally marked when Jacaw 1, under Paasegeni, built an *wuut* of its own at Neeworoor (700–400).

Some time before this, the future Jacaw 3 lineage had been established as a distinct descent line of Jacaw 2. The lineage had grown numerically beyond the capacity of its house at Nëwynareg. Weejires (U4), a husband of one of its women, built a separate house for his wife and daughters at Wiiton (720–390), a plot to which his lineage held full title. This, the Wuwäänyw 4 lineage, was numerically weak at the time, with more land than its members needed. As its *mwääniici*, therefore, Weejires provided for his own children, not only with the aforementioned plot and house, but with the *niffag* of other plots as well: namely, a part of Fääsöton (750–300), Neejimwetiw (720–350), Neejimwowu (500–

[1]The history of the Pwereka lineages, already discussed above, is not included in this appendix.

173

470), Neetin (800–320), and parts of Neewa (750–320). The new household was joined by Nikon, next oldest woman of Jacaw 2, who became its *finniici*, while her older sister, Nijäämën, remained at Nëwynareg. The time of this move was either shortly before or shortly after the assassination of Nusumwacej (P1) by the men of Wiitëë 3. Both descent lines of Jacaw 2 continued to share the same *wuut* and *fanag*, preserving their over-all corporate unity as a single lineage.

Shortly before 1900, the descent line at Nëwynareg moved its house to Neepiru (500–360) next to the lineage *wuut* at Neepëëk, later moving to Neejimwafë (350–350) on land acquired two generations earlier in *niffag* from an Jeffeg father, Cyynik. Here it remained until shortly before the second World War. The descent line at Wiiton, meanwhile, moved its house to Fäätuutu (850–230) on land which its *mwääniici*, Wup-wene (A3), had got from his father Meejiwen (P1). Around 1930 the two groups formally separated into the present Jacaw 2 and Jacaw 3 lineages, the former under Simiron (A2) with an *wuut* at Neeripwyyg (520–350), and the latter under Weejita (A3) with its *wuut* at Wiicuk (850–370). Lineage lands held under full title were divided according to the new affiliation of members currently holding them under provisional title within the lineage. Lands to which only residual title was held were divided according to the descent line affiliation of the last person to hold them before they were alienated by *niffag*. Lands which were already distinct as the corporate property of one or the other group presented no problem. As a result of this division Jacaw 2 now lists as its *sööpw* lands (those to whose soil it holds full or residual title): the group of *jejif* comprising Nuukan and consisting of Neeggë (250–480), Nëwynareg (250–360), Nykiisöton (200–530, 200–550), Piijessic (200–510), Wäännap (260–520), Winijaas (250–450), Winipwëw (300–420, Winipwökur (200–450), Wönaggat (350–410), and Wuroroor (220–410); the *jefif* of Neejimwonö *(550–370)*, Neejinacaw (550–320), Neepëëk (510–380), Neepiru (500–360), Neepwöötög (540–340), Neeripwyyg (520–350), Neewyr (460–370), and part of Nëëry (820–170). The *sööpw* lands of Jacaw 3 consist of the *jejif* of Fääggypë (540–200), Fään Cuuk (880–440), Fääneettow (600–300), Neemäsä (750–440), Neepwör (940–370), Neeröötiw (900–320), Neewëwyyn (750–480), and Wiicuk (850–370). It also includes in its *sööpw* the holdings obtained by *niffag* from Weejires (U4) as given above, since Wuwäänyw 4 has forgotten its residual title rights to them.

Jacaw 2 and Jacaw 3 now operate closely as a ramage. During the war they temporarily merged their households at Nömwuccu (430–200) when the Japanese took over the bulk of Romonum's land for military purposes. They have since separated again. One of the Jacaw 3 women is now living with subsib mates in Jepin district on Pata, where she went after being divorced by her husband. The other surviving adult woman is living in virilocal residence. The Jacaw 2 lineage has split into two well-defined descent lines, one with a cluster of houses at Fääggypë (540–200) and the other with two houses on the adjacent plots of Nëwyyfë (510–200) and Neepwörö (460–200). The former inherited considerable property not long ago from the extinct Jeffeg lineage. When the writer left the field, the Jacaw 3 woman and her newly married, fourteen-year old daughter were talking of moving their house to Fääggypë and joining the group there, possibly remerging the two lineages.

The Jacaw 1 lineage, because of few suitable lands,[2] continued to reside at Fëwywepeep until after the recent war. In order to satisfy the requirements of living near the shore, it has since moved to its present location, where by makeshift arrangements it has a cluster of houses at the point of intersection of the three *jejif* Fäätuutu (850–230), Janapa (810–240), and Neefanag (780–200).

JEFFEG

At present there is but one old woman left from the Jeffeg sib, and she has lived for years on Moen Island among her husband's kin. For all practical purposes, therefore, this sib, never represented by more than one lineage, is extinct. According to their traditions, the Jeffeg people were originally members of the Sowupwonowöt sib and came to Romonum from Puluwat. They came to be called locally by the collective name for their lineage lands, Jeffeg, the older sib name being almost completely forgotten. The Jeffeg lineage was already flourishing at the time when Pwereka took the chiefship away from Jimwö. Before dying out, it reckoned as its *sööpw* lands one of the largest aggregations of *jejif* held by any of Romonum's lineages.[3]

The first Pwereka chief of Romonum, Jöku (P3), was married to an Jeffeg woman. When he was killed by Jaamew (P2), his children in Jeffeg were drawn into the feuds which resulted. As we have seen already, they were forced to flee the island together with the members of Pwereka 3a. On their return they built their lineage house at Neemes (430–340) and *wuut* at Nömwuccu (430–200), where they were located when Krämer (1932) visited Romonum in 1908. By 1930 the extinction of Jeffeg was imminent. Jineettiw, its oldest surviving woman (all its men were dead) adopted some of the members of that descent line in Jacaw 2 which is now located at Fääggypë (see above under the Jacaw lineages). To them she made a *niffag* of a number of Jeffeg holdings, which since her death they now hold under full title.[4] It was reported that Jineettiw took this action because the Sowupwonowöt sib from which Jeffeg came considered itself a local manifestation on Puluwat of the Jacaw sib. Simiron (A2) asserted that because of this supposed relationship the Jeffeg people would not marry into Jacaw, but the genealogies show one such marriage as having taken place about 100 years ago.

[2] Its *sööpw* lands are limited to the three *jejif* comprising Wunuugëwyg, and consisting of Fäänifac (730–440), Fëwywepeep (700–420), and Neeworoor (700–400), and the two additional *jejif* of Fääneejö (810–400) and Neejö (790–410).

[3] Jeffeg proper consisted of the *jejif* of Jepinifäässic (280–250), Neefëwyfëw (400–230), Neejimwafë (350–350), Neejöpwös (430–220), Neekköötiw (470–280), Neemään (380–310), Neemes (430–340), Neeniga (420–240), Neeppiijenefen (270–240), Neepwörö (460–200), Neerup (450–300), Neewoota (380–200), Neewuunö (450–250), Nëwynëëmaw (400–290), Nömwuccu (430–200, 500–150), Nuuken Fëny (480–400), Pwööjeew (320–320), Winimejë (370–270), Winipisin (320–270), Winipisipis (460–220), Wonosop (270–300), Wukupw (410–390), and Wunuupwan (400–180). Residual title to soil was also held in the two *jejif* of Cëësinifë (130–500) and Säärec (170–480).

[4] These are the *jejif* of Neejöpwös (430–220), Neekköötiw (470–280), Neewuunö (450–250), Winimejë (370–270), and parts of Nömwuccu (430–200) and Winipisipis (460–220).

PWËËN

At about the time when Pwereka took the chiefship of Romonum from the Jimwö lineage, a man, Pwöriitipw, and his sister, Nösaryn, of the Pwëën sib came to Romonum from Pulap Atoll. They were taken in as clients of the Jacaw 2 lineage, which allotted them some land. Given in *niffag* to Nösaryn were the island of Fenessic and the plot called Neewyr (460–370), while Pwöriitipw received Neeggë (250–480) from Cööpwa, who was then *mwääniici* of the Jacaw 2 lineage.

Nösaryn married an Jeffeg man, Nööfejin, with whom she lived in virilocal residence. From Nööfejin her children received a *niffag* of additional lands: the lagoon part of Nömwuccu (500–150), Wunuupwan (400–180), and parts of Säärec (170–480) and Winipisipis (460–220). These they added to the holdings their mother had obtained, but Pwöriitipw passed on Neeggë to his own children in Wuwäänyw 1. Nösaryn's daughter, Ninnä, married Wupweewyn of Wiitëë 3 by whom she had six children, two of them girls. From Wupweewyn they received more lands, to which they acquired full title after the annihilation of Wiitëë 3. These were the *jejif* of Neejäsep (820–470), Neepwyg (500–410), and Nëëwuwë (360–520). The husbands of Ninnä and her daughters built a separate house for them at Neepwyg and an *wuut* was constructed at Neewyr, the young Pwëën lineage now being strong enough to stand on its own feet, its members no longer operating as clients of other lineages.

As *jëfëkyr* of Wiitëë 3, the members of the Pwëën lineage supported Pwereka 3a (also *jëfëkyr* of Wiitëë 3) and Jeffeg in their feud with Pwereka 2, and followed Pwereka 3a into the district of Winisi when Romonum was subsequently divided. The brothers, Jetir and Wynööreg, managed to protect their lineage interests against Pwereka 2 after the latter's victory, but on their death the Pwëën lineage fell on evil days. Its sole survivors were Jinäärejög, a young woman who had to move in virilocal residence with her Wiitëë 1 husband, her son, Setin, and her infant daughter, Nejimär. With no one strong enough to protect their interests, one of their lineage's *jëfëkyr* in Pwereka 2, Jerenög, who had been given some Pwëën lands in *niffag* by his father, seized the island of Fenessic.[5] At the same time, Wunnunö (P1), as the island chief, seized the lagoon of Nömwuccu.[6]

Pwëën has not functioned as an independent lineage since. When Nejimär married, she lived in virilocal residence until her husband's death. She and her thirteen-year old daughter now reside with Sitoon (W1), their nearest classificatory father, actually a sister's daughter's daughter's son of Nejimär's father. He is exercising the responsibility of a "father" to care for his dependent "children." Pwëën's only man, Setin, has meanwhile continued with his deceased wife's lineage, Jacaw 2, where he looks after the interests of his young son and step-daughters, who are without adult men in their descent line.

[5]At the beginning of the Japanese administration, taking advantage of new powers given to district chiefs, Nijap (P3a), as chief of Winisi, seized Fenessic in turn from Jerenög.

[6]This section of lagoon has since been inherited by Wunuunö's children in Jacaw 1 and is held in the name of Kekin, their *mwääniici*.

PWUKOS

When the Germans came to Truk in 1902–03, they were accompanied by a Chinese trader whom the natives called Siko. He had formerly lived at Jaluit in the Marshall Islands, where he had left the American ship on which he served as cook in order to marry a Marshallese woman. On her death, he moved to Truk under the auspices of the German trading company at Jaluit. He stopped at Moen Island long enough to marry two sisters of the Pwukos sib from Tuunnuuk district in a polygynous union. He then proceeded to Romonum, landing at Corog (850–150). Since Romonum's chief, Wunnunö (P1), had recently died, this section of lagoon had been placed under the *röög* taboo by Sëwynyk (P1), his successor. By landing here, Siko violated the taboo, and Sëwynyk only refrained from killing him when he realized that the violation was through ignorance. Siko obtained permission to establish a trading post on Pwereka 1 land at Neminaany (770–160). In time he acquired additional lands in the immediate vicinity in payment of debts to his store. He built a large, two-story house for his wives and children, imported livestock, had natives working in his employ on his trading sloop, churning butter in his dairy, etc. With sand fill and by building retaining walls, he extended the shore-line out about 30 or 40 feet into the Corog lagoon, and planted this reclaimed land in coconut trees.

Siko had had a son by his Marshallese wife. When the boy was six or seven years old, he was brought to Romonum, where he grew up as *mwääniici* of Siko's Trukese children. On nearby Udot Island, meantime, an English trader named Irons was similarly acquiring property and had several daughters by a Trukese wife. The oldest daughter was married to Siko's Marshallese son, who took over the management of his father-in-law's estate along with his last name, being known to Americans as Ayster Irons. The immediate management of the affairs of Siko's other children, who now form the Pwukos lineage on Romonum, devolved upon Söön (John), oldest of Siko's Trukese children[7] and locally *mwääniici* of their lineage.

Söön has added to Siko's holdings through additional purchases[8] and runs the local retail store on Romonum for the sale of trade goods. Under the Japanese, Ayster became administrative chief of the Udot area, to which Romonum belongs. This has helped to keep the Pwukos lineage politically independent of Romonum's two districts, the local chiefs being faced with Söön's more direct access to higher administrative authority. Under the American administration, Ayster was raised to the position of assistant atoll chief of Truk. He owned a Japanese diesel fishing boat, which Söön operated for him with a crew of Romonum men.

---

[7] Söön's half brother, Riikar, appears to be a month or two older, but he spends little time on Romonum and is less aggressive than Söön.

[8] Lands presently held by Pwukos and spoken of as its *sööpw* lands are the cluster of *jejif* comprising Neminaany (770-160), Neepijenap (750-180), Nëëry (820-170), Söpwunifëw (710-150), Sowujëëwyr (710-120), and parts of Neefanag (780-200) and Neefäreen (870-190). Also held are Neerup (450-300), Wuroroor (500-320), Wuroroor (220-410), and parts of Neepwör (940-370), Neepwörö (460-200), Nëwyyfë (510-200), Winijaas (250-450), and the coconut trees on Winifej Römönum (670-150).

One of Siko's daughters married a prominent native on Polle, where a new lineage of the Pwukos subsib in the form of her several sons has been established. Siko's other children have married locally on Romonum. They operate as a typical Trukese lineage, though with a somewhat higher standard of living derived from their business interests. Already one of them, Puruuta, has made over his house and the surrounding land to his young children in the Jacaw 2 lineage.

As has been pointed out earlier, partly because of its economic and higher political connections, and partly because of its lack of kinship ties, other than through marriage, with Romonum natives, the Pwukos lineage has occupied an anomalous position politically on Romonum, being considered, properly speaking, a part of neither the Winisi nor Corog districts. In another generation or two, however, its integration with the rest of Romonum's population should be complete as its present land holdings become dispersed to its *jëfëkyr* and its members, in turn, become *jëfëkyr* of local lineages. Already the Pwukos people are almost completely acculturated, deviating from traditional patterns no more than do other native lineages which have come to positions of more than usual power through their connections with the German, Japanese, or American administrations.

SÖÖR 1

This lineage is now represented by only two men. It has never been associated with Söör 2 in a ramage, belonging to a different subsib, nor has it had a long history on Romonum. The Söör 1 lineage got started at about the time of Jöku's chieftaincy, or perhaps a little earlier, when Cööpwa (A2) married a woman of the Söör sib from the district of Mwäänitiw on Udot. When he became lineage and later ramage chief (see above under the Jacaw lineages), he brought his wife to Romonum in virilocal residence, where she functioned as a client member of Jacaw 2. They had three children, to whom Cööpwa gave a part of the land plot called Nëwynareg (250-360), where the Jacaw 2 house was then located. Their one daughter, Nefi, married Mwënefëw of Pwereka 1, with whom she apparently lived in virilocal residence at Mwej, since she and her brothers were not sufficiently numerous to have a lineage house of their own. The brothers Fenetej and Jatëëw attended the *wuut* of Jacaw 2, their father's lineage, Jatëëw subsequently attending the *wuut* of Pwereka 1, his children's lineage. Nefi had two daughters, one of whom married Seger of Jeffeg, from whom her children acquired the land plot Winipisin (320-270). Here Seger built a house in which Nefi and her two daughters were installed. The latter's sons subsequently built a *wuut* at Fääjiccyk (850-320) on land belonging to the wife of Kunun, Söör 1's *mwääniici*, and the lineage house was moved from Winipisin to Nëwynareg. Never rich in land on Romonum, the members of this lineage had to rely on holdings in Mwäänitiw. Many of them returned to live permanently with subsib mates there and married Mwäänitiw people. When all the women but Suuken died, she went to live in virilocal residence with her husband of Pwereka 2, in which lineage her two sons, the only survivors, now operate as client members.

SÖÖR 2

One of Romonum's oldest lineages, Söör 2 was already established before the defeat of the Jimwö lineage, having sired Jacaw 2 from Pata well before this (see under the Jacaw lineages above). At the time when Jöku gained the chieftaincy on Romonum, Söör 2 had one lineage house, located at Neepiitä (580–470), and a *wuut* at nearby Fënykytiw (630–310).[9] Shortly thereafter it had grown sufficiently so that the husbands of three of its women (Nikiim, her daughter Notup, and her niece Nëwuwer) built a new house for them a stone's throw away at Neettow (620–350), establishing what was to become the Söör 2c descent line.

Remaining in the older house were two sisters, Nijeejice, who was married to Cëëppywn (P3a), and Nijeejinen, who was married to Mwaatejinyk (P2a). In the feud between Pwereka 2 and Pwereka 3a following the murder of Jöku, Cëëppwyn and Mwaatejinyk were on opposing sides, and the former was eventually forced to flee Romonum, going to live for a time on Moen. When Mwaatejinyk became island chief he gave his children the plots of Neemwëc (720–470), Neeceemej (420–460), Neejimwetä (390–450), and Neeram (460–490), and built a house for his wife and daughters at Neeceemej, thereby establishing the Söör 2a descent line. Full or residual title to the soil of these plots is now considered the property of this descent line. When Cëëppwyn returned from exile, he gave his children the land plot Neejöör (540–470), where he, too, built a house for his wife and daughters, who founded the present Söör 2b descent line. All three descent lines continued to operate as a single lineage with one *wuut*—the old one at Fënykytiw was moved to Neetupw (580–350)—and one *fanag*, forming an over-all corporation holding full or residual title to the old *sööpw* lands collectively called Pwowunög.

Each descent line continued to reside in its separate house until recently, when Söör 2a and Söör 2b had too few adult women to maintain separate households. Nataanija (S2a) went in virilocal residence with her husband of the Wiitëë 1 lineage. After his death she moved with her daughters to Neeppiijenefen (270-240), to a portion of which plot she holds provisional title, and where the Söör 2c descent line had already moved from Neettow shortly before the war. Nëwynys, the only surviving woman of Söör 2b, went in virilocal residence with her Jacaw 3 husband. Her oldest daughter married Jemwor of Wiitëë 1, whose descent line was also without women, and who was himself living with his father's lineage (P3). She moved in, therefore, with the women of Pwereka 3. When she died, Jemwor married her sister via the sororate, and she, with the now wid-

---

[9] Its *sööpw* lands included the cluster of *jejif* comprising Pwowunög and consisting of Fënykytiw (630–310), Fëwysep (680–310), Neepiitä (580–470), Neettow (620–350), Neetupw (580–350), Nëëmëgy (570–190), Nëwyyfë (510–200), and Penipat (600–190). The *jejif* of Neepwinijepwin (180–270) was also said to be a part of Söör 2's *sööpw* lands, but it is located in the midst of what appears to have been originally Wiitëë 3 land, and is traced back in the genealogies to Kokkan (S2c), whose father belonged to Wiitëë 3. It, like the other lands Kokkan is known to have received from Wiitëë 3 (Neeceece, Neejör, and Fäänifac), was passed to Kokkan's children in Pwereka 2b, who in turn passed it to one of their sons, Weejita, in Jacaw 3. It is significant that a younger informant gave Weejita as the present residual title holder of the soil of this plot.

owed Nëwynys, lives today with the Pwereka 3 women in what is best characterized as virilocal residence.[10]

WIITËË 1

There are at present two lineages of the Wiitëë sib on Romonum, Wiitëë 1 and Wiitëë 2.[11] They do not form a ramage, having different origins and belonging to different subsibs.

Wiitëë 1 is perhaps Romonum's oldest surviving lineage, being at one time united with Wiitëë 3 in a single lineage. The latter became independent, however, either prior to or more probably in connection with its inheritance of some of the former Jimwö lineage lands, as we have seen in connection with the history of Romonum's chiefship. Not long thereafter Wiitëë 1, outgrowing its house at Wiinen (360–470), established a second one at Neejimwowu (500–470). It was built by Nëwyta (A3), husband of one of the Wiitëë 1 women, on land he had received from his father in Wuwäänyw 4 (which holds residual title to the soil), and which he in turn gave to his children along with the house. Both of Wiitëë 1's descent lines continued as a single lineage, with their over-all *sööpw* lands collectively called Jinyykywu[12] and attending one large *wuut* at Neejagery (450–440) while maintaining another for canoes at Fäässic (320–220). Wiitëë 1 at this time also maintained close subsib ties with a Wiitëë lineage on the island of Param (Perem), as the genealogies show.

Not long after 1900 the two descent lines consolidated into one large house at Neekuc (360–440). Here the women of one descent line (that of Jijowanes) died out, and the women of the other (Sitoon's) dwindled until there were but two left shortly before the second World War. The house at Neekuc was then abandoned, the two surviving women now maintaining a joint household at Neemasan (120–300). The survival of this lineage now rests with the two small daughters of these women.

[10]Normally these women would be living with the women of Wiitëë 1, Jemwor's lineage, but since his descent line is without women and includes only one other man, Jemwor has been raised by his father's lineage as one of its dependents. Söör 2b is also without coastal land at present on which it could establish itself independently, so its women are living in the only arrangement possible for them under existing residence rules. See Appendix D.

[11]Wiitëë 3, already discussed, has long been extinct, while Wiitëë 4 is not an independent lineage, but functions as a part of Wuwäänyw 2.

[12]The *jejif* comprising Jinyykywu proper are Fääneecë (400–470), Neejä (300–500), Neejin Acaw (320–450), Neekuc (360–440), Negenimwär (300–460), and Wiinen (360–470). Wiitëë 1's *sööpw* lands also include Fääjinömw (500–290), Fäänimwacag (200–320), Fäänimwön (820–350), Fäässic (320–220, 250–160), Mëkyr (340–220), the eastern half of Mwyyn (190–220), Näämärew (500–450), Neejagery (450–440), Neemwar (550–280), Neettijööc (860–340), Neettimaras (230–240), and Söpwunuwar (270–210). An elderly informant stated that he was under the impression that Wiitëë—whether Wiitëë 1 or Wiitëë 3 was uncertain—had at one time controlled the additional *jejif* of Neeceemej (420–460), Neefëwynap (350–490), Neejimwetä (390–450), Neenisäpiwu (420–530), Neeram (460–490), and Neettifëw (440–520), residual title to all of which is now the property of Söör 2a or Pwereka 2.

WIITTËË 2

The Jacaw 2 lineage on Romonum at one time gave rise to an Jacaw lineage in Moen Island's district of Jiräs. Close subsib ties are maintained between them, with much visiting back and forth. Thus it happened that two men of Jacaw 2, Mënyka and Nikicciw, married women of a Wiitëë lineage in Jiräs and brought them home with them to Romonum. Shortly afterwards, Kyymec of Wuwäänyw 4 married another woman of the same lineage. From these three women are descended the members of the present Wiitëë 2 lineage, the most populous of all Romonum's lineages today.

To his children Mënyka made a *niffag* of the plots of Neepwöötög (540–340) and Piijessic (200–510), both of them too small to be of much value. Nikicciw gave his children the more substantial plot of Winipwökur (200–450), while Kyymec appears not to have provided for his children at all. By consolidating their holdings, the children of all three men were able to get along and became established as a poor but incipient lineage on Romonum, although the children of Kyymec found it necessary to spend much of their time with their relatives on Moen. One of Menyka's daughters married Sööpi of Jacaw 1, who gave his children the plots of Neettifëw (440–520) and Neenisäpiwu (420–530), which had previously been given to Jacaw 1 by the wife of Sööpi's sister's son. Here Sööpi built a house for his wife and daughters. Mënyka's remaining two daughters married Nitej and Jecag of Pwereka 1. Jecag gave his children the plots of Fään Öför (180–450) and Neetëttën (180–390), which he had apparently taken over from the defeated Wiitëë 3 lineage. He built a house for his wife and the daughter and granddaughter of Nikicciw at Fään Öför. Nitej gave his children the plot of Wiiseejinyk (410–420), of which he was guardian for his Wuwäänyw 5 kinsmen, where he built a house in which the rest of Wiitëë 2's women took up residence. The three branches of Wiitëë 2 which were thus established have never come together in common residence. Moreover, in recent times the descendants of Kyymec, whose women had been shifting around in virilocal residence or living on Moen for protracted visits, have acquired the plots of Mëkyr (340–220) and Fäässic (320–220), where they now reside in two adjacent houses. The Neettifëw group has moved to Neefäreen (870–190), acquired from a father, Mwures, of Pwereka 1, where it now resides. Of the three surviving women of the Fään Öför and Wiiseejinyk groups, two are so old and feeble as to be wholly dependent on others for care and are attached to households in which the son of one and sister's son of the other now reside, while the remaining woman operates a household at Neemasan (120–300), helped by an unmarried classificatory daughter from the Jacaw 2 lineage. As the Wiitëë 2 lineage has grown in numbers, its members have, with each generation, picked up more land holdings from fathers, so that in proportion to their numbers they now hold provisional title to as much land on Romonum as do most lineages (see above, Table 15).

WUWÄÄNYW 1 AND 4

The oldest of the Wuwäänyw lineages on Romonum are Wuwäänyw 1 and Wuwäänyw 4, which have recently become united in a single lineage. They were distinct lineages joined in a ramage at the time when the Pwereka sib gained the island's chiefship from the Jimwö sib. Which of them is older is difficult to guess, nor is it certain as to how they became separated from the one lineage in which they are said to have once belonged. They may have been a new, comparatively landless group shortly before the annihilation of Jimwö, with the Wuwäänyw 4 group getting a sizable portion of Jimwö lands through inheritance and thus becoming established as a separate lineage. At any rate, memory begins with Wuwäänyw 4 solidly established with extensive *sööpw* lands,[13] a lineage house at Jinipw (750-360), and an *wuut* at Neetin (800-320), while the women of Wuwäänyw 1 were apparently scattered in virilocal residence, the men of the latter group attending the *wuut* of their ramage mates.

One of the Wuwäänyw 1 women was married to the immigrant Pwëën man, Pwöriitipw, who had been given the plot of Neeggë (250-480) by Cööpwa of Jacaw 2. Here Pwöriitipw built a house for his wife and some of the other Wuwäänyw 1 women,[14] giving Neeggë, with Jacaw 2's permission,to his children. Pwöriitipw's sister's son, Jesennan (Pw), had also married a woman of Wuwäänyw 1, for whom he built a house at Wuroroor (500-320).[15] As these two descent lines of Wuwäänyw 1, the children of Pwöriitipw and the children of Jesennan, expanded in numbers, they built an *wuut* of their own at Wäänap (660-440) on land acquired in *niffag* from a father in Pwereka 2. They continued to reside in their separate houses until around 1930 (?), when the group at Neeggë moved to Mwönon (150-340), to which it obtained rights in the merger of Wuwäänyw 1 with Wuwäänyw 4, and a new *wuut* was built at Neeggë.

At about the time when Winisi and Corog were established as separate districts, Wuwäänyw 1 affiliated with the former and Wuwäänyw 4 with the latter. While the circumstances are not too clear, the termination of the ramage organization between these two lineages appears to have been associated with this event. Around 1930, however, the Wuwäänyw 4 lineage was reduced to one adult man, Keseer, one adult woman with an infant son, and one young girl. Keseer arranged for the merging of his lineage with Wuwäänyw 1 at this time, in order to insure that the property interests of the woman and children would be properly cared for. Accordingly he brought in Kinöwus, *mwääniici* of Wuwäänyw 1, as a sibling with himself in the land plot of Mwönon, uniting the property interests of the two lineages in this way, and arranged that Kinöwus should be guardian of the other Wuwäänyw 4 properties, thus further integrating the two groups as a single corporation.

[13]The *sööpw* lands of Wuwäänyw 4 are collectively referred to as Jinipw, after the *jejif* name of its old house site, and were composed of the cluster of *jejif* called Fääsöton (750-300), Fënywejipap(700-080), Jinipw (750-360), Mesekajinömw (650-180), Neejimwetiw (720-350), Neetin (800-320), Neewa (750-320), Wiiton (720-390), Winifej Römönum (670-150), Winijä (700-330), Winipiru (800-360), and Wynynaw (620-140). Wuwäänyw 4 is also said to hold full or residual title to the soil of Mwönon (150-340), Neejimwowu (500-470), and Neemasan (120-300)

[14]These women were Pwöriitipw's daughters, Weran and Säräkö, and also Neejifi and her daughter, Nëwynan.

[15]This plot is said to have been held under full title by the Wuwäänyw 1 lineage, its other plot being Winifëw (200-490), but it is quite possible that Jesennan got it as a *niffag* from his Jeffeg father and made a *niffag* of it in turn to his Wuwäänyw 1 children.

At present the surviving members of both descent lines of the old Wuwäänyw 1 lineage are located in a group of houses at Mwyyn (150–220), land which Kinöwus received in *niffag* from his father in Pwereka 2b. There are now two adult women of the old Wuwäänyw 4 lineage. One of them, Necep, is married to the lay head of the Catholic congregation and lives with him in the mission house next to the Catholic church next door to his sisters of Söör 2c in what amounts to a virilocal residence, for she works with these women who are her immediate neighbors. The other woman, Toni, is married to Sitoon of Wittëë 1. He has built a house at Söpwötä (130–430), which land he holds under provisional title, and which he has already made over to his young children in *niffag*. Also living there as Sitoon's dependent "daughters" are the two surviving Pwëën women, who together with Toni manage to operate a household.[16]

WUWÄÄNYW 2 AND 5

These two lineages are unrelated to Wuwäänyw 1 and Wuwäänyw 4, as far as can be told, and definitely belong to a different subsib from that of Wuwäänyw 3. Originally one, they were founded at about the time when the Pwereka sib gained Romonum's chiefship, a Wuwäänyw woman coming from another island in virilocal residence, though who her husband was is no longer remembered. From him, however, her three children acquired the *jejif* of Nykynyför (400-500), Wiiseejinyk (410-420), and Wunuupw (360-390), full or residual title to which is now considered the property of Wuwäänyw 5. One of these children, a daughter, had in her turn a daughter and a son, Jitimä (U5). The latter married Nepitag of Pwereka 1 and fathered the hot-headed pair, Nitej and Jätäna (P1), who gave Jöku so much trouble. Since Jitimä's lineage was not sufficiently strong to justify an *wuut* of its own, he attended that of his sons' lineage (P1) and closely supported Pwereka 1 in its various feuds against Wiitëë 3 and later against Pwereka 3a and Jeffeg. This separated him and his sister sharply from the children of their mother's sister, who founded Wuwäänyw 2. The father of the latter was an Jeffeg man with whom their mother had lived in virilocal residence, and from whom they received a *niffag* of the plots of Wukupw (410-390), Nuuken Fëny (489-400), and Neeppiijenefen (270-240), which, since the extinction of Jeffeg, are now held under full or residual title by Wuwäänyw 2. Their diverse affiliation in Romonum's feuds, for Wuwäänyw 2 supported Jeffeg against Pwereka 1, separated these two lines as independent lineages, Jitimä's line retaining the older lands, and the other line establishing itself on the basis of the plots acquired from Jeffeg, losing all rights in the others.

As the Wuwäänyw 2 group increased in numbers, it established a lineage house at

---

[16] It is recognized by Romonum's natives that Sitoon has heavier than average responsibilities with his two dependent Pwëën relatives and wife and three small children in a household which boasts no other husbands. His younger brother lived with him until he got married, which helped considerably. But now Sitoon is excused from labor quotas, which the island occasionally has to fill, and from such modern public offices as island secretary, for which he is considered the best qualified man. His 12-year old son already is given work responsibilities which are not assumed ordinarily until 16 or 17 years of age. This case illustrates the practical necessity for Truk's extended family organization, which despite some modification from its old form, has persisted in the face of strong Japanese pressures (according to informants) to break it down.

Wukupw and a *wuut* at Nuuken Fëny. It has recently moved its house site to Neeppii-jenefen (270–240), where its women occupy a cluster of adjacent huts. Around 1900, one of its men, Meneki, married a woman of the Wiitëë sib on Moen Island. When he became *mwääniici* of Wuwäänyw 2, he brought his wife, wife's brother, and two daughters to Romonum, in virilocal residence. His wife and brother-in-law acted as client members of Wiitëë 1, by virtue of common sib membership, but his daughters were treated as client members of Wuwäänyw 2, and continued to live with the women of their father's lineage after marriage. Their daughters are doing the same, so that this Wiitëë group (W4) is now an integral part of the Wuwäänyw 2 lineage. This has been facilitated by two factors: Wuwäänyw 2 never controlled enough land to give it away to its Wiitëë offspring, but in order to provide for them has had to keep them on as clients; and the women of Wuwäänyw 2 are now reduced to one, who is past the child-bearing age, so that both groups have had to hold together in order to maintain themselves as a distinct social unit. Wiitëë 4 is already showing signs of losing its identity, its members being classed with the Wuwäänyw sib. In another generation's time Wuwäänyw 2 will be extinct, at which time Wiitëë 4 will emerge as a distinct Wiitëë lineage in possession of the Wuwäänyw 2 lands or will carry the old lineage on under the old name, its Wiitëë origins being forgotten.

Wuwäänyw 5 never had enough members to become independent of Pwereka 1. For a short time it had a small house for its women at Nykynyför (400–500), but when they were reduced to one survivor, the latter moved back into the Pwereka 1 house. Continued close association with Pwereka 1 was in part, at least, determined by the paucity of men in Wuwäänyw 5, there being no male members for three consecutive generations. By the time Jitimä died, it was represented by only two women, neither of whom ever married, but both of whom bore illegitimate daughters. Responsibility for the latter, perforce, continued with the sons of Jitimä in Pwereka 1, who acted as guardians of Wuwäänyw 5 property and thus took these women into the Pwereka 1 corporation, since they were without fathers to care for them. Prolonged association with Pwereka 1 has thus led to Wuwäänyw 5's complete integration within it. Now that Taapen is Pwereka 1's sole survivor, Jerinis of Wuwäänyw 5 is looked upon by many as his proper successor to the chiefship of Corog district. Jerinis' identification with the Pwereka sib is so close that he married a fellow sib mate in Wuwäänyw 3 without its arousing much criticism. All of the women of Pwereka 1 are now dead, and there is only one woman, past child-bearing age, left in Wuwäänyw 5. She is now living in the Wuwäänyw 3 household at Fään Acapar (140–390), where her brother, Jerinis, is a husband.[17]

WUWÄÄNYW 3

Unrelated to the other Wuwäänyw lineages, Wuwäänyw 3 was started when a Wuwäänyw woman from Polle came to Romonum in a virilocal marriage to Wysejë of Söör 2. This event, like the founding of some of Romonum's other lineages, took place around the time when Jimwö lost the chiefship to Pwereka. Six children resulted from

[17]This is not in violation of the taboo against a brother and sister sleeping in the same house, for the household consists of a cluster of houses, Jerinis sleeping in one and his sister in another.

this marriage, two daughters and four sons. Wysejë was not, apparently, in a position to give them any land, so that they would have been forced to remain as clients either of Söör 2 or of the lineages into which they married, or they would have had to return to their mother's lineage in Polle. The oldest of the two daughters, however, married Jaamew of Pwereka 2, who later became island chief of Romonum. It will be recalled that when he succeeded in annihilating the Wiitëë 3 lineage, Jaamew took over much of what had been its *sööpw* lands. To his young children he gave a large number of these and other plots[18] which came under the guardianship of his wife's brothers. With this property and its already populous membership, Wuwäänyw 3 was able to establish itself solidly as an important lineage on Romonum, its importance enhanced by the position of its younger members as heirs to Romonum's chiefship *(jëfëkyren sömwoon)*.

Wuwäänyw 3's first lineage house was at Neewoonö (640–380), where Jaamew built it near that of his own lineage at Neewuukec. An *wuut* was built somewhat later at Neesöpworeg (130–370). As its numbers increased, and the danger of attack from other islands was removed by the new German administration, the lineage moved its house around 1905 to Fään Acapar (140–390), next to its *wuut*, where it was located when Krämer visited Romonum in 1908. Wuwäänyw 3 has since split into two distinct descent lines, one of them still located in a cluster of houses at Fään Acapar.[19] The other is now located in a group of houses, three of which are at Neepwinijepwin (180–270), given to Wyryw (U3) by her father Weejita (A3). The remaining house is hard by at Jepinifëny (100–250) by permission of Pëwytaw (P2b), whose father by adoption, Simiron (A2), is married to a Wuwäänyw 3 woman.

[15]The plots received in *niffag* from Jaamew included the reef of Faajë, Fään Acapar (140–390), the island of Kyny, Neemaji (090–350), Neesöpworeg (130–370), and Söpwötä (130–430), which had been seized from Wiitëë 3; also Söpwutiw (090–450), which Jaamew later seized from Pwereka 3a; and finally the *jejif* of Neekkar (800–280), Neewoonö (640–380), Pisiinaakkic (720–210), Winimwër (600–500), Wocamwoc (090–280), and parts of Fäänippan (690–500), Neepiiköw (680–570), Neemwon (650–450), and Söpwonotow (620–550). The collective name for Fään Acapar, Neemaji, Neesöpworeg, and Söpwötä is Neemwön, which is sometimes used as a *sööpw* name for the Wuwäänyw 3 lineage or that descent line of it now resident at Fään Acapar. It is also used to designate what might be called Jaamew's personal *sööpw*.

[19]The present members of this descent line are Nejoomi, Nesewe, Janannaw, Namiko, Jijowici, and Jisaje.

APPENDIX D: HOUSEHOLD BY HOUSEHOLD ANALYSIS OF RESIDENCE ON ROMONUM

THE QUESTION of residence on Romonum has been critically reexamined in an article that has been frequently cited for the issues raised (Goodenough, 1965a). The case by case analysis of residence summarized in that article is herewith presented.

For this analysis the types of residence descriptive of the possibilities in Truk may be summarized as:

1. Residence with the extended family associated with the lineage or descent line of which the wife is a member or dependent *(uxorilocal residence,* termed "matrilocal" in the first edition).

2. Residence with the extended family associated with the lineage or descent line of which the husband is a member or dependent *(virilocal residence,* termed "patrilocal" in the first edition).

3. Residence by arrangement with a specific kinsman in an extended family in which one is otherwise without residential right.

4. Residence independent of any extended family—apparently only a hypothetical possibility until after the imposition of colonial rule, now involving church officials and a few persons seeking to break with traditional ways.

The first two of these types are the ones that have been important in the past. Provided the enabling conditions are met, the uxorilocal choice has been preferred. But if the wife's lineage is unable to maintain a household because of small numbers or unsuitable land, if the husband is too urgently needed to look after his own lineage sisters, or if the wife's lineage is located too far from the husband's (especially if the husband has valuable land to give to his children), then the virilocal choice is preferred. The exercise of these options is exemplified in the household analyses.

The map of Romonum in Figure 4 shows the location of all of the houses on Romonum as of January 1, 1948. On the map groups of houses are numbered, each numbered group representing a localized lineage or descent line or a nuclear family in independent residence. The analysis of residence presented here deals with each numbered house group in turn. The reader who wishes to check this analysis should consult the genealogies (Charts 3-22) and the lineage histories given in Appendix C. The results of our analysis are tabulated in Table 16.

HOUSE GROUP NO. 1

One house and one married couple at Söpwötä (Fig. 7: 130-430).

Occupants: Sitoon (WI), his wife Toni (U4), their three unmarried sons; the widow Nejimär (Pw) and her unmarried daughter.

Discussion: Sitoon got the land from his father and is giving it to his children. The only other woman in Toni's lineage, Necep (U4), is married to the lay catechist and lives with him in the house reserved for whoever is catechist (House Group

186

No. 11). If Necep's husband should give up his office, she and her family would presumably move here also. It would then be clear that this is the Wuwäänyw 4 lineage household installed on land supplied by a husband. From this point of view Sitoon and Toni are in uxorilocal residence. They cannot be in virilocal residence, because the women of Sitoon's lineage are localized in House Group No. 4. Nejimär is the only surviving Pwëën woman and lived virilocally with her husband until he died. She then came to live with Sitoon, who is genealocally her nearest "father" and hence responsible for her food and shelter. Because there is only one married couple living here, this may also be regarded as a case of independent residence.

Conclusion: One ambiguous case of independent residence or residence with the wife's lineage.

HOUSE GROUP NO. 2

Four houses, five married couples, at Fään Acapar (Fig. 7: 140-390).
Occupants first house: Jerinis (U5) and Wi Nejoomi (U3).
Occupants second house: Siiwo (S2a) and Wi Namiko (U3, Da of Jerinis and Nejoomi), Netiw (U5, Si of Jerinis and FaSi of Namiko), Kojici (U5, So of Netiw) and Wi Pereesen (A1).
Occupants third house: Jijowanes (W1) and Wi Nesewe (U3, Si of Nejoomi).
Discussion: The land belongs to the descent line of Wuwäänyw 3 of which Nejoomi is *finniici* and is under her control. All the women of this descent line live here, and this is clearly their descent line's household. Netiw has no father's lineage (her Fa came from Udot). She is a client member of Pwereka 1, but it has no other women and no lineage house. She is perforce dependent on her Br Jerinis and her BrDa Namiko. Kojici has no father or father's lineage. He and Pereesen are newly married in temporary residence with the husband's parents (in his case Netiw and Jerinis) in what passes as the closest equivalent to the husband's lineage before moving into uxorilocal residence with Pereesen's lineage (A1).
Conclusion: Four cases of residence with the wife's lineage and one case of temporary residence with the husband's lineage.

HOUSE GROUP NO. 3

One house, one married couple, at Neemasan (Fig. 7: 120-300).
Occupants: Rëfajin (A1) and Wi Jijaana (W2), Wymiko (W4, BrDa of Jijaana), Cënyn (P3a, distant FaBr of Jijaana), Tarajimen (A2, Da of Cënyn).
Discussion: The land is owned by Raany (W2, Br of Jijaana). Raany and Jijaana are the only survivors of their descent line, and regard this house as their descent line household. Cënyn is an old man; the only man in his father's lineage is Wejita (A3), equally old and weak, so Cënyn must depend for shelter on remoter relatives. His need is supplied here, for Raany and Jijaana are *jëfëkyr* of his lineage, and Rëfajin is a distant "father," being a ramage mate of Cënyn's father.
Conclusion: one case of residence with wife's lineage.

HOUSE GROUP NO. 4

One house, two married couples, at Neemasan (Fig. 7: 120-300).

Occupants: Komonu (A1), Wi Neejöönen (W1), and two children; Mijagi (U1), Wi Wojite (W2, Si of Neejöönen), and one child.

Discussion: The land is owned by Jijowanes (W1), who is *mwääniici* of the lineage to which Neejöönen and Wojite belong. These two are its only adult women, and this is clearly their lineage household.

Conclusion: Two cases of residence with wife's lineage.

HOUSE GROUP NO. 5

Three houses, three married couples, at Neemasan (Fig. 7: 120-300).

Occupants first house: Maateewus (P2a), Wi Neejisijop (A1), and Jiciwo (A1, orphaned Siso of Neejisijop).

Occupants second house: Jösög (W2) and Wi Sipeer (P2a, lineage SiDa of Maateewus).

Occupants third house: Wurijen (A1, SiSo of Neejisijop), Wi Niina (P2a, Si of Sipeer), and two children.

Discussion: The land is controlled by Maateewus. He, Sipeer, and Niina are the surviving adults of the Pwereka 2a descent line, and this is their descent line household.

Conclusion: Two cases of residence with the wife's lineage, one of residence with the husband's lineage.

HOUSE GROUP NO. 6

One house, one married couple, at Jepinifëny (Fig. 7: 100-250).

Occupants: Seneti (W2) and Wi Naasy (P2b); Pëwytaw (P2b, unmarried Br of Naasy).

Discussion: The land is controlled by Pëwytaw. Naasy is one of two surviving women of Pwereka 2b. The other, Nijoniina, is living virilocally with her husband (House Group No. 19) in order to be near the home of Söön (Pu), her husband's employer, and on land supplied by Söön. When this employment terminates, Nijoniina will presumably move here. This would make it clear that this is the location of the Pwereka 2b household, but this can also be construed as a case of independent residence.

Conclusion: An ambiguous case of independent residence or residence with the wife's lineage.

HOUSE GROUP NO. 7

Three houses, two married couples at Mwyyn (Fig. 7: 150-220, western half).

Occupants first house: Cyyw (P3a) and Wi Marijena (U1), Take (U1, unmarried So of Cyyw and Marijena); Pwinipwinin (S2a) and Wi Meniita (A1, BrDa of Marijena adopted by her).

Occupants second house: Nefici (U1, widowed MoSi of Marijena), Tamijan (U1, psychotic lineage Br of Marijena), Ketten (U1, unmarried SiSo of Marijena).

Occupant third house: Niinmwëgë (P3a, lineage Br of Cyyw).

Discussion: The land is controlled by Kinöwus, *mwääniici* of the U1 lineage, and this is regarded as the U1 lineage household. Meniita and her husband may be construed as living with Meniita's lineage by adoption or her father's lineage. Old Niinmwëgë is single, and his father's lineage (A3) is without men able to shelter him.

Conclusion: Two cases of residence with the wife's lineage (of which one can be interpreted as a case of residence with the wife's father's lineage).

HOUSE GROUP NO. 8

Four houses, three married couples, at Neepwinijepwin (Fig. 7: 180-270) and the adjacent corner of Jepinifëny (Fig. 7: 100-250).

Occupants first house: Jaatoonif (S2c), Wi Wyryw (U3), and unmarried Da.

Occupants second house: Siipen (W2), Wi Simako (U3), two children of Siipen and Simako's dead sister Pwowune (U3).

Occupants third house: Jana (U3, widow and Mo of Simako), Sacko (U3, SiDa of Jana).

Occupants fourth house: Simiron (A2) and Wi Napac (U3, lineage sister of Jana), Japinis (U3, Br of Napac), Jejipu (U3, lineage SiSo of Napac), and Teriwo (U3, Siso of Jana).

Discussion: The first three houses are on land controlled by Wyryw, given to her by her father. The third house is an old meeting house on land belonging to Pëwytaw (P2b), who was raised as a son by Simiron and his former wife. Pëwytaw has given permission to Simiron to live here next door to his wife's other lineage mates, and the unmarried men of his wife's lineage have moved in to share the house with him. One descent line of U3 is localized elsewhere (House Group No. 2); all the remaining U3 women live here, except Soofi (Si of Jana and Mo of Sacko), who is temporarily residing with her husband in a special arrangement (House Group No. 20). Fischer's census two years later shows that Soofi had then moved back here with her husband. This is the lineage household of U3 (except for the descent line in House Group No. 2).

Conclusion: Three cases of residence with the wife's lineage.

HOUSE GROUP NO. 9

Two houses, one married couple, at Mwyyn (Fig. 7: 190-220, eastern half).

Occupants first house: Nuukas (W2) and Wi Neseg (A3).

Occupant second house: Pwuset (W2, widow and Mo of Nuukas).

Discussion: The land is controlled by Nuukas. He and his wife work closely in domestic matters with Nuukas' brother Jemma, who lives next door in House Group No. 10. There are no young women in Nuukas' descent line of the W2 lineage, only the aged Pwuset and Naaton, who lives with Jemma. Nuukas' wife, Neseg, and her adopted daughter (House Group No. 20) are the only women of A3 left on Romonum. Is this to be construed then as the locality of the A3 lineage on land supplied by a husband, the locality of Nuukas' descent line of W2, a case of independent residence, or something else? Another possibility is that Nuukas is affiliated with House Group No. 10, the localized Pwereka 3a descent line. He received this land from the former *mwääniici* of P3a, which was also his own father's lineage. The fact that he and his wife cooperate closely with the other houses in House Group No. 10 is also suggestive. From this point of view Nuukas can be seen as living with his Fa's lineage household but on his own land. Within the next two years this couple joined Neseg's ramage mates in House Group No. 17.

Conclusion: Ambiguous, best treated as a case of independent residence.

HOUSE GROUP NO. 10

Eight houses, nine married couples, at Mwyyn (Fig. 7: 190-220, eastern half) and an adjacent section of Neettimaras (Fig. 7: 230-240).

Occupants first house: Cajimen (U1 formerly, now a client of P3a) and Wi Jinepas (S2c), Peesa (adopted So of Cajimen); Makareeta (P3a, a widow) and her two children.

Occupants of second house: Jemwor (W1), Wi Perna (S2b), Minsijor (S2b, So of Jemwor and Perna), Kaniisto (S2b, So of Jemwor and Perna's dead sister), Nëwynys (S2b, widowed Mo of Perna).

Occupants of third house: Jantonijos (P3a, a widower), Kasijan (S2a, a widower, see House Group No. 13).

Occupants of fourth house: Jakim (U3) and Wi Nuusijaana (P3a), Jisitaro (U2) and Wi Jasinoki (P3a, Da of Jakim and Nuusijaana), Samiina (P3a, Da of Jakim and Nuusijaana).

Occupants of fifth house: Tawywe (W4), Wi Rufiina (P3a), and three children; Mijäri (U3), Wi Sysyme (P3a, lineage SiDa of Rufiina, Da of Kiriis in the sixth house), and child.

Occupants of sixth house: Jemma (W2) and Wi Kiriis (P3a, Mo of Sysyme in fifth house), Nejira (W2, widowed Mo of Jemma), Naaton (W2, widowed MoSi of Jemma).

Occupants seventh house: Riiken (W2), Wi Nejisi (P3a) and child; Jijoona (P3a, widowed Mo of Nejisi).

Occupants eighth house: Mwijegas (W1), Wi Jinätipin (P3a) and four children.

Discussion: The last five houses are on land belonging to Rufiina (P3a, fifth house), and all the wives in them are P3 women. The first three houses are more heterogeneous, but contain a P3a widow, a P3a widower, and are on land controlled by Mwäär, who is *mwääniici* of P3a and the entire P3 lineage. Clearly we are dealing with the Pwereka 3 household group. In the first house, Cajimen is a client member of Mwäär's lineage, and the widow Makareeta is Mwäär's own sister's daughter. An immigrant from the Mortlocks, Cajimen is in what amounts to virilocal residence with his adopted lineage household. In the second house, Perna and Nëwynys are the only women of S2b, which has no household at present; and Nëwynys father's lineage (A3) has no men able to look after their *jëfëkyr* nor a lineage household of its own. Jemwor, similarly, is one of only two surviving men in his descent line and is an jëfëkyr of P3b. There being no men in P3b, the *mwääniici* of the entire P3 lineage, Mwäär, becomes Jemwor's nearest "father". His wife being without a locality, Jemwor has brought her virilocally to live with his father's lineage, of which he is himself a dependent for purposes of shelter.

Conclusion: Seven cases of residence with wife's lineage, one case of residence with husband's lineage, one case of residence with husband's father's lineage.

HOUSE GROUP NO. 11

One house, one married couple, at Neettimaras (Fig. 7: 230-240).
Occupants: Peeta (S2c), Wi Necep (U4), and three sons.
Discussion: This house is on land owned by Jaatoonif, *mwääniici* of S2c, but it is the house intended for the use of church officials. Peeta is the catechist and conducts the church services. He and his wife cooperate for domestic purposes with the S2c household next door (House Group No. 12). They operate as if in virilocal residence with the husband's lineage household, but they live here for occupational reasons.
Conclusion: Best considered as one case of independent residence.

HOUSE GROUP NO. 12

Two houses, three married couples, at Neeppijenefen (Fig. 7: 270-240)
Occupants first house: Mwäär (P3a) and Wi Jeniina (S2c), Riikar (Pu) and Jemeter (S2c, Da of Mwäär and Jeniina), two children of Riikar and Jemeter.
Occupants second house: Taapen (P1) and Wi Rekiinija (S2c), Jijajeko (U4, BrDa of Rekiinija and Da of Peeta and Necep in House Group No. 11).
Discussion: The land belongs to Rekiinija and her siblings in S2c. All S2c women live here except Jinepas, who is living virilocally in House Group No. 10.
Conclusion: Three cases of residence with the wife's lineage.

HOUSE GROUP NO. 13

One house, one married couple, at Neeppijenefen (Fig. 7: 270-240).
Occupants: Jejimwun (S1) and Wi Jines (S2a); Nataanija (S2a, widow and Mo of Jines); Jiciro (S2a, SiSo of Nataanija), Misente (S2a, Br of Jiciro); Kasijan (S2a, widower, Br of Nataanija) takes his meals here but sleeps with another widower in House Group No. 10.
Discussion: The land belongs to Jiciro and is controlled by Pwinipwinin, So of Nataanija, who is guardian. This is clearly the household of the S2a descent line, as is further attested by the fact that Nataanija and Jines were already living here before Jejimwun married Jines and moved in. There seems to be a close relationship between this household and House Group No. 14, immediately next door, where Raany (W2) is a "father" of Nataanija and where Naako (P3b) is Nataanija's MoBrDa and a *jëfëkyr* of S2a.
Conclusion: One case of residence with the wife's lineage.

HOUSE GROUP NO. 14

Four houses, four married couples, at Neeppijenefen (Fig. 7: 270-240).

Occupants first house: Raany (W2), Wi Piin (W4), and three children; Pissija (U3), Wi Naako (P3b), and Jecko (P3b, Da of Naako's dead sister).

Occupants second house: Mënyken (P2a), Wi Jinecen (W4), and two children.

Occupants third house: Jesefär (Al), Wi Masako (W4, Da of Jinecen by former marriage), and child.

Occupants fourth house: Reesi (U2, widow) and Macko (W4, Da of Jinecen and Mënyken in second house).

Discussion: The land is jointly held by Piin and her FaSiSo Sepinon (U2, Br or Reesi in fourth house). The W4 and U2 groups operate as a single lineage, Piin and Jinecen being *jëfëkyr* of U2 and without brothers while U2 has no women of childbearing age to perpetuate it. This is clearly the place where U2 and W4 are localized. The case of Pissija and Naako in the first house is not clear. Naako is the only adult survivor of the P3b descent line. It would be logical for her to live with the S2a household next door in House Group No. 13, since her father was an S2a man; instead she is living with Raany and Piin. Raany is himself a *jëfëkyr* of the P3a descent line and hence Naako is his remote "mother." Pissija's lineage is localized (House Group No. 8), so we would expect that he and Naako would live with his lineage. It is crowded for space, however, on the land available. Raany is head of the same descent line from which Pissija's mother's father came, so that Raany is a fairly close "father" to Pissija. Pissija's real father, Wejita (A3), is very old, and there are no other men in the A3 lineage, so that Pissija must have recourse for functioning fathers to his mother's father's lineage. My judgment is that Naako and Pissija are really associated with Nataanija in House Group No. 13, but are sleeping in Raany's house because there is more room for them there and they have close kinship ties with Raany as a basis for making such an arrangement. If this is so, then we must see Pissija and Naako as really living with the wife's father's lineage.

Conclusion: Three cases of residence with the wife's lineage (of which two may be regarded as residence with the wife's father's lineage), and one case of uncertain diagnosis, best treated as a case of residence by special arrangement.

HOUSE GROUP NO. 15

Two houses, three married couples, at Fäässic and Mëkyr (Fig 7: 320-220 and Appendix A).

Occupants first house: Wyres (S2b) and Wi Pereta (W2); Jisikar (Al), Wi Ceejina (W2, Da of Wyres and Pereta), and child.

Occupants second house: Rosu (P3a) and Wi Kari (W2, Si of Pereta); Kari's three children by a former husband, of whom the eldest is Manas (W2).

Discussion: The land was given to Manas (W2) by his father and came under the guardianship of Siipen, So of Wyres and Pereta and *mwääniici* of this descent line of W2. All the women of this descent line are living here.

Conclusion: Three cases of residence with the wife's lineage.

HOUSE GROUP NO. 16

One house, one married couple, at Neepwörö (Fig. 7: 460-200).
Occupants: Siro (Maasanë), Wi Perek (Wiitëë), and their two children.
Discussion: Siro is the protestant minister, and this is the house reserved for whoever is minister. He and his family come from Tol and function here as client members of P1 lineage, which controls the land. For domestic purposes they cooperate with their neighbors in House Group No. 17.
Conclusion: One case of independent residence.

HOUSE GROUP NO. 17

Four houses, eight married couples at Neepwörö (Fig. 460-200), Nëwyyfë (Fig. 7: 510-200), and Fääggypë (Fig. 7: 540-200).
Occupants first house: Pwuna (Pu), Wi Kasija (A2, SiDa of Jijoopa in House No. 3), Tatajici (A2, Br of Kasija).
Occupants second house: Nikommy (U3) and Wi Jijoopa (A2), Siro (P1) and Wi Fuciko (A2, Da of Nikommy and Jijoopa) Akawo (W1) and Wi Aruko (A2, Da of Nikommy and Jijoopa), two unmarried sons of Nikommy and Jijoopa.
Occupants third house: Taan (U3) and Wi Cajippwej (A2), Symijer (A1) and Wi Namako (A2, Si of Nesäw in fourth house, and lineage SiDa of Cajippwej).
Occupants fourth house: Japen (S2c), Wi Naapi (A2), and two children; Jejiwe (U1) and Wi Nesäw (A2, Si of Naapi), Kawajici (A2, Br of Nesäw), Setin (Pw, widowed Fa of Kawajici).
Discussion: The first two houses operate as one domestic unit and the second two as another, but all four cooperate closely as a larger overall household entity. The first house is on land belonging to Söön, *mwääniici* of Pwuna's lineage, but Pwuna and his wife live here to be with his wife's lineage mates. The second house is on land owned by Taapen (P1), who is adopted father of Siro, a husband in this house. Siro has gotten his father's permission for his wife's family to live here. The last two houses are on land given to Kawajici by his father Setin and controlled by Nesäw as guardian. All the women in this group belong to the A2 lineage and this is definitely regarded as the place where it is localized.
Conclusion: Eight cases of residence with the wife's lineage.

HOUSE GROUP NO. 18

Three houses, eight married couples, at Sowujëëwyr (Fig. 7: 710-120), Söpwunifëw (Fig. 7: 710-150), and Neefanag (Fig. 7: 780-200).
Occupants first house: Puruuta (Pu, So of Neejipwin in second house), Wi Sitaje (A2), and two children; Pijo (Pu, So of Neejipwin) and Wi Rosaanija (W4), Teriwo (U3, FaSiSo of Pijo).
Occupants second house: Neejipwin (Pu, widow), Söön (Pu, So of Neejipwin) and Wi Nemesej (S2a), Santijako (S2a, So of Nemesej's dead sister), Rooke (P3a) and Wi

Keneeta (Pu, SiDa of Neejipwin, Da of Niimw in third house); Sojino (U3, FaSiSo of Pijo in first house) and Wi Nesepic (A2).

Occupants third house: Sepinon (U2) and Wi Niimw (Pu, Si of Neejipwin); Jijoosef (Pu, So of Niimw) and Wi Kinnako (W2); Jeniisa (Pu, Da of Niimw), Jeniisa's two children; Jakiwo (A2) and Wi Fytaako (Pu, Da of Sepinon and Niimw), Tokiko (Pu, Da of Fytaako).

Discussion: All the land is controlled by Söön in the second house, *mwääniici* of the Pu lineage. This is said to be this lineage's *sööpw* or locality. Either the husband or wife of every married couple living here belongs to the Pu lineage. All wives of Pu men living here have households associated with their own lineages. But the Pu lineage was sired by a Chinese trader and has business interests which make it important for its men to live here as well as its women. Sojino and his wife in the second house were employees of Söön and living here in connection with their employment, until they moved away to live with Nesepic's lineage mates on Moen Island.

Conclusion: Three cases of residence with the wife's lineage, four cases of residence with the husband's lineage, and one case of special arrangement.

HOUSE GROUP NO. 19

Four houses, four married couples, at the junction of Neefanag (Fig. 7: 780-200), Fäätuutu (Fig. 7: 850-230), and Janapa (Fig. 810-240).

Occupants first house: Kinöwus (U1), Wi Teni (A1), and child

Occupants second house: Taamisin (A1), Wi Nijoniina (P2b).

Occupants third house: Suuta (U3) and Naanu (A1).

Occupants fourth house: Miciwo (A1), Wi Jajiko (Maasanë), and child; Pwöpwo (Maasanë, Mo of Jajiko), Jijosiwo (Maasanë, Br of Jajiko).

Discussion: The second house is on land controlled by Söön (Pu, House Group No. 18). Taamisin works for Söön and has been given permission by him to build a house here near his lineage mates. The land of the first house is controlled by Pwinipwinin (S2a) who is married to the Da of Kinöwus and Teni (see House Group No. 7). He has given his wife's parents permission to live here. The land for the third house has been owned by Suuta, who has given it to his BrSo Wurijen (A1). As for the fourth house, the land is controlled by Refä (A1), a childless widower and MoBr to Miciwo. Miciwo's wife and wife's family come from Dublon Island and have no lineage here. They are client members of A1 at present. The house group is, with the help of some make-shift arrangements as far as land is concerned, the A1 lineage household. Within the next two years, all except the occupants of the second house moved to Nömwuccu (Fig. 7: 430-200), land controlled by members of the A1 lineage.

Conclusion: Two cases of residence with the wife's lineage and two cases of residence with the husband's lineage.

HOUSE GROUP NO. 20

Two houses, four married couples, at Neefäreen (Fig. 7: 870-190).

Occupants first house: Woopet (A1), Wi Rejikiina (W2), and four children; Neejeta (W2, widowed Mo of Rejikiina, died in 1947); Jepwer (S2b), Wi Jannako (W2, SiDa of Neejeta, Da of Kekin in second house), and two children.

Occupants second house: Kekin (A1) and Wi Soofi (U3); Tosiso (W2, So of Kekin, Br of Jannako in first house) and Wi Jaruko (A3); Teriwo (W2, So of Kekin), Renipu (W2, So of Kekin).

Discussion: The first house stands on land controlled by Rejikiina, who got it from her Fa Mwures (P1). Rejikiina is *finniici* of her descent line of W2 and brought the women of her descent line together here to form a household. These included her mother's sister Wukan (W2), who was married to Kekin. After Wukan died, Kekin continued to reside with his children, and when he recently married Soofi, he was allowed to bring her here so that he might continue with his children. By 1950 this arrangement terminated, however, and Kekin is shown in Fischer's census as living with House Group No. 8, his wife's descent line of U3. The land of the second house is under dispute between Söön (Pu) and Rejikiina. Tosiso's wife comes from a lineage that lacks a lineage household.

Conclusion: Two cases of residence with the wife's lineage, one case of residence with the husband's lineage, and one case by special arrangement.

TABLE 16. TABULATION OF RESIDENCE TYPES

House Group	No. Cases	Wi's lin.	Hu's lin.	WiFa's lin.	HuFa's lin.	Ind.	Spec. Arr.	Ambi- guous
1	1	(1)	-	-	-	(1)	-	1
2	5	4	1	-	-	-	-	-
3	1	1	-	-	-	-	-	-
4	2	2	-	-	-	-	-	-
5	3	2	1	-	-	-	-	-
6	1	(1)	-	-	-	(1)	-	1
7	2	2	-	(1)	-	-	-	-
8	3	3	-	-	-	-	-	-
9	1	-	-	-	-	1	-	-
10	9	7	1	-	1	-	-	-
11	1	-	-	-	-	1	-	-
12	3	3	-	-	-	-	-	-
13	1	1	-	-	-	-	-	-
14	4	3	-	(2)	-	-	1	-
15	3	3	-	-	-	-	-	-
16	1	-	-	-	-	1	-	-
17	8	8	-	-	-	-	-	-
18	8	3	4	-	-	-	1	-
19	4	2	2	-	-	-	-	-
20	4	2	1	-	-	-	1	-
Totals	65	46	10	0	1	3	3	2
Percent	100	71	15	0	1.5	5	5	2.5

Note: These figures are the same as those published elsewhere (Goodenough, 1956a) except that one case (House Group No. 6) there classed as independent is here classed as ambiguous. Residence is there typed as matrilocal (with wife's lineage), avunculocal (with husband's lineage), amitalocal (with wife's father's lineage), patrilocal (with husband's father's lineage), and neolocal (independent).

APPENDIX E: CHANGING SOCIAL ORGANIZATION ON ROMÓNUM, TRUK, 1947-1965*

IDEALLY, ETHNOGRAPHIC accounts of cultural change should be based on a record of continuous observation over an extended period. Anthropologists are rarely in a position to obtain such records, however, and commonly resort to the next best strategy, which is to make ethnographic studies of the same community at two or more different times. A comparison of the separate ethnographic records will presumably indicate how the local culture has changed in the interim. To control for the possibility that recorded differences reflect differences in the ethnographic observers rather than changes in the culture, it is preferable to have later studies done by the ethnographers who did the earlier ones. Repeat studies of this kind are regarded with favor by anthropologists as an appropriate strategy for examining change.[1] In 1964 I had an opportunity to return to the small island of Romónum in Truk, Micronesia, where I had been a member of an ethnographic team seventeen years earlier.[2] I did not have a study of change as my principal concern when I went back, but I tried to check my understanding of Romónum's social organization as I had published it in 1951 by such further inquiry as my other research responsibilities allowed me.

This report recounts such changes in family and kinship as I was able to observe and calls attention to some problems that can arise in the course of doing return studies.

MATERIAL EVIDENCE OF CHANGE

In 1947, Romónum's large interior plateau was covered largely by vegetation that was only two years old. This area had been completely cleared by the Japanese during the war and the population settled entirely along the island's coastal flats (Fig. 4, p. 134). All but one of the dwelling houses were constructed of sawn lumber, largely salvaged from the Japanese barracks, with floors raised off the ground on piles and

*Reprinted by permission from Robert J. Smith, editor, *Social Organization and the Applications of Anthropology: Essays in Honor of Lauriston Sharp,* Ithaca: Cornell University Press, copyright 1974 by Cornell University. The orthography for Trukese used here differs from that in the original monograph, and accords with that adopted at a conference on orthography held in Truk in 1972. The difference is that an accent mark (´) replaces the dieresis on vowels, the symbol *y* replaces *j* as a semivowel, and *ú* replaces *y* as the high central vowel. The personal names here rendered Boutau and Eiue appear as Pëwytaw and Jejiwe in Charts 9 and 19.

[1] Examples are Margaret Mead's return to the Manus in the Admiralty Islands, Raymond Firth's return to Tikopia, and Lauriston Sharp's return to the Yir Yoront in Australia.

[2] In 1947 I spent seven months in Romónum as a member of a research group from Yale University, led by Professor G.P. Murdock, sponsored by the Pacific Science Board of the National Research Council, and financed by the Office of Naval Research. My return in 1964 was made possible by a research grant from the National Science Foundation (NSF-GS-340).

corrugated iron roofs from which rain water was caught in fifty-gallon gasoline drums, and in many cases with sliding glass windows.

In 1964 the interior plateau was fully planted in breadfruit and coconut groves. The sweet-potato and manioc gardens that had dotted the bush here in 1947 were entirely gone. About half of the population had moved its dwellings up onto the plateau (Fig. 8.) where all dwellings had been located in precolonial times. Most houses were now of traditional frame and thatch construction, corrogated iron being used only for siding, especially on sides exposed to the wind. Houses, moreover, were more widely scattered. The main path along the south shore had fallen into disrepair and in two places had been entirely destroyed by the sea. In other ways, the people seemed to be a little more prosperous than in 1947. The food supply was somewhat better, and there was more cash, mainly from the sale of copra. Several people had boats powered by outboard motors. In effect, the things that had resulted from or been made possible by the Japanese presence, such as roadways and houses with raised floors, had disappeared or were in a state of advanced decay; but the resources of the island were now being much more fully exploited, and the overall standard of living showed a corresponding modest improvement.

In 1947, Romónum's resident population was 242 persons, including some who were not members of lineages based on Romónum.[3] Residing elsewhere were eighteen persons who were members of lineages or sublineages based on Romónum. In 1964, Romónum's resident population had grown to 296 persons, and the number of Romónum-based individuals residing elsewhere had increased to forty-seven. The increase of 22 per cent in the resident population is small in comparison with the increase of approximately 60 per cent in Truk's total population during the seventeen-year period (from c. 10,000 to c. 16,000). Although there were many more births (148) than deaths (89) on Romónum,[4] the island lost more residents through emigration (24) than it gained through immigration (19). I cannot say that the rate of population movement to and from Romónum has changed since before World War II, for I lack information for earlier periods. Table 17 gives a detailed picture of populaion changes since 1947.

These physical and demographic changes do not in themselves imply any significant change in Romónum's social organization. To show what seems to be happening here it will be necessary first to give a sketch of the traditional social system.[5]

[3]A lineage (or sublineage) is said to be based on Romónum if its members have permanent rights in land there.

[4]Given an average population of 266 and average number of births per year of 8.7 and deaths per year of 5.5, the average crude birth rate for the period 1947-1964 is 33 per thousand per year, and the average crude death rate is 21 per thousand per year.

[5]The picture of Romónum's social organization outlined in my earlier report (Goodenough 1951) seems to have been reasonably accurate as far as it went. I was able to add considerably in 1964 to my understanding of its workings. The account given here takes advantage of this additional information.

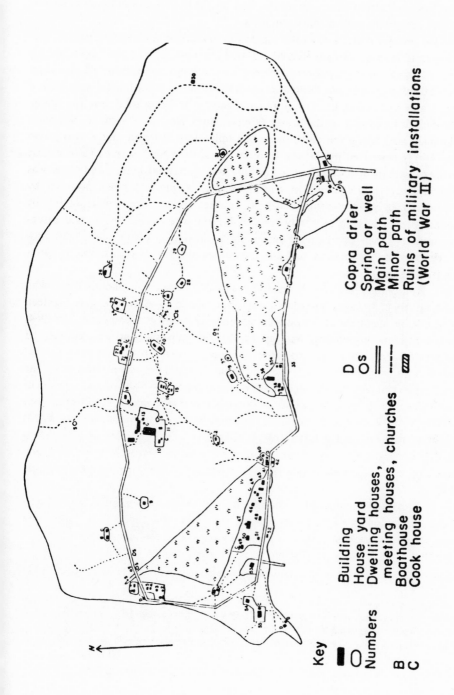

Key

Building
House yard
Dwelling houses,
meeting houses, churches
Boathouse
Cook house

Numbers

B
C

D   Copra drier
Os   Spring or well
═══   Main path
------   Minor path
▨▨▨   Ruins of military installations
           (World War II)

Fig. 8 Romónun Island, Truk, 1964-65

TABLE 17. CHANGES IN ROMÓNUM'S POPULATION BETWEEN DECEMBER 1947 AND DECEMBER 1964

Lineage or sublineage*	1947 On Rom.	1947 Off Rom.	1964 On Rom.	1964 Off Rom.	Died On	Died Off	Born On	Born Off	Born & Died†	Emigrated	Immigrated
Acaw 1	19	0	16	3	6	0	5	0	3	3	1
(Maasané)	4	-	9	-	0	-	6	-	0	1	0
Acaw 2	21	0	36	1	3	0	19	0	1	1	0
(Fesinimw)‡	0	-	5	-	0	-	3	-	0	0	2
(Sóór)§	0	-	4	-	0	-	3	-	0	0	1
Acaw 3	2	2	8	1	1	0	6	0	0	0	1
Pwereka 1	1	0	0	0	1	0	0	0	0	0	0
Wuwáánúúw 5	3	1	2	1	1	0	0	0	0	2	0
(Fesinimw)‡	2	-	0	-	0	-	0	-	0	4	0
(Maasané)	4	-	0	-	1	-	0	-	0	-	0
Pwereka 2a	6	0	9	1	1	0	5	0	0	1	0
Pwereka 2b	3	0	2	0	0	0	0	0	0	0	0
Sóór 1	2	0	0	0	0	0	0	0	0	0	0
Pwereka 3a	32	0	37	0	14	0	19	0	3	0	0
Pwereka 3b	2	0	2	0	0	0	0	0	2	0	0
(Wuwáánúúw)	1	-	0	-	0	-	0	-	0	1	0
Pwéén§§	3	0	2	0	2	0	1	0	0	0	0
Pwukos	16	8	23	23	4	1	13	14	1	2	0
Sóór 2a	9	0	5	1	4	0	1	0	0	1	0
Sóór 2b	5	0	4	0	1	0	0	0	0	0	0
Sóór 2c	10	0	4	2	5	0	1	0	0	2	0

Wiitéé 1	10	0	16	0	1	0	7	0	0	0	0
Wiitéé 2a#	13	1	22	1	4	0	13	0	0	0	0
Wiitéé 2b	6	0	3	0	3	0	0	0	0	0	0
Wiitéé 2c	2	5	2	0	2	2	3	7	0	2	1
Wiitéé 2d	8	–	8	10	0	2	3	–	0	0	–
(Pwéén)	0	–	1	–	–	–	0	–	0	0	1
Wuwáánúúw 1	8	0	3	0	5	0	0	0	0	0	0
Wuwáánúúw 4	10	0	15	3	1	0	9	0	0	3	0
Wuwáánúúw 2	3	1	2	0	2	0	0	0	0	0	1
(Wiitéé 4)	12	–	22	–	1	–	10	–	7	1	2
Wuwáánúúw 3a	14	0	9	0	6	0	1	0	0	0	0
Wuwáánúúw 3b	11	0	13	0	3	0	5	0	0	0	0
(Nuuken Fénú)§	0	–	2	–	0	–	0	–	0	0	2
(Maasané)§	0	–	7	–	0	–	1	–	0	0	6
Affil. unknown	0	–	1	–	0	–	0	–	0	0	1
Totals	242	18	296	47	72	3	131	21	17	24	19

*Lineages and sublineages are grouped according to their association together in a *fanag* (hearth). Each *fanag* is a political unit within a *sóópw* (district), its members working together to prepare first fruits for presentation to the district chief. Lineages are listed here as in my earlier report (Goodenough 1951) by their sib names. A number is added when a sib is represented by more than one lineage, and letters designate important sublineages. Sib names in parentheses represent groups or individuals who belong to lineages that are not based on Romónum. For reckoning purposes, all adopted persons are counted with their lineages or sublineages of birth except when the adopted person came from another island. In the latter event the adopted person is counted with his lineage of adoption and reckoned as a birth on Romónum, if he was born after 1947, rather than as an immigrant.

†On Romónum only.
‡These two groups of Fesinimw outsiders are from the same lineage on Uman Island.
§Members of these sibs make a related group of immigrants from Losap.
§§Associated with Wiitéé 1 in 1947 and with Sóór 2a in 1964.
#This had become a separate lineage, Wiitéé 5, by 1964.

TRADITIONAL SOCIAL SYSTEM

In precolonial times, property in land was held both individually and corporately by lineages and sublineages *(eterekes)*. In the case of individually owned property, full title (Goodenough 1951) passed to a man's or a woman's children and became their corporate property. If a woman had children by different husbands, the children pooled whatever holdings they acquired from their respective fathers into a single estate, which they held collectively. Illegitimate children had equal rights with legitimate ones in this corporate estate.[6] The resulting corporation of siblings became the beginning of a sublineage, the children of the sisters among them being added to its membership. If title passed to an only child, the property remained, in effect, under individual rather than corporate ownership.

Under corporate ownership the rights of individuals derived from their membership in the owning group. The corporation held title and there was no inheritance until the group was without childbearing female members. Heirs to the corporation's property were the children of its male members, its *éfékúr,* who were regarded as the corporation's children. Authority over the corporation's property lay with its senior male member. He was the eldest brother among a group of uterine siblings, and the eldest son of the eldest woman in the senior female line in the case of groups several generations deep. In such groups, however, if he was not the lineage's eldest male, he shared the authority with that individual, the latter serving as the group's executive head and the former as its symbolic head until he reached middle age and thereby became old enough to assume executive as well as symbolic leadership.

Whoever exercised authority over the corporation's landholdings was called the *sowuppwún* (lord of the soil). No one else could harvest anything from it without his permission. At the same time he was responsible for the needs of his junior kinsmen within the corporation. This responsibility is dramatized in a story about the demigod Wonofáát, who selfishly refused to allow his sisters and their children access to food on their corporate property. One of his sisters lured him into incestuous relations with her, declaring that if he did not treat his sisters as kin then they need not treat him as kin either, so shaming him into more responsible behavior. Thus, failure to provide for one's junior *eterekes* mates was portrayed as a violation of kinship responsiblility on a par with incest.

The *sowuppwún* might allocate certain properties to junior members of the owning group for their personal use. He might also make such properties available to a junior male member's own children, who were not members of the corporation. In the latter case, the children continued to enjoy the use of the land after their father's death, holding it collectively as a matrilineal corporation subject to the residual authority of the *sowuppwún* of their father's corporation. They had to use the land and not leave it idle; they had to look after it; and, most important of all, they had to render gifts of

---

[6]The minimal familial unit in Romónum reckoning is the *owunnun,* consisting of an adult woman, all of her children, and her current husband. The closest possible sibling bond is between the children of one mother.

first fruits *(mmwen ppwún)* to the head of their father's corporation, who continued to hold the title of *sowuppwún* for these lands. Any improvements they made on the property were theirs under full title. If they failed to render first fruits and the *sowuppwún* decided to exercise his right to demand return of the property, he was required to render compensation for the labor represented by the improvements.

In theory, such grants or gifts of land to a corporation's children required the consent of all its members; but in practice strong corporation heads often acted on their own and sometimes favored their own children with such grants at the expense of their junior corporation mates. Indeed, when a man died, the legal status of the properties subject to his authority was likely to be disputed by his surviving children and corporation mates. To prevent such disputes, a dying man customarily issued a "death instruction" *(emwirimá)* to his assembled kinsmen so that his intentions and desires regarding the land under his authority would be clear to all.

Grants of land to a corporation's children, as the foregoing indicates, resulted in two corporations having interests in the same land. One, the grantee, had the rights and privileges that went with physical possession. The other, the grantor, had right to the first fruits, to the title of *sowuppwún,* to confiscate if the grantee misused the property, and to the ultimate return of physical possession upon extinction (in the female line) of the recipient corporation. As children and heirs of the granting corporation, the recipient corporation had the right to acquire full title in the event that the granting corporation died out. Either party might prevent such dying out by resort to adoption.[7]

This grantor-grantee relationship between corporations, in which the grantee acquires a provisional title (which may eventually become a full title) and the grantor retains a residual title (which may eventually revert to a full title), is the key to understanding much of Romónum's traditional social organization and, consequently, to understanding how it has been changing in recent years.

Traditionally, Truk's islands were divided into small districts *(sóópw* or *sópwun fénú).* A district was a territory with a matrilineal corporation holding residual title to its space, as distinct from tracts of soil, *ppwún,* within it. The head of this corporation was chief of the district, the *sómwoonun fénú.*[8] In theory a group of siblings had established a full title to the space when the island was first inhabited and held this title thereafter as their corporate property. Rights to portions of the space were then granted to the children of men in this corporation. By developing their grants, they acquired full title to tracts of soil. The resulting junior corporations, sired by the chiefly one, owed first fruits to the chief for their use of the space. They, in turn, sired other corporations to which they gave grants of soil *(ppwún)* and from which their

[7] Adoption on Romónum is described at length by Ruth Goodenough (1970).

[8] This expression is now used for the elected office of mayor of Romonum Municipality under the Trust Territory government, and *sómwoonun sóópw* now refers to the traditional district chief. If the symbolic chief and executive chief were not the same person, they were distinguished as the *sómwoonun mwëgë* (chief of food) and the *sómwoonun kkapas* (chief of talk), respectively. The word *sómwoon* (chief) seems originally to have meant "top father" or "big father," being derivable from a Proto-Micronesian *tama-ulu.* For the shift of *T to s, *l to n, *au to oo, and *a to ó, see Dyen (1949).

respective *sowuppwún* were entitled to first fruits as well. Intermarriages among these corporations and successive grants of soil back and forth resulted in a number of larger and smaller corporate groups, some contained within others. Twc corporations might be independent with respect to some recently acquired properties but be part of a larger one with respect to holdings acquired many generations earlier. A maximal corporation of the latter kind, one that is not part of a larger one, I have called a lineage (Goodenough 1951).

The active-use rights people had in land were as likely to come from holdings whose soil they held under provisional title as from holdings whose soil they held under full title, even when they were members of long-established lineages. What distinguished the older corporations from the younger ones was the extent of holdings to which they had a residual (or full) title—holdings, that is, of which their head could claim to be *sowuppwún*. The chiefly corporation was entitled to first fruits from all holdings within the district. The older corporations were entitled to first fruits from extensive tracts of soil. The most junior corporations were entitled to no first fruits at all, holding only provisional title to tracts of soil. The size of these provisional holdings was important for their economic well-being but irrelevant for reckoning their political rights within the district.

Only corporations with full or residual rights to soil, whose heads could claim to be *sowuppwún* of some land within the district's territory, could claim full membership in the district. They were the corporations that owed first fruits to the chief directly. The others owed first fruits to these and were called upon by them to assist in preparing presentations of first fruits to the district chief. Junior lines in older corporations remained joined in common lineages with the senior lines down which the title of *sowuppwún* descended, even though these junior lines might be corporations in their own right with extensive provisional holdings. A junior line might declare itself independent of the senior line when it acquired full title to soil in its own name, thus becoming a new lineage. A new minor corporation resulting from an interdistrict or interisland marriage associated itself with the corporation of its local founding father, the grantor group taking in the grantee group as its political client. Without full or residual title to soil, the client group could not render first fruits directly to the chief in its own name, thereby presenting itself as a fullfledged constituent of the district.

A lineage with full political rights maintained a *fanag* (hearth, lit. ashes), where it prepared food for presentation of first fruits to the district chief. Dependent corporations and in-married residents from other districts attached themselves to the *fanag* of their father's, spouse's, sibmate's, or other available kinsman's lineage. Lineages with a right to their own *fanag* temporarily joined with other lineages with which their members had kinship ties if their numbers were too depleted to enable them to mobilize an effective work force. The *fanag,* then, were the immediate constituents of a district, each consisting of an established lineage with full or residual title to soil in the district's territory, together with attached individuals and lineages lacking such title.

With its rights to first fruits, its reversionary rights, and its right to district membership, residual title to soil obviously played a key role in the workings of the precolonial social order. It provided incentive for lesser corporations to stay together as larger lineages, even when all use rights to common holdings had been given to other groups under provisional title.

The members of a corporation often acquired holdings in more than one district. It was not uncommon for a group to function as a major corporation, a lineage, in one district while at the same time enjoying membership rights with sibmates in another district in a corporation with more ancient land holdings there. Such extended lineages, or subsibs as I have called them (Goodenough 1951), resulted both from inter-district marriages and military conquest.

When one district defeated another in war, the chiefly lineage of the conquering district might expropriate all of the holdings of the chiefly lineage in the defeated district, the members of the defeated group taking refuge with kinsmen in other districts and islands. Other lineages in the defeated district might be allowed to remain on their lands as before, in return for which favor they now owed first fruits to the chief of the conquering district. Members of the conquering lineage might take up residence in the defeated district and function locally as the new chiefly line, but they remained a junior line within the larger, extended lineage that wielded the chiefship in both districts. The new local chief was expected to render first fruits on behalf of his entire district to the head of the senior line in the conquering district. In this way, the chiefly lineage of Núkúnúféw District on Udot Island once claimed overlordship of neighboring Peniya District and of the whole of Romónum Island, which comprised another district.

Extended family households were the standard domestic form in precolonial Romónum (Goodenough 1951, 1956a). Ideally, all the women of a lineage or sublineage lived together in one house with their husbands and children. The number of adult women per household seems not to have been large, ranging from a minimum of two to as many as five or six. It was important that there be at least one middle-aged woman, for it was felt that two or three young women in their late teens and early twenties, relatively inexperienced in the care of children, ought not to form a separate household by themselves. When there were only one or two younger women left in a household, they went to reside with the women of their father's lineage, or they resided in a separate house near the women of their respective husbands' lineages, with whom they cooperated in a single domestic economy. In the latter case, the separate dwelling was required by a tabu against lineage brother and sister sleeping together in the same house except when the brother was ill and under his sister's nursing care. A house was identified with the lineage or sublineage whose women resided in it. The lineage's men kept their valuables there in the care of their mothers and sisters.

A lineage entitled to maintain its own *fanag* might also maintain an *wuut* (meeting house, or men's house), where its unmarried young men slept and where the lineage head might himself reside with his wife and children in a small apartment at one end. If for any reason a lineage lacked a meeting house, its young men slept in the meeting houses or dwellings of their respective fathers' lineages. A chiefly lineage regularly

206

maintained a meeting house. Fig. 3 (p. 133) shows the distribution of houses and meeting houses on Romónum circa 1900 as remembered in 1947 by a man who was about fifteen years old when Germany established its administration in 1903.

The classification of kinsmen reflected the corporate organization of property relationships. The relationship between grantor and grantee was commonly between a corporation and the children (or descendants) of its men. It was understood to result from a father's obligation to provide for his children. The corporation as provider was therefore in a collective parental relationship to the children of its men. These same children were the corporation's children in another sense: they were heirs to whatever it held under full title, and would actually inherit if the corporation died out in its female line. From this perspective, a person regarded all members of his or her father's lineage as belonging to the parental generation of kinsmen. Complementarily, all children of men of one's own lineage were regarded as belonging to a junior generation, and all children of men of one's father's lineage were equated with one's own generation.

The resulting system of kinship classification (Goodenough 1951, 1956a), as reflected by the use of kinship terms for reference purposes, was one of "Crow" type (Murdock 1949; Lounsbury 1964). The conceptual model of the system, however, remained one of "generation" and "Hawaiian" type (Murdock 1949), for informants gave as a general principle that all relatives in a senior generation were "father" or "mother," all those in a junior generation were "child," and all those in one's own generation were "sibling of the same sex," "sibling of the opposite sex," "spouse," or "sibling-in-law of the same sex." What accounted for the Crow pattern was not a skewing rule based on on equivalence of kin types, as discussed by Lounsbury (1964), but a rule regarding the reckoning of generation membership in the context of lineage membership (Goodenough 1956b).[9]

Social Change since 1947

The beginnings of change away from the traditional social system go back to the imposition of the German administration in 1903, which put an end to warfare. This made it more difficult for chiefs to enforce their hegemony over districts on other islands.[10] It was the German administration, apparently, that settled the long-standing

[9]Lounsbury's skewing rules can, of course, be used, together with merging and other appropriate rules, to account for the distribution of Romónum kinship terms. The Romónum system can, therefore, be placed in Lounsbury's typology of Crow and Omaha systems when there is reason to do so for comparative purposes. Within the framework of Romónum culture, however, the Crow skewing is an artifact of the following rule: In any collateral relationship involving a common ancestress and the presence of one or more male links in either or both lines of descent, all female links between the ancestress and the first descendant male link in each line are ignored for purposes of reckoning generation distance. Thus people recognize generation distance throughout the genealogical structure but operate with a rule as to when generations will and will not be counted for purposes of classifying kin.

[10]This had been difficult before. At about the time when Germany took over Truk, for example, the local chief of Romónum murdered emissaries from Núkúnúféw on Udot—his own extended lineage mates—who came to inquire about his failure to keep up with Romónum's first-fruits obligations to Núkúnúféw.

quarrel among the several Pwereka lineages on Romónum as to which was senior and hence entitled to Romónum's chiefship and the first fruits and other perquisites that went with it. Their division of Romónum into two districts, each with its own chief, was still in effect in 1964. The island continues to be a single community, however, with land holdings and residences scattered all over it to such an extent that the chiefly line of one district has its own major land holdings and its household in what is physically regarded as the other district.

The effect of the division was to award to each of two political factions control of half the traditional spoils. When Romónum was made a single municipality by the American administration after World War II, with elected island officials, a new set of spoils came into existence. The two districts now function in some ways as political parties or organized voting blocks, competing for control of the islandwide municipal offices.

The German administration also made a registry of land holdings. The registry was incomplete, and corporation titles were registered in the names of the corporation heads, the *sowuppwún*. Often thereafter they were treated as if they were individual rather than corporate holdings, the written deed being used as evidence of individual ownership in court. These deeds are still important legal documents in Truk's courts today, serving as crucial evidence in many disputes, although the courts, now well aware of the fraudulent use to which these deeds were sometimes put in the past, seek to investigate each case as best they can. The Japanese encouraged transmission of property from parent to child and apparently sought to weaken the matrilineal lineages, looking with little favor upon matrilineality as a principle of organization.

In 1947, only two years after the Japanese surrender of Truk to the United States, the American government was still an unknown quantity to Romónum's people. Administrative policy held that local custom was to be respected unless it seriously conflicted with American conceptions of justice and fair play or created especially difficult problems for effective administration. Romónum, a small island on the other side of the Truk lagoon from administrative headquarters, was left almost entirely to itself. The policies, prejudices, and ignorance of the administration could not be exploited as a means of bypassing the requirements and obligations of the traditional social and property system, except by a very few people who did not live on Romónum. The Japanese had gone, and the changes they had instituted were presumably no longer in force. The traditional system was functioning with minimal interference.

As soon as courts were re-established, they were deluged with property disputes. The Japanese had treated grants of corporation land to the children of one of its men as if they were an inheritance by a man's children of his individually owned land. The result was that many disputes coming before the American high court were between the members of a corporation and the children of its men. The latter were disputing the residual title of the former and claiming full title for themselves and the former were asserting their confiscatory and reversionary rights under traditional residual title. The court undertook seriously to follow local custom, but some witnesses presented the rulings of the Japanese courts as representing local custom whereas others presented the traditional system as local custom, depending on which representation was to their immediate advantage.[11] The high court, I am told, chose to follow the precedent set by the Japanese and ruled that if it could be established that a corporation grant to the children of one of its men had been made with the consent of the corporation's members, then the children had the same rights as if it had been their father's personal property.

The effect of this ruling was to deprive the granting corporation of its residual title; once the grant was made, the grantee had full title. The grantee need not now render first fruits or obtain the grantor's approval for transactions he wished to arrange. The head of the granting corporation could no longer claim to be *sowuppwún*; this title now belonged to the head of the recipient corporation if he wished to claim it. Some people on Romónum continue to follow traditional practice and continue to render gifts of first fruits to the traditional *sowuppwún* as a matter of courtesy, and there are some who still try to assert their right to first fruits under the traditional system. No one is compelled to follow traditional practice and a number of people no longer do so. It is my impression that scarcely anyone would do so if he felt that he would be seriously inconvenienced by it.

The value of residual title to tracts of "soil" had helped to hold lesser corporations of immediate siblings together in lineages in the traditional social system. Except as other interests countervail, Romónum's traditional lineage organization has been weakened. Indeed, before I learned about rulings of the courts, I had gained an impression that Romónum's lineages were less frequently a unit of reference in community affairs than they had been in 1947. Talk of dissension within the lineages led me to the intuitive judgment that the lineage organization was weaker and looser than it had been. I cannot pretend to have examined all the different possible causes of this, but if my impression was correct, the court's ruling regarding the jural relations of grantor and grantee in land transactions seems likely to have been an important contributing factor.

Old lineages, whose corporate assets consisted largely of holdings under residual title, derived their cohesion in good part from the value of a residual title. The ruling of the court has not only deprived the traditional residual title of much of its former value, but it has also made it possible for junior and dependent corporations to acquire full title to what they had formerly held only under provisional title. They are

[11]Trukese terminology makes it difficult to distinguish between individually owned land that has passed to the owner's children by right of inheritance and corporately owned land that has been given as a grant to the children of one of the corporation's male members. The Trukese refer to either as *fenúwen naaw* (land of the child) or *fenúwen saam* (land of the father)—depending on whether they are looking at it from the father's of child's viewpoint—adding *seni eterekes* (from the matrilineal corporation) when they wish to make it clear that the holding is a grant from a corporation. The Trukese manner of speaking emphasizes not the difference in the nature of the children's title but the fact that in each case control of use rights lies with the children rather than with their father's lineage or with other members of their own lineage.

[12]Thus Boutau, chief of Corog District, comments on the residual title to several plots that the two major sublineages within the Neepiikóów lineages (Pwereka 2) hold in common. "Today it does not really

now freer than they formerly were to establish themselves as independent lineages with their own *fanag* and with full political rights within the district. What was a sublineage within a large one on Romónum in 1947 had taken this step by 1964, establishing itself as a constituent lineage of the district other than the one to which its parent lineage belonged.[13] In this, it was acting in a thoroughly traditional manner. Some of Romónum's older lineages were established in the same way. The point remains that sublineages now have more options and seem to be functioning with somewhat greater autonomy than before. The effect of the court's ruling has not been and will not be to do away with corporate ownership of land. What it has done is diminish the importance of the larger corporations with considerable generation depth, the lineages, and enhance the relative importance and autonomy of sibling sets and sublineages with shallower generation depth.

In 1964 the lineages were still looked upon as the constituent units of Romónum's two districts. The lineages sent representatives to meetings called by the chiefs, for example, but the heads of sublineages within them might all attend and argue with one another in public over matters at issue, something regarded as distinctly bad form by traditional values.

The traditional chiefs still wielded authority in 1964 over the conservation of food resources in their districts, tabooing for a time the harvesting of coconuts for copra in one district, for example, and controlling the times when harvesting and eating fresh breadfruit, preserved breadfruit, and taro might begin. There were, however, no ceremonial presentations of first fruits to either district chief in 1964-65, as there had been in 1947. The chiefs of the two districts consulted with one another to coordinate the timing of the opening of the different harvest seasons, but they were free to act independently and did so when they felt the occasion required it.

There has been little modification in the selection of traditional chiefs on Romónum. The executive, as distinct from the symbolic, office is now filled by election in Corog District. Those elected have been of chiefly rank, however, and Corog's executive chief in 1964 was also its proper symbolic chief according to traditional principles of primogeniture. According to him, the people of Corog have agreed to regard only persons of chiefly rank (men in the chiefly lineage or their sons) as eligible for the executive chiefship. In Winisi District, the succession has followed the same principles. In 1964, the chiefly office was divided between the symbolic chief and a somewhat older cousin in his lineage who functioned as executive chief. For a time the executive chiefship had been held by the son of a former chief, but he later stepped down in favor of maturing members of the chiefly lineage.

---

mean anything, because the *éfékúr* ɪchildren of Neepiikóów menɴ have taken all these plots and under present law control them outright. Under traditional law, the Neepiikóów lineage would still control *ppwún* ɪsoilɴ and Maateewus ɪsenior in age of the two sublineage headsɴ would be *sowuppwún* of these lands."

[13]The main holdings that made this move possible had come to them from lineages in Corog District including its chiefly lineage, whereas the other sublineages of the parent lineage were intimately tied through marriage and grants of property with lineages of Winisi District.

Romónum's municipal government, created in 1952, was responsible for the upkeep of paths, keeping the peace, and providing a school (but not for teachers' salaries). The municipal chief or mayor was elected by those who had registered their names on Romónum's electoral roll, rather than on some other municipal roll. These were people who regarded Romónum as their continuing place of residence. A municipal judge was nominated by the electorate and his appointment confirmed by the District Administrator of the Truk District.[14] In 1964 responsibility for the maintenance of paths had been delegated by the municipal chief to the two traditional district chiefs. What was used as the school building was in fact the traditional meeting house of the chiefly lineage of which the principal and other teacher were both members. The municipal chief confined his activity to making occasional reports to the District Administrator's office and to collecting personally the municipal taxes, the spoils of office. The traditional political organization and the Protestant and Catholic churches were the effective institutions for community action and social control on Romónum.[15]

Household composition seemed to me to have changed considerably in the interval between 1947 and 1964. Already in 1947 the extended families associated with lineages and sublineages were not housed under one roof to the extent that they seemed to have been earlier. A house usually contained a woman and her daughters or several uterine sisters, together with their husbands. If the older women of a lineage or sublineage tended to have separate houses of their own, their several adjacent houses formed clusters. In 1964 the individual houses tended to have the same composition, but they were much more scattered and did not so frequently cluster by lineage and sublineage. I interpreted this as further evidence of the weakening of lineage cohesion on Romónum. Consideration of other evidence, however, has forced me to abandon this interpretation. When I counted up the number of distinct households as recalled in 1947 by Simiron of Romónum for around the time the Germans first came to Truk in 1903 (Fig. 3, p. 133), it turned out that there were very nearly as many as in 1964 (Table 18). It is difficult to imagine that Romónum's population was any larger in 1900 than it was in 1964. Consequently, I conclude that the average number of persons to a household in 1900 was as small as in 1964. The situation in 1947, when the house clusters seemed larger, represented the adjustments Romónum's poeople had made to the Japanese military having taken over much of their island. The people had been crowded into the beach areas. They built near their lineage mates, because it was through them that they could get access to land on which to build. When the interior of the island was rehabilitated after the war, there was then a return to former conditions rather than a change toward new ones. What had changed between 1900

[14]Under American administration, the Trust Territory of the Pacific Islands is divided into six administrative districts. The Truk District is the largest in population (but not in land area), with about 26,000 inhabitants in 1964, and includes Truk, the Mortlock Islands to the southeast, the Hall Islands to the north, and Namonuito, Pulap, Tamatam, Puluwat, and Pulusuk Islands in the west.

[15]Another man has since been elected municipal chief. By 1967 there was a new municipal school building, obtained under a building program of the Trust Territory, and a school lunch program.

TABLE 18. LINEAGES, HOUSE CLUSTERS, AND MEETING HOUSES ON ROMÓNUM, 1900, 1947 AND 1964

Lineage	Distinct houses or house clusters			Meeting houses		
	c. 1900	1947	1964	c. 1900	1947	1964
Acaw 1	1	1	3	1	0	0
{ Acaw 2*	1	1	4	{ 1	0	0
{ Acaw 3	1	0	0		0	0
Effeg	1	-	-	1	-	-
{ Pwereka 1	1	0	-	{ 2	} 0	} 0
{ (Wuwáánúúw 5)	1	0	0			
Pwereka 2	2	2	3	1	0	1
Pwereka 3a	1	1	3	1	1	1
Pwereka 3b	1	0	0	1	0	0
Pwukos	-	1	1	-	0	1
Sóór 1	1	0	0	1	0	0
Sóór 2	3	2	2	1	0	0
Pwéén	1	0	0	1	0	0
Wiitéé 1	2	1	1	2	0	0
{ Wiitéé 2	2	3	3	{ 1	} 1	1
{ Wiitéé 5†	1	1	2			0
Wiitéé 3	-	-	-	-	-	-
Wuwáánúúw 1	2	1	0	1	0	0
{ Wuwáánúúw 2	1	} 1	} 1	1	} 0	} 1
{ (Wiitéé 4)	1			-		
Wuwáánúúw 3	1	2	2	1	0	0
Wuwáánúúw 4	1	1	1	2	0	0
Maasané	-	-	1	-	-	0
	25	18	27	19	2	5

*Brackets indicate shared meeting houses.
†A sublineage of Wiitéé 2 in 1947.

and 1964 was the distribution of population among the lineages. There had earlier been more smaller ones with houses of their own, and in 1964 some lineages had grown considerably in numbers while others had become too reduced to maintain distinct households at all. It is evident from this analysis that it is methodologically unsound to draw conclusions regarding social trends from only two observations in time. Interpretation of the apparent change between 1947 and 1964 was entirely altered when data from 1900 were taken into account.

One change in residential practice was clear, however. In 1947 I knew of no instance in which an adult brother and sister (uterine or classificatory) were domiciled together under the same roof.* Informants agreed that such an arrangement was

*This statement is in error. Review of the census shows two such cases, one where an elderly widower slept in the same large *wuut* as his elderly married sister, and another involving a young unmarried man who worked on Moen but whose local residence was listed as where his sister and sister's husband lived on his land. See house groups 6 and 8 (fourth house) in Appendix D.

taboo. In 1964 there were several cases in which uterine and lineage brothers and sisters were so housed. Informants recognized them as definite departures from older customs and as reflections of a changing attitude toward the traditional code governing relationships among kinsmen.

A truly difficult problem of interpretation, which confronted me at the outset of my return in 1964, was what appeared to be a change in the use of kinship terminology. In 1947 I had systemically worked through the genealogies with an elderly informant, Simiron, obtaining from him the "Crow" pattern of usage that I subsequently published (Goodenough 1951, 1956b). With another informant, Eiue, who was then in his early thirties, I had called the name of every resident of Romónum, asking him to tell me for each name what category of kinsman, if any, the indicated person was for him. On the basis of the genealogies I had already collected I predicted what his response would be for every name. My predictions were realized without exception, and in every instance his usage conformed with the Crow pattern. I used kinship terms and had them used to me constantly by many people without my encountering, or at least registering, a single instance in which cross-cousins were classed as siblings. The behavior I observed between young men and women who were cross-cousins was entirely different from that I observed between those who were parallel cousins and siblings. I should add, moreover, that the contexts in which the Crow pattern of usage was obtained were unstructured and devoid of any reference to property, and the contexts in which I experienced the use of kinship terms in everyday affairs were varied. Moreover, when lineages as corporate bodies were the objects of reference, kinship terms were used with first-person-plural possessive pronouns rather than with first-person-singular pronouns.

I stress this because a few years later, Swartz (1960, 1962) observed instances in which cross-cousins on Romónum were referred to as "siblings" rather than as "parents" or "children." He concluded that the Crow pattern of usage obtains only in contexts in which the inheritance of property or corporate relations are involved, but that "in all other contexts" (1962: 359) cross-cousins are referred to in the Hawaiian pattern as "siblings." This conclusion, derived from two observations (Swartz 1960), simply did not accord with what I had observed. That there were certain situations in which a Hawaiian pattern of usage might occur seemed reasonable, but that it was the prevailing pattern in all contexts except those where property was a consideration was controverted by my own data and experience.

In 1964, within the first week of my return to Romónum, I heard my landlord's wife refer to a classificatory father's sister's son as her "brother" rather than as her "father." Startled, I questioned her usage. An older man present agreed that the man in question might also be classed as her "father," but she, a young woman of twenty-five, expressed herself as having no knowledge of any such possibility. The kinsman in question was her "brother" and nothing else. Satisfied with confirmation of my understanding by the older man, I dismissed the incident as indicative of youthful ignorance by a young woman who had spent some years in mission boarding school. Two weeks later her husband, Boutau, a man in his middle forties, the adopted son of my former elderly informant Simiron, and the symbolic as well as executive chief of Corog District, also casually referred to a cross-cousin as his "brother." I expressed my surprise and he replied that one normally referred to cross-cousins as siblings. As *éfékúr* (heirs) of one's lineage, mother's brother's children might be refered to as one's "*éfékúr*-children," but otherwise they were to be classed as "siblings." He went on to say that this was the way it had always been done on Romónum and that his father, Simiron, must have been deliberately misleading me if he had told me otherwise.

What was I to believe now? In consternation I asked Eiue about it, for it was from him that I had earlier obtained the complete roll call of Romónum that had accorded perfectly with my predictions. He replied that, of course, the Hawaiian pattern was an alternative usage and always had been. "Look at me and Teriwo," he said. "Teriwo is a member of my father's lineage, but I prefer to deal with him as my 'brother.'" Teriwo was in fact Eiue's father's sister's daughter's son and specifically listed by Eiue as his "father" in the 1947 roll call. By the Hawaiian pattern he would have been Eiue's "child" rather than his "brother." But Teriwo was now also Eiue's wife's younger sister's husband and, as such, his "brother" by marriage (*winipwúnú*). The significance of this latter fact did not strike me until after Eiue's death a few months later, and for the moment I could only conclude that somehow I had managed to miss a common alternative pattern of usage in my earlier study.

But I was still troubled, for I could not see how I could have missed it if it had been at all common. I had been confronted with it quickly enough on my return and had had ample opportunity to be similarly confronted with it before. I decided to repeat the roll-call approach I had used earlier with Eiue. This time I did it with Boutau, asking him to tell me his relationship, if any, to every person on Romónum as I called off his or her name. The result was a perfect Hawaiian pattern. Since the matter had already become an issue between Boutau and me, this was not too surprising. Even so, I had hoped that I might catch him out in some inconsistencies, but he was ready for me. Whatever the truth regarding past usages might have been, there was no doubt that Boutau was able to conceive of the entire terminological system according to Hawaiian principles and do so accurately and consistently. I then decided to try the same procedure with Suuta, one of Romónum's oldest living men. What I got from him was even more baffling. The bulk of his answers conformed to the Crow pattern of usage, except that he switched to the Hawaiian pattern for his father's most immediate matrilineal kin. His father's more distant matrilineal kinsmen, in whose property he had *no* interest as an heir, he classed as "fathers" and "mothers" without regard to generation. He could not explain why he classed his father's more immediate sister's children (nearly all of whom were dead) as "siblings" and the more distant ones as "parents." That was just the way they had been and were to one another. At least I was reassured that the Crow pattern was a reality, but it was also apparent that various considerations affecting individuals could produce Hawaiian patterns of usage as well. What these considerations were, however, remained obscure.

In the meantime, I was becoming increasingly aware of a problem in my relations with Boutau, who was working closely with me as one of my principal informants. The problem arose from the fact that the brief history of Romónum Island that I had published (1951) was based almost entirely on information supplied me by Simiron, Boutau's father by adoption. Included in this account were names and alleged facts with which Boutau was unfamiliar. I had been privileged to receive information from his father that he had not received himself. This, it became apparent, was disturbing to Boutau. He had personal reasons for wanting to question the truth of what his father had told me. By bringing his father's name into my original query about his use of kinship terms, I had injected into the situation this more basic issue of our rivalry in relation to his father.

When I became aware of this problem between us, I asked Boutau to review with me my version of Romónum's history with the object of correcting its mistakes and getting the record straight. He decided whom we should consult as the presumed most knowledgeable living person. The upshot of our deliberations was Boutau's finally saying that he could see that none of the versions of Romónum's history that contradicted the one Simiron had given me was acceptable when projected against my genealogical records. These other versions were obviously much more fragmentary. Boutau finally said that he could see now that my version of Romónum's history would have to stand, for whatever the mistakes in it, there was now no one alive who knew enough to be able to correct them. He also told me that he now knew enough from other things we had discussed that Simiron had not lied to me, even in connection with some land holdings where it might have been in his personal interest to have done so.

Shortly after this I began with Boutau to make an inventory of behaviors that were obligatory or taboo in at least some social relationships. I also prepared a list of the social relationships in which some behavior was obligatory or taboo with the object of examining how obligations and taboos were distributed in these relationships. Boutau agreed that it would be proper to look at cross-cousins as being both in a sibling relationship and in a parent-child relationship when we charted the distributions of obligatory acts. When cross-cousins were classed as siblings, he invariably indicated that the obligations between them were those of classificatory siblings (parallel cousins), and when cross-cousins were classed as parents and children, he invariably indicated that the obligations between them were those of classificatory parents and children (that is, parents' siblings and siblings' children). After we had listed these alternatives, I regularly asked Boutau which pattern of obligation was the more binding one. He invariably answered that the pattern for the parent-child relationship took precedence over the sibling pattern. In other words, when behavioral considerations came into the picture, the Crow pattern of kinship took priority over the Hawaiian pattern. Boutau remarked in relation to this one day that Simiron had often reminded him when he was young that it was important to remember that cross-cousins were also like siblings and that it was appropriate to treat them as such. In other words, cross-cousins were basically in another category, but were also like siblings.

My wife, meanwhile, was gathering detailed information about every case of child adoption that she could find. It turned out that adoption had been very common.

There were a great many cases of which I had been quite unaware. There was a tendency, moreover, for younger people to be unaware that older people had been adopted. In one instance a woman did not know that her own older sister had been adopted by the same woman who had adopted her. The reason is that the adopting parent is almost always a close relative of the child. Furthermore, adoption transfers primary parental rights from the original to the adopting parents, but it in no way alters the child's right to membership in his natal lineage or his place in his natal sibling set, nor does it remove all parental rights from the original parents. Only primary parental rights (as against secondary rights such as are held by parents' siblings) are transferred and only for the lifetime of the adopting parents. Older persons who were adopted in childhood are usually functioning as members of their natal lineages just as if they had not been adopted at all. Adopted persons, however, grow up looking upon the members of their adopted mother's lineage as lineage mates and regarding their siblings by adoption as siblings. In many cases the adopting mother is already a member of the child's lineage, for example, the child's mother's sister, but often she is the child's father's sister. In the latter case, the child's paternal cross-cousins become lineage mates by adoption and "siblings" instead of "parents." Thus Boutau's two maternal cross-cousins (mother's brother's sons) had been adopted by Boutau's mother and mother's sister. Since they were the last surviving members of their natal lineage, they continued to operate as members of Boutau's lineage as adults and to regard him as an older sibling. The significance of all of this for the problems of kinship usage that I had encountered did not strike me until I had returned home from Truk. The young woman who had insisted that her paternal cross-cousin was her "brother" and nothing else, it turned out, was quite right, because she had been adopted by her father's sister.[16] Adoption by a father's sister would explain the peculiar pattern of usage I had obtained from Suuta, who referred to his immediate paternal cross-cousins as "siblings" but to the remote ones as "parents." But he was one of Romónum's oldest inhabitants and beyond the age limit for which we had information for adoption in childhood.

There remained, of course Boutau's own stated preference for dealing with his paternal cross-cousins as "siblings" rather than as "parents," except when the roles were in conflict. It also remains that Swartz encountered the use of sibling terms as an alternative usage, although I cannot corroborate his statements regarding the contexts for it.[17] I should add that in 1966, Trukese instructors at a Peace Corps training program with which I was associated in Key West, Florida, used sibling terms as the translation for English *cousin* as well as for *brother* and *sister*. When I called attention

[16]I did not know that she had been adopted, even in 1947, when she was yet a child. She had been assigned to her natal lineage in our census.

[17]Swartz tells me in personal correspondence that according to his recollection one of his two examples involved Isitaro, himself adopted. Isitaro is one of two last surviving members of a lineage that has incorporated in it as client members the descendants of one of its men. They were first reported to me as belonging to Isitaro's sib in 1947, although Isitaro's was Wuwáánúúw and theirs was Wiitéé.

to the Crow pattern of usage, they acted surprised that an American should understand this peculiar Trukese way of classifying kinsmen.

What are we to make of all of this? Is kinship usage changing from a Crow to a Hawaiian pattern? Have there been alternative patterns of usage right along? If so, is the Hawaiian pattern being used in a wider range of contexts than before? And if so, does this reflect a shift toward what Romónum's people regard as an American pattern? Or does it reflect the changing relations people have with the members of their fathers' lineages now that property relations have been changed by action of the courts? I cannot answer these questions.[18] My main concern in 1964 was simply to reassure myself that what I had understood in 1947 was, indeed, true: the Crow pattern was the common pattern at the time on Romónum at least, whatever alternative patterns may also have existed. It was a familiar pattern on other islands in Truk too, but Hawaiian usage could have been common there without my knowing it. On this last point, however, Tolerton and Rauch (n.d.: 39-40) report a Crow pattern of usage of the same terms for Lukunor in the Mortlock (Nomoi) Islands to the southeast of Truk; and in 1947 two different sets of informants from Puluwat, to the west of Truk, gave me the Crow pattern as the standard one there, also.

I must leave the matter there. I cannot say what change in usage of kinship terms has actually taken place on Romónum, but I can report a considerable change in how certain I am about my knowledge of usage. I can also illustrate how personal relationships on return studies can be affected by relationships in earlier studies in ways that make the assessment of change very difficult indeed.

[18]Information on kinship usage is, unfortunately, too ambiguous in the earlier ethnographic sources (Krämer 1932: 266-267, Bollig 1927: 103-104) to clarify matters.

APPENDIX F: GLOSSARY OF NATIVE TERMS

cöö, lineage; subsib.

fääjiro, special greeting reserved for chiefs and *jitag*.

faameni, lineage; subsib.

fanag, hearth, the lineage cooking place.

feefinej, my sister (man speaking).

finniici, oldest sister; head woman of lineage.

futuk, a bilateral kin group; literally "flesh."

jääj mwään, my older brother (man speaking); my older sister (woman speaking).

jejif, subsection; plot of land; lineage.

jejinag, sib; ramage.

jetereges, lineage; subsib.

jëësej, my sibling-in-law of same sex.

jëfëkyr, heirs, the children of the men of a matrilineal kin group.

jëkkëës, behave to someone as to an *jëësej*.

jiimw, dwelling house.

jinej, my mother.

jinejin, behave to someone as to an *jinej* or *fefinej*.

jinejisemej, my father's sister.

jitag, specialist in law, diplomacy, war, and rhetoric.

kiis, gift (recipient under no obligation).

kinissëw, beholden, obliged; obligation.

määräär, remote kinsman; kinsmen collectively.

mwääni, my brother (woman speaking).

mwääniici, oldest brother; head man of lineage.

mwääninyk, younger brothers of *mwääniici*.

mwääninyki, my younger brother (man speaking).

neji, my child.

nëwynëw, behave to someone as to a *neji*.

niffag, gift (recipient under obligation).

pin me wöön, taboo from above.

pisek, movable goods.

pisekin sööpw, lineage owned movables.

pwiij, my sibling of same sex.

pwiipwi, siblings of same sex; behave to someone as to a *pwiij*.

pwiipwii cëk, lineage siblings; own siblings.

pwiipwi winipwyny, husbands of sisters; wives of brothers.

pwiipwi winisam, children of brothers; *jëfëkyr* of same lineage; children of same father by different mothers.

pwynywej, my spouse.

pwyppwyny, behave to someone as to a *pwynwej*.

roog, magic.

röög, taboo or "no trespass" sign on property.

samasam, behave to someone as to a *semej*.

semej, my father.

217

218

setipwitur, youngest sibling.

soojëny, a form of sorcery utilizing the ghost of a man slain in battle.

sömwoon, chief.

sömwoonun fëny, district chief.

sömwoonun ejinag, ramage chief.

söpwun faameni, lineage; lineage territory.

söpwun fëny, district; district as a territory.

sööpwun fëny, district; district as a territory.

tetten, rank, line, file; descent line; lineage; generation; age group.

wuut, meeting house; canoe house.

wutten sömwoon, chief's meeting house.

BIBLIOGRAPHY

ADAM, LEONARD
    1947. *Virilocal and Uxorilocal* (American Anthropologist, n.s., vol. 49, p. 678, Menasha).

ALKIRE, WILLIAM H.
    1977. *An Introduction to the Peoples and Cultures of Micronesia* (Menlo Park).

ARENSBERG, CONRAD M.
    1937. *The Irish Countryman: An Anthropological Study* (New York).

BARTON, R. F.
    1949. *The Kalingas* (Chicago).

BLOCH, BERNARD, AND GEORGE L. TRAGER
    1942. *Outline of Linguistic Analysis* (Special Publication of the Linguistic Society of America, Baltimore).

BLOOMFIELD, LEONARD
    1933. *Language* (New York).

BOLLIG, LAURENTIUS
    1927. *Die Bewohner der Truk-Inseln; Religion, Leben und kurze Grammatik eines Mikronesiervolkes* (Anthropos Ethnologische Bibliothek, vol. 3, no. 1, Münster i. W.).

BRYAN, E. H., JR.
    1946. *Area of Islands in Micronesia* (Map of the Islands of Micronesia, pp. 1-5, United States Commercial Company, Washington).

CAHB
    1944. *East Caroline Islands* (Civil Affairs Handbook, No. 5, compiled by G. P. Murdock, C. S. Ford, and J. W. M. Whiting, Office of the Chief of Naval Operations, Navy Department, Washington).

CAPELL, A.
    1949. *The Concept of Ownership in the Languages of Australia and the Pacific* (Southwestern Journal of Anthropology, vol. 5, pp. 169-189, Albuquerque).

COOK, W. W.
    1933. *Ownership and Possession* (Encyclopaedia of the Social Sciences, vol. 11, pp. 521-525, New York).

DYEN, ISIDORE
    1947. *Interim Report on Language and Education, CIMA, Truk* (Interim Reports, Coordinated Investigation of Micronesian Anthropology, pp. 133-138, Pacific Science Board, National Research Council, Washington).
    1949. *On the History of the Trukese Vowels* (Language, vol. 25, pp. 420-436, Baltimore).

ELBERT, S. H.
    1947. *Trukese-English and English-Trukese Dictionary* (U. S. Naval Military Governmen, Washington).

EVANS-PRITCHARD, E. E.
    1940. *The Nuer* (Oxford).

FINSCH, OTTO
    1893. *Ethnologische Erfahrungen und Belegstucke aus der Südsee* (Wien).

220

FIRTH, RAYMOND
1946. *We, the Tikopia* (New York).
FISCHER, JOHN L.
1957. *The Eastern Carolines* (Behavior Science Monographs, New Haven).
GOODENOUGH, RUTH G.
1970. *Adoption on Romónum, Truk (In* Adoption in Eastern Oceania. Vern Carroll, ed. Honolulu. p. 314-340).
GOODENOUGH, WARD H.
1949. *Premarital Freedom on Truk: Theory and Practice* (American Anthropologist, n.s., vol. 51, pp. 615-20, Menasha).
1951. *Property, Kin and Community on Truk.* (Yale University Publications in Anthropology, No. 47, New Haven).
1956a. *Residence Rules* (Southwestern Journal of Anthropology 12:22-37, Albuquerque).
1956b. *Componential Analysis and the Study of Meaning.* (Language 38: 195-216).
HALL, EDWARD T., JR., AND KARL J. PELZER
1946. *The Economy of the Truk Islands: An Anthropological and Economic Survey* (Mimeographed, Honolulu). [Republished, 1964, by Human Relations Area Files.]
HOEBEL, E. ADAMSON
1949. *Man in the Primitive World* (New York).
HUDSON, ALFRED E.
1938. *Kazak Social Structure* (Yale University Publications in Anthropology, no. 20, New Haven).
KRAMER, AUGUSTIN
1908. *Die Medicin der Truker* (Archiv fur Schiffs- und Tropen-Hygiene, vol. 12, Leipzig).
1932. *Truk* (Ergebnisse der Südsee-Expedition 1908-1910, ed. G. Thilenius, Series II, subseries B, vol. 5, Hamburg).
KROEBER, A. L.
1909. *Classificatory Systems of Relationship* (Journal of the Royal Anthropological Institute, vol. 34, pp. 77-84, London).
KUBARY, J. S.
1889. *Ethnographische Beiträge zur Kenntnis des Karolinen-Archipels* (Leiden).
KUBARY, J. S., AND R. KRAUSE
1889. *Ein Beitrag zur Kenntniss der Ruk-Inseln* (Mittheilungen der Geographischen Gesellschaft in Hamburg, 1887-1888, pp. 53-63, Hamburg).
LEBAR, FRANK M.
MS. *Trukese Material Culture* (Published in 1964, Yale University Publications in Anthropology, No. 68, New Haven).
LEVI-STRAUSS, CLAUDE
1945. *L'Analyse structurale en linguistique et en anthropologie* (Word, vol. 1, no. 2, pp. 1-21, New York).
LESSON, P.
1839. *Voyage autour du monde entrepris par ordre du gouvernment sur la corvette "La Coquille"* (vol. 4, Bruxelles).
LINTON, RALPH
1936. *The Study of Man* (New York).
1945. *The Cultural Background of Personality* (New York).

LOUNSBURY, FLOYD G.

    1964. *The Formal Analysis of Crow- and Omaha-Type Kinship Terminologies* (In Explorations in Cultural Anthropology, Ward H. Goodenough, ed, New York).

LOWIE, ROBERT H.

    1920. *Primitive Society* (New York).

    1928. *A Note on Relationship Terminologies* (American Anthropologist, n.s., vol. 30, pp. 265-6, Menasha).

    1929. *Relationship Terms* (Encyclopaedia Britannica, 19th edition, vol. 14, pp. 84-6, London).

    1948. *Social Organization* (New York).

MARSHALL, MAC, AND JAMES D. NASON

    1975. *Micronesia 1944-1974: A Bibliography of Anthropological Source Materials* (New Haven).

MORRIS, CHARLES

    1946. *Signs, Language, and Behavior* (New York).

MURDOCK, GEORGE P.

    1940. *Double Descent* (American Anthropologist, n.s., vol. 42, pp. 555-61, Mensha).

    1948. *Anthropology in Micronesia* (Transactions of the New York Academy of Sciences, ser. 2, vol. 2, no. 1, pp. 9-16, New York).

    1949. *Social Structure* (New York).

MURDOCK, GEORGE P. AND WARD H. GOODENOUGH

    1947. *Social Organization of Truk* (Southwestern Journal of Anthropology, vol. 2, pp. 331-43, Albuquerque).

NIDA, Eugene

    1946 *Morphology: The Descriptive Analysis of Words* (University of Michigan Publications, Linguistics, vol. 2, Ann Arbor).

OSGOOD, CORNELIUS

    1940. *Ingalik Material Culture* (Yale University Publications in Anthropology, no. 22, New Haven).

PELZER, KARL J.

    1947. *Agriculture in the Truk Islands* (Foreign Agriculture, Vol. 11, no. 6, pp. 74-81, Office of Foreign Agricultural Relations, U. S. Department of Agriculture, Washington).

RIVERS, W. H. R.

    1906. *The Todas* (London).

    1914. *History of Melanesian Society* (2 vols., Cambridge).

    1926. *Social Organization* (New York).

ROUSE, IRVING

    1939. *Prehistory in Haiti: A Study of Method* (Yale University Publications in Anthropology, no. 21, New Haven).

SPIER, LESLIE

    1925. *The Distribution of Kinship Systems in North America* (University of Washington Publications in Anthropology, vol. 1, Seattle).

STOUFFER, SAMUEL A., ET AL.

    1950. *Measurement and Prediction* (Studies in Social Psychology in World War II, vol. 4, Princeton).

222

SWARTZ, MARC J.

1960. *Situational Determinants of Kinship Terminology* (Southwestern Journal of Anthropology, vol. 16, pp. 393-97, Albuquerque).

1962. *Recruiting Labor for Fissionary Descent Lines on Romonum, Truk* (Southwestern Journal of Anthropology, vol. 18, pp. 351-64, Albuquerque).

TOLERTON, BURT, AND JEROME RAUCH

1950. *Social Organization, Land Tenure and Subsistence Economy of Lukunor, Nomoi Islands* (Final report, The Pacific Science Board, National Research Council, mimeographed, Washington).

UCHIDA, KANICHI

1930. *The Problem of the Relation between Climate and Clothes in Our South Sea Islands* (Historical and Geographical Essays, Commemorating Dr. Okawa's Sexagenary Celebration, pp. 643-739, Tokyo; in Japanese, translated extracts in files of Human Relations Area Files, Inc., New Haven).

VOEGELIN, C. F., AND Z. S. HARRIS

1945. *Linguistics and Ethnology* (Southwestern Journal of Anthropology, vol. 1, pp. 445-65, Albuquerque).

YANAIHARA, TADAO

1940. *Pacific Islands under Japanese Mandate* (London and New York).

GENEALOGICAL CHARTS

EXPLANATION OF CHARTS

CHARTS 1, 2. *Correlation of Numbered Status with Kinship and Behavior Terms.*
1, Status on scale of *pin me wöön*. 2, Status on scale of sexual distance.

CHARTS 3–22. *Romonum's Genealogies.*
These genealogical charts are given by lineage in the following order: 3, Pwëën. 4, Jacaw 1. 5, Jacaw 2. 6, Jacaw 3. 7, Jeffeg. 8, Pwereka 1. 9, Pwereka 2. 10, Pwereka 3. 11, Pwukos. 12, Söör 1. 13, Söör 2. 14, Wiitëë 1. 15, Wiitëë 2. 16, Wiitëë 3. 17, Wiitëë 4. 18, Wuwäänyw 4. 19, Wuwäänyw 1. 20, Wuwäänyw 2. 21, Wuwäänyw 3. 22, Wuwäänyw 5.

The names of all members of the lineage in question are given in capital letters, while those of their spouses and other related non-members are given in small letters. Underneath the name of each spouse is given the lineage to which he or she belongs. Sex is indicated by the position of the marriage symbol (=), which is always to the left of a man's name, to the right of a woman's, or, in the case of single persons, by the symbols "m" and "f" under the name. The names of living persons are underlined. Lineage designations are abbreviated to A, Jacaw (e.g., A2 for Jacaw "); E, Jeffeg; P, Pwereka; Pu, Pwukos; Pw, Pwëën; S, Söör; U, Wuwäänyw; W, Wiitëë. Solid lines indicate consanguineal descent, and broken lines descent by adoption. Numbers before the names of spouses indicate order of marriage, single parentheses after such names indicating polygynous unions.

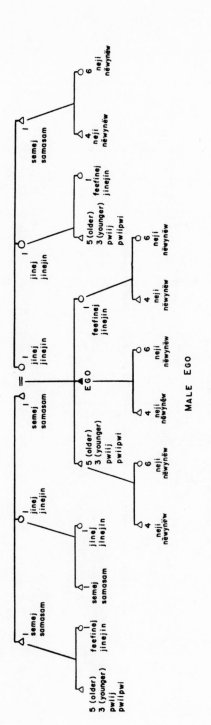

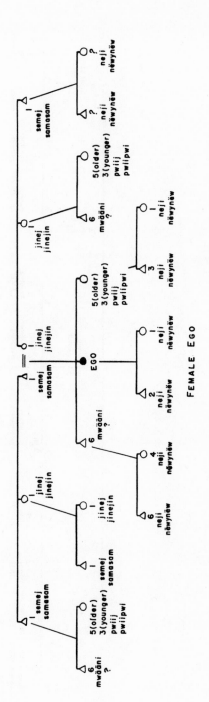

GENEALOGICAL CHART CORRELATING NUMBERED STATUS ON SCALE OF *PIN ME WÖÖN* WITH KINSHIP AND BEHAVIOR TERMS

225

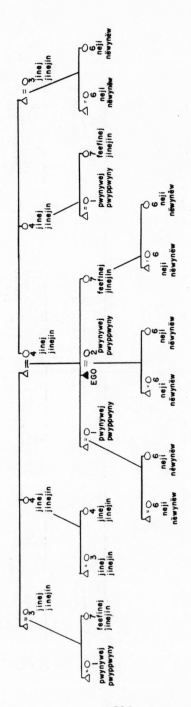

GENEALOGICAL CHART CORRELATING NUMBERED STATUS ON SCALE OF SEXUAL DISTANCE WITH KINSHIP AND BEHAVIOR TERMS

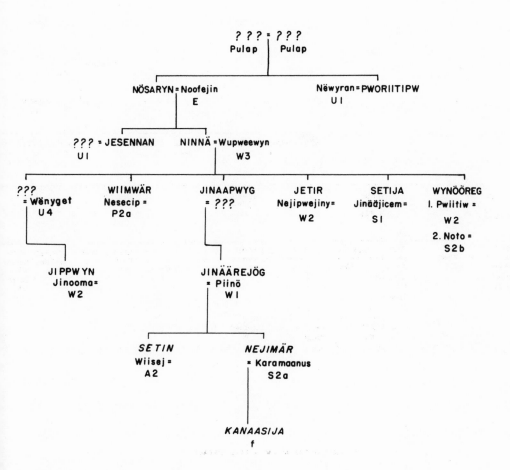

GENEALOGY OF THE PWËËN (Pw) LINEAGE

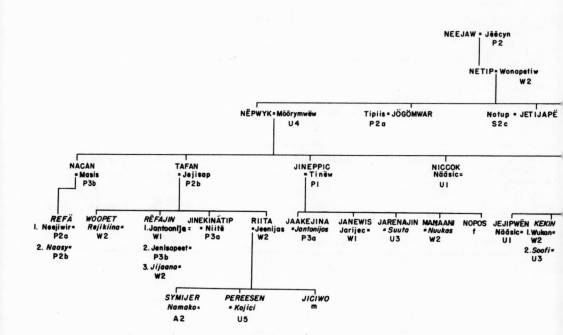

GENEALOGY OF THE JACAW I (AI) LINEAGE

228

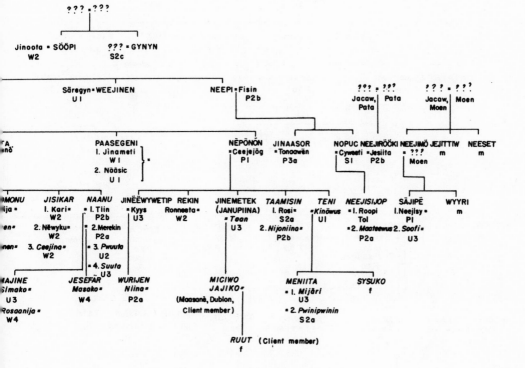

GENEALOGY OF THE JACAW I (AI) LINEAGE (CONT)

229

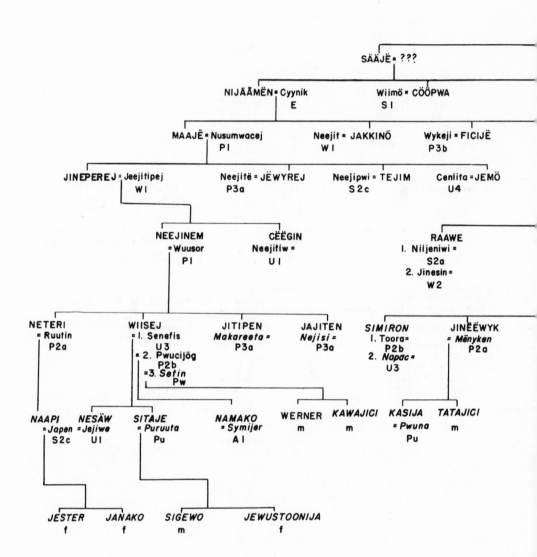

GENEALOGY OF THE JACAW 2 (A2) LINEAGE

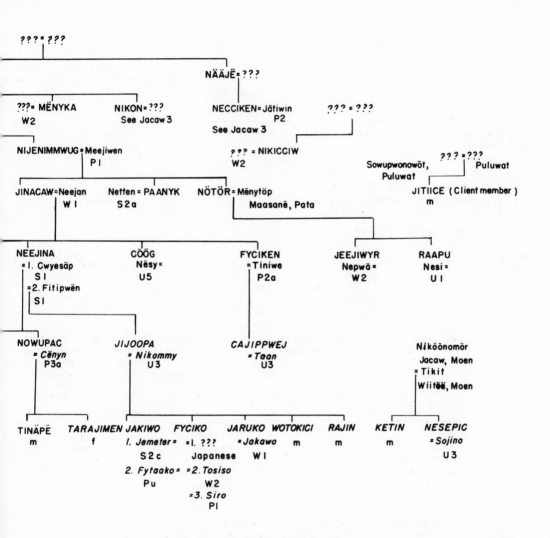

GENEALOGY OF THE JACAW 2 (A2) LINEAGE (CONT.)

231

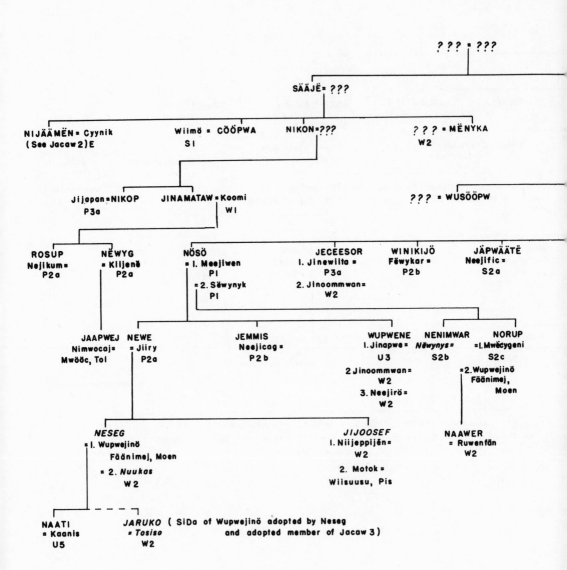

GENEALOGY OF THE JACAW 3 (A3) LINEAGE

232

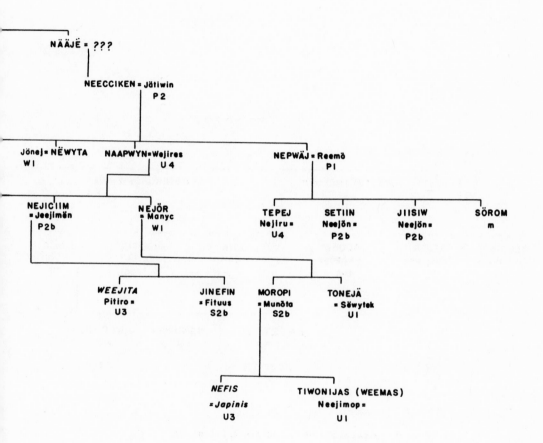

GENEALOGY OF THE JACAW3 (A3) LINEAGE   (CONT.)

233

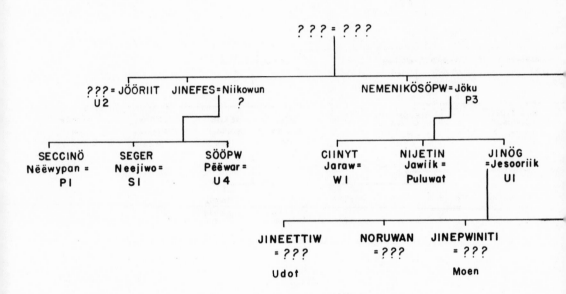

GENEALOGY OF THE JEFFEG (E) LINEAGE

Nijäämën = CYYNIK
A2

Jaraw = KININ
WI   (believed to have been a brother to
              Jööriit and Cyynik)

NÖÖFEJIN   JIITYN   PÄSÖNÖ   MEJICËW
Nösaryn=   ??? =   Nejikeciw=   Neejicë=
Pw   P3a   U2

(These four men are believed to have been real or
  classificatory sister's sons of Jööriit and Cyynik.)

KÖÖNIS
= ???
Moen

GENEALOGY OF THE JEFFEG (E) LINEAGE (CONT.)

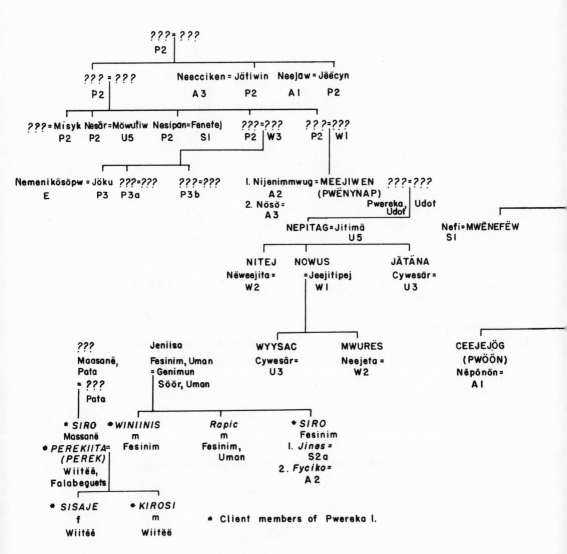

GENEALOGY OF THE PWEREKA I (PI) LINEAGE

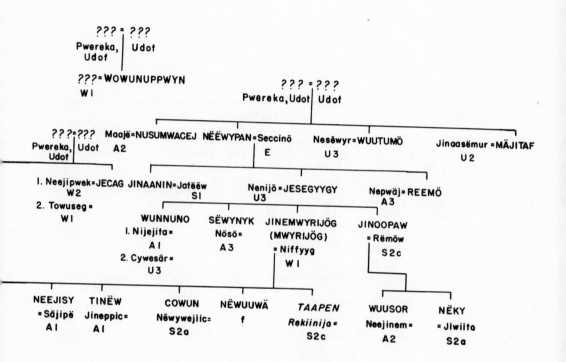

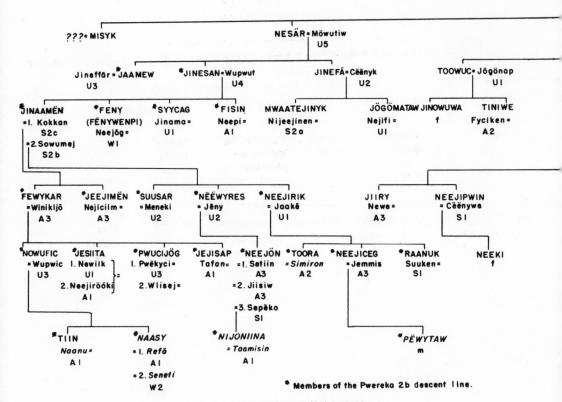

GENEALOGY OF THE PWEREKA 2 (P2) LINEAGE

238

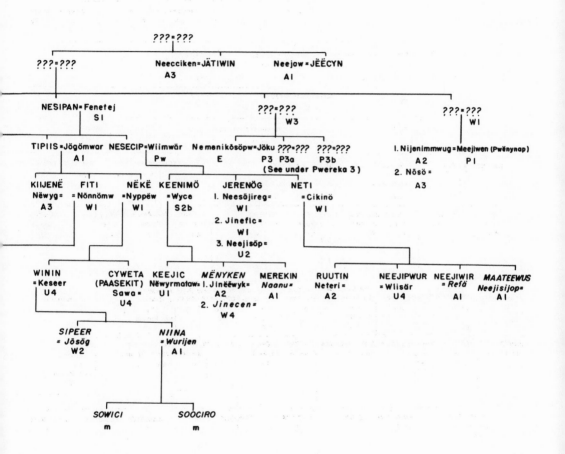

GENEALOGY OF THE PWEREKA 2 (P2) LINEAGE   (CONT.)

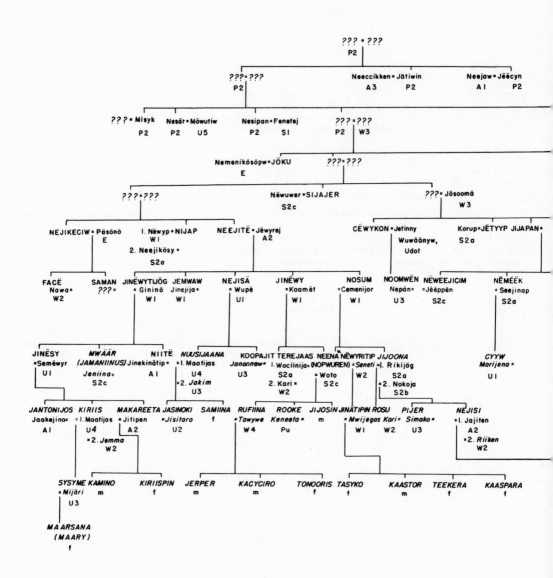

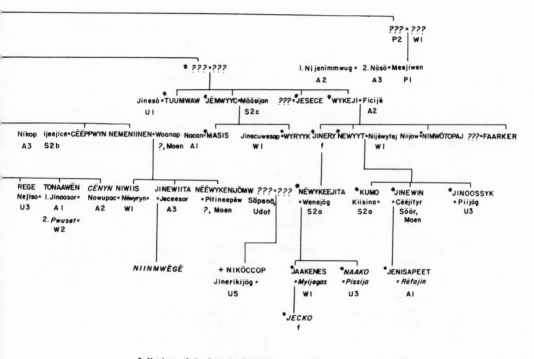

* Members of the Pwereka 3b descent line.
+ Client member of Pwereka 3a descent line.

GENEALOGY OF THE PWEREKA 3 (P3) LINEAGE (CONT)

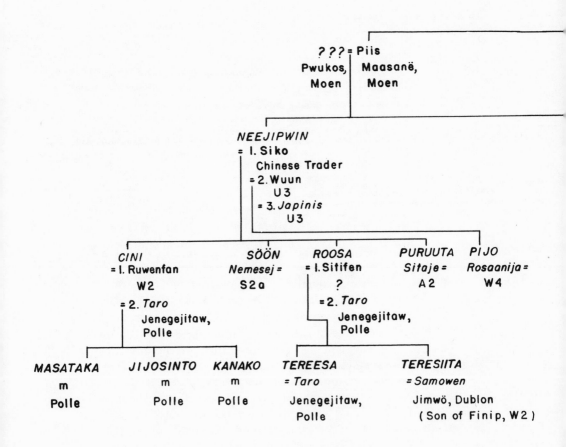

GENEALOGY OF THE PWUKOS (PU) LINEAGE

242

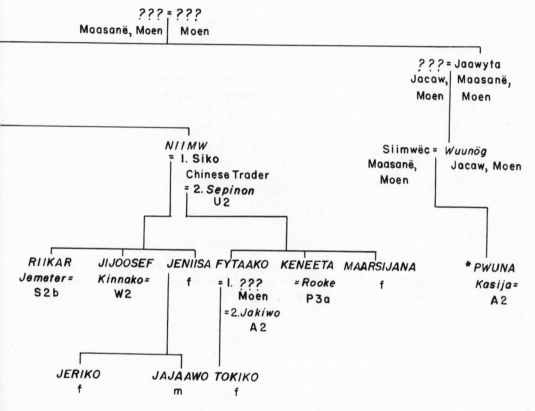

* Client member of Pwukos lineage.

GENEALOGY OF THE PWUKOS (PU) LINEAGE (CONT.)

243

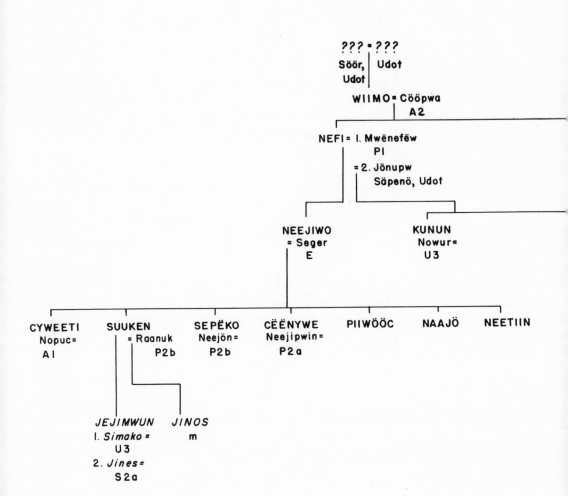

GENEALOGY OF THE SÖÖR I (SI) LINEAGE

244

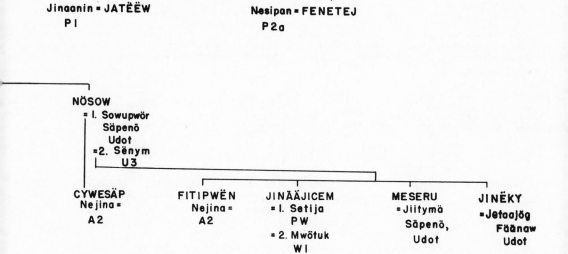

Jinaanin = JATËËW
P I

Nesipan = FENETEJ
P2a

NÖSOW
= I. Sowupwör
Säpenö
Udot
=2. Sënym
U3

CYWESÄP
Nejina =
A2

FITIPWËN
Nejina =
A2

JINÄÄJICEM
= I. Setija
PW
= 2. Mwötuk
WI

MESERU
=Jiitymä
Säpenö,
Udot

JINËKY
=Jetaajög
Fäänaw
Udot

GENEALOGY OF THE SÖÖR I (SI) LINEAGE (CONT.)

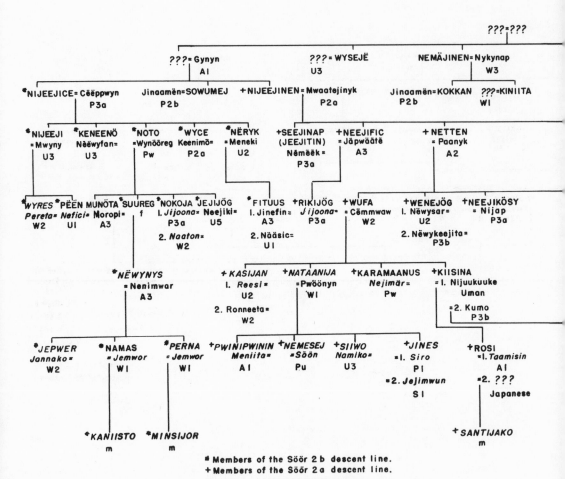

*Members of the Söör 2b descent line.
+Members of the Söör 2a descent line.

GENEALOGY OF THE SÖÖR 2 (S2) LINEAGE

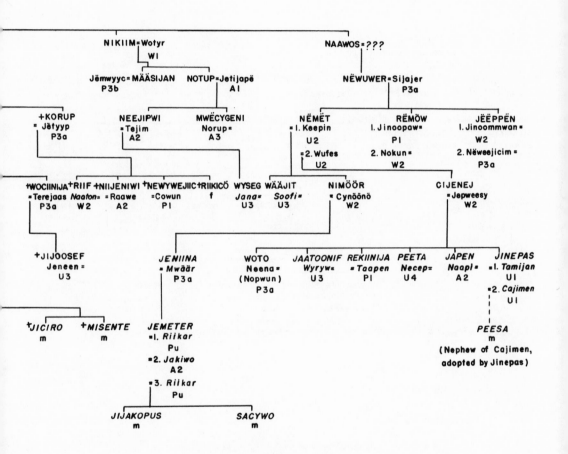

GENEALOGY OF THE SÖÖR 2 (S2) LINEAGE (CONT.)

247

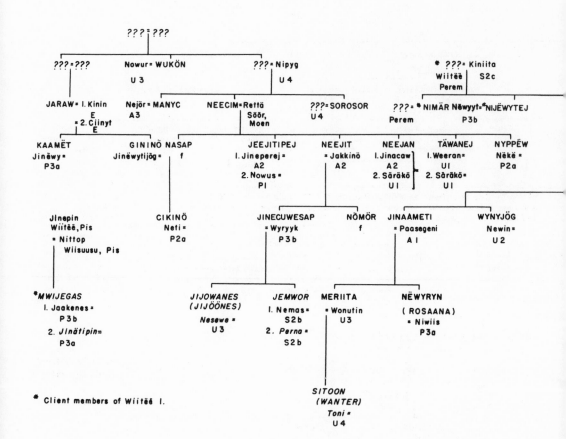

GENEALOGY OF THE WIITËË I (WI) LINEAGE

248

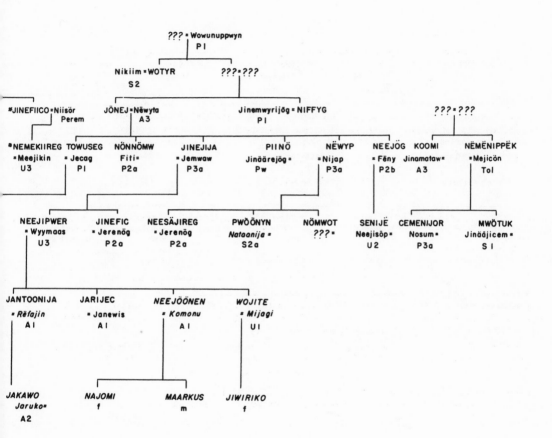

GENEALOGY OF THE WIITËË I (WI) LINEAGE (CONT.)

249

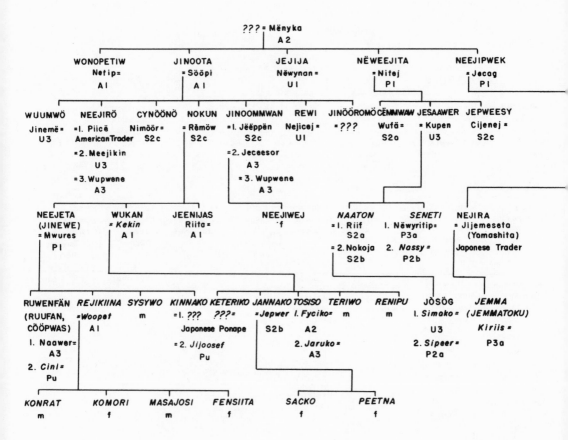

GENEALOGY OF THE WIITËË 2 (W2) LINEAGE

250

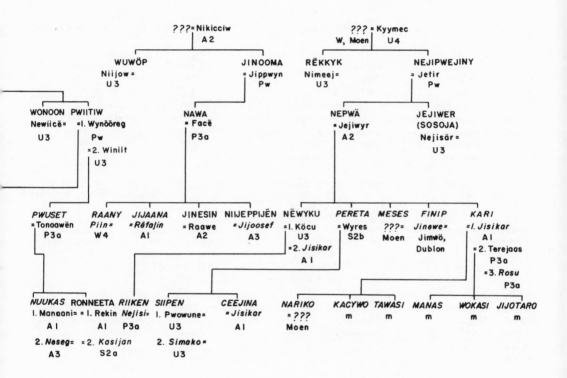

GENEALOGY OF THE WIITÉË 2 (W2) LINEAGE (CONT.)

251

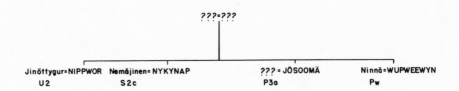

GENEALOGY OF THE WIITËË 3 (W3) LINEAGE

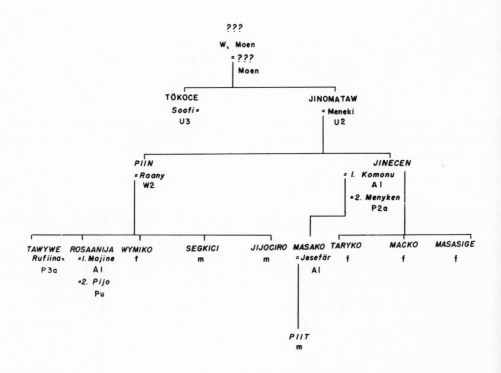

GENEALOGY OF THE WIITËË 4 (W4) LINEAGE

252

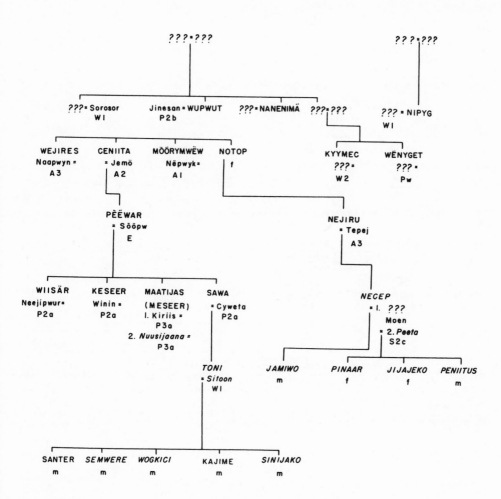

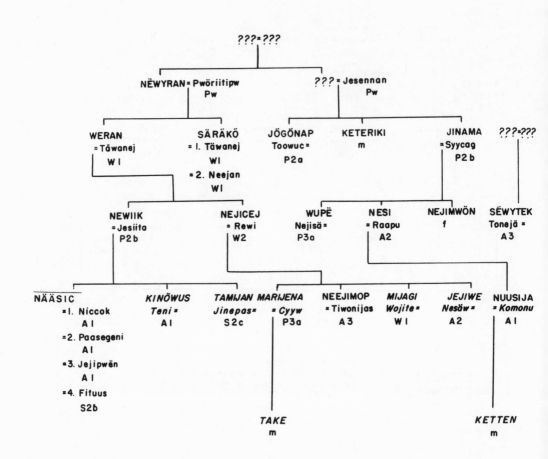

GENEALOGY OF THE WUWÄÄNYW I (UI) LINEAGE

254

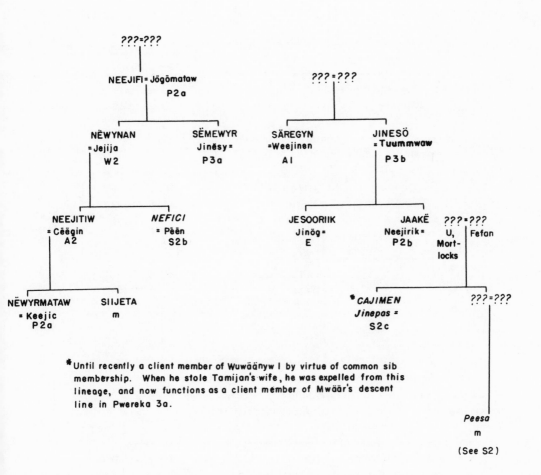

*Until recently a client member of Wuwäänyw I by virtue of common sib
membership. When he stole Tamijan's wife, he was expelled from this
lineage, and now functions as a client member of Mwäär's descent
line in Pwereka 3a.

GENEALOGY OF THE WUWÄÄNYW I (UI) LINEAGE (CONT.)

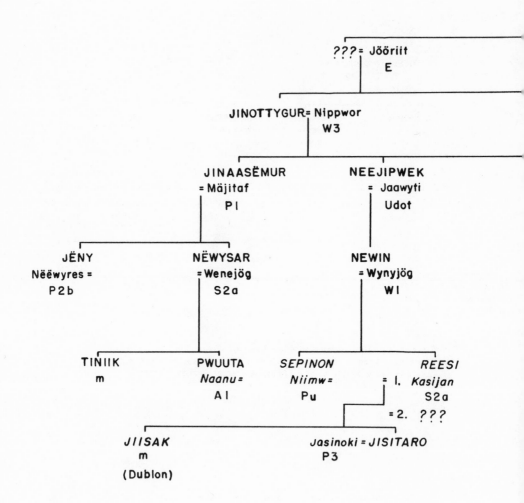

GENEALOGY OF THE WUWÄÄNYW 2 (U2) LINEAGE

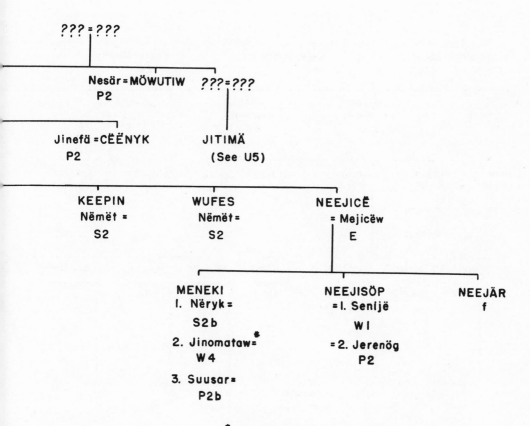

*The children of this woman have been
adopted into the U 2 lineage.   See W 4.

GENEALOGY OF THE WUWÄÄNYW 2 (U2) LINEAGE (CONT.)

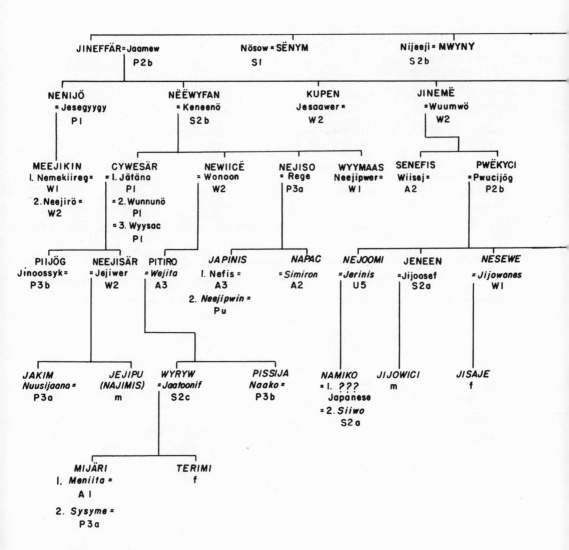

GENEALOGY OF THE WUWÄÄNYW 3 (U3) LINEAGE

258

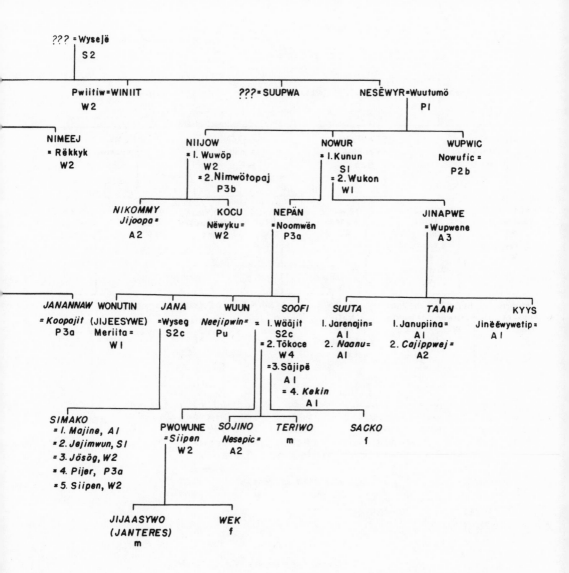

??? = Wysejë
S 2

Pwiitiw=WINIIT
W 2

??? = SUUPWA

NESĒWYR=Wuutumö
PI

NIMEEJ
▪ Rëkkyk
W 2

NIIJOW
▪ I. Wuwöp
W 2
▪ 2. Nimwötopaj
P 3 b

NOWUR
▪ I. Kunun
S I
▪ 2. Wukon
W I

WUPWIC
Nowufic ▪
P 2 b

NIKOMMY
Jijoopa▪
A 2

KOCU
Nëwyku▪
W 2

NEPÄN
▪ Noomwën
P 3 a

JINAPWE
▪ Wupwene
A 3

JANANNAW
▪ Koopajit
P 3 a

WONUTIN
(JIJEESYWE)
Meriita ▪
W I

JANA
▪Wyseg
S 2 c

WUUN
Neejipwin▪
Pu

SOOFI
▪ I. Wääjit
S 2 c
▪ 2. Tökoce
W 4
▪3. Säjipë
A I
▪ 4. Kekin
A I

SUUTA
I. Jarenojin▪
A I
2. Naanu▪
A I

TAAN
I. Janupiina▪
A I
2. Cajippwej ▪
A 2

KYYS
Jinëëwywetip▪
A I

SIMAKO
▪ I. Majine, A I
▪ 2. Jejimwun, S I
▪ 3. Jösög, W 2
▪ 4. Pijer, P 3 a
▪ 5. Siipen, W 2

PWOWUNE
▪Siipen
W 2

SOJINO
Nesepic ▪
A 2

TERIWO
m

SACKO
f

JIJAASYWO
(JANTERES)
m

WEK
f

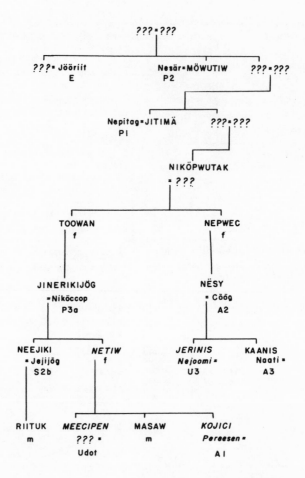

GENEALOGY OF THE WUWÄÄNYW 5 (U5) LINEAGE

INDEX

262